THE CHURCHES AND RAPID SOCIAL CHANGE

Paul Abrecht

THE CHURCHES
AND RAPID
SOCIAL CHANGE

Doubleday & Company, Inc.
Garden City, New York
1961

To the members of the Working Committee (1955–1961) of the Department on Church and Society, World Council of Churches.

Grateful acknowledgment is made to the World Dominion Press for permission to reprint material from THE SPONTANEOUS EXPANSION OF THE CHURCH by Roland Allen, London, 1927 and 1959.

CONTENTS

1160555

6   *Contents*

Part IV: CONCLUSION

PREFACE

This book is the outcome of my work for the World Council of Churches as director of its six-year study program on "The Common Christian Responsibility Towards Areas of Rapid Social Change." I must add immediately, however, that the conclusions and judgments expressed here are my own, and are not the responsibility of the World Council of Churches nor of the expert group of laymen and church leaders who have participated so faithfully and effectively in this study.

A subject of this breadth and substance is an almost impossible assignment, and some limitation in the topics considered has been inevitable. The choice of subjects may appear highly arbitrary. Throughout I have been guided by the issues which formed the core of the World Council study: Responsible Citizenship, Urbanization and Industrialization, Rural Change, and the Impact of the West, for these seemed to deserve attention in a book which could not in any case be comprehensive. Some topics have been omitted because they are dealt with fully elsewhere. Problems of population are the subject of a recent book by one of my World Council colleagues,[1] and I have treated very briefly the problems of rural life because these are examined so fully in the companion volume in this study by Professor Egbert de Vries.

Some areas of rapid social change receive scant attention here. This is due in part to the fact that in some of these, and particularly in the Middle East, the study program has developed very slowly. I also realize that I have scarcely done justice to the awakening concern for social questions in Latin America, particularly in Brazil. The Latin American Evangelical Consultation on Social Questions held in Lima, Peru, in July 1961, reveals the spreading interest throughout the continent.

The basic problem confronted in writing in this field is that the discussion of Christian ethics in relation to society in Africa, Asia, and

[1] Richard M. Fagley, *The Population Explosion and Christian Responsibility*. Oxford University Press. New York, 1960.

Latin America has been so very much neglected. There is even yet surprisingly little writing on these issues: no Troeltsch has yet appeared to analyze the social teaching of missions and younger churches over the last 150 years. Standard histories of missionary work are surprisingly silent on its social witness and its involvement with Western political and social domination, as well as with movements of national economic and social liberation. Here is a fruitful and important field for research which is fundamental to the Church's efforts to find its way in a time when old patterns of Christian relationships are disintegrating. I have had to write in anticipation of that necessary basic research.

A book of this kind owes much to a great many people, and I acknowledge with gratitude the help I have received from Christian workers, missionaries, and colleagues in the ecumenical movement. A special word of appreciation is due to Dr. W. A. Visser 'tHooft, General Secretary of the World Council of Churches, and to Dr. Robert S. Bilheimer, an Associate General Secretary and director of the Division of Studies, who have read and criticized the manuscript and whose advice and interest has been a constant encouragement. My particular thanks goes also to Professor de Vries who, as both chairman of the Working Committee of the Department on Church and Society and author of the companion volume, has given me the benefit of his wide-ranging knowledge of the subject of our common study. I owe thanks also to my secretaries who have faithfully and patiently typed the various drafts of this book, and I am especially grateful to my wife for her invaluable editorial assistance.

Paul R. Abrecht

Geneva, Switzerland
June 1, 1961

Part I

THE PROBLEMS CONFRONTING THE CHURCH

Chapter 1

THE INVOLVEMENT
OF THE CHURCH

*Social change is a medium through which God acts to
awaken the world anew.*

—Statement from the World Christian Study Conference
on Rapid Social Change, Thessalonica, 1959

The rapid social change now taking place in Africa,
Asia, and Latin America is a vast revolutionary movement of ideas,
institutions, and peoples which in its immensity and complexity seems
to defy analysis and description. And Christians ask today, what is the
explanation of this amazing awakening of the peoples of the non-
Western world and how are we involved?

The situation of the Church in relation to rapid social change in
the non-Western world is often like that of an African audience watching a movie in some regions of southern Africa. In Rhodesia, for example, Africans in a public movie theater can see only films that have
been censored by an all-white committee appointed by the government.[1] It must remove all scenes of "immorality" and "violence," and
the definition of these is so broad that when the film is rejoined great
gaps are left in the dialogue and story. The African audience watching
this hopelessly patched-up result of the censors' work sees only dis-
connected snatches of action. It observes the developing tensions and
the mounting struggle between individuals and groups, but there is no
continuity and little meaning. It is fascinated and amazed, but not
enlightened. So the Church today is frequently the spectator of an
exciting, fast-moving world which, however, only mystifies it and frus-

[1] In July 1960 the government of Northern Rhodesia removed the restrictions
on Africans in movie theaters, cafés, and restaurants. In Southern Rhodesia
segregation in theaters, hotels, and eating places is still maintained.

trates its desire for understanding. It too is bewildered as it tries to discover a meaning where none seems to exist.

This is the general conclusion which must be drawn from a survey of the response of the Church to the vital drama of rapid social change. For some Christians this situation raises no serious problems. They see their role in the world as essentially that of onlookers rather than of participants. The world is in rebellion against God and they feel no obligation to assume any responsibility for it. But the greater number of Christians today are concerned about the way in which the Church should respond to the challenge of change. How has it been involved in change in Africa, Asia, and Latin America in the past? How is it to interpret the phenomenon of change today, and how can we explain its failure to react more alertly and adequately to a changing world? Is this inertia due to some defect in its theology or structure? On what specific problems should it focus its attention and what are the ethical issues which it must face? These are some of the questions which will concern us here.

I. *The Universal Spiritual and Ethical Problem of Change*

The Church may, with some justification, plead that it is confronted with an impossible task. It may be argued that we are not dealing with social change but social changes, and that each situation must be judged according to its own characteristics. And indeed the great variety in the issues as they appear in different countries of Africa, Asia, and Latin America, often seems more striking than their similarities. Each of these countries is at its own stage of political and economic reconstruction. Land reform and agricultural change raise different questions in countries on the same continent; the obstacles to economic development are different even between neighboring countries; and the impact of the West varies in form and intensity from region to region.

Similarly, is it possible to generalize about a *common* Christian responsibility when the Church itself is at such different stages of development and has such a varying relationship with society in these areas? In Asia, the churches are beginning to feel a new sense of solidarity with each other and already have had some experience in speaking together about the problems of social change; but in Africa, the common responsibility of Christians to witness to their peoples has only recently been launched and is still struggling for support and reality. And both these situations contrast very markedly with that in Latin America, where the obstacles to Christian witness in society are quite different and where, because of the unique historical background, the whole conception of "Christianity" has to be seen in a completely different context. The task of the Church in relation to rapid social change is bound to differ greatly from one country to another.

Paradoxically, however, the more we consider the differences in the Church's experience with rapid social change the more the similarities of Christian concern and responsibility appear. In all these varied situations, common human problems arise which present similar dilemmas and opportunities for the Church. This solidarity of Christian concern emerges very clearly in relation especially to the fundamental ethical problems of change: the moral impact of economic and political change on the human situation, the struggle to discover the moral criteria for determining what is desirable in change, and the need to clarify the common moral assumptions on which a new social order can be built.

Rapid social change means for all the countries of Africa, Asia, and Latin America the revolutionary transformation of their life, politically, economically, socially, and culturally. Politically it often takes the form of a new national state and community. Economically it means industrialization and economic development on a vast scale carried out in most cases by means of long-range government planning. Socially it means tremendous community development and programs to bring public education, health, and welfare to great new sectors of the population. Social change also leads to a re-evaluation of the traditional cultural life of these countries and a questioning of old customs and attitudes to man and the world. The specific reasons for this revolution vary from region to region, but in nearly all situations the following elements seem to encourage the desire for change:

(1) new ideas about social justice and human rights, and especially the conviction that such evils as hunger and misery can be overcome by the reorganization of society and political life and new methods of production;

(2) the technological revolution introduced from the West, which has had the double effect of promising economic growth and development and making necessary new patterns of community and family life, or at least the radical modification of old patterns;

(3) the idea of national unity based on democratic principles and the rule of law, and supported by a universally literate and informed citizenry.

The Christian in these areas is inevitably deeply involved in the whole process of change. He has a responsibility as a citizen to help define the goals of a new political and social life; he must contribute to thinking about the pattern and structure of the new institutions; he can help to elaborate the conception of man and society which is needed to make these new patterns workable; and he must perform a ministry of love and service to those who find that they are more the victims than the masters of social change. In every situation, there are practically unlimited opportunities for the Church to help men discover the meaning of God's rule over man and society in terms of the realities of their present political and social experience. The demand for such help must be regarded as a fundamental challenge to any Church which claims to be faithful to its Lord, and these demands are presented today with tremendous urgency in Africa, Asia, and Latin America.

II. *The Christian Encounter with Social Change*

A. IN AFRICA

In West Africa today the first question asked by youth about everything, old and new, which they encounter in their life is, "Is it African?" This does not mean "old African," but "new African." It means, in the first instance, does it help them to achieve freedom from Western political and economic domination? Does it give them a status of equality with the rest of the world? A sense of being master of their own affairs? They are searching for forms of society and culture which are congenial to them and which express their desire to be rid of the frustrating experience of Western superiority and domination. These are not easy to discover. In the first place their world is permanently changed, and they themselves are not what they once were. It is impossible to reconstruct traditional African culture and society, and to try to do so would be to disrupt or destroy the national revolution for which they have been fighting. In the second place, the social revolution of Africa must inevitably bring more change; the economic and political revolution on which these countries have embarked has a momentum, a dynamism, which sweeps them along and which seems irresistible. They must industrialize, they must become more efficient, they must have a more educated population, and they must be nationally united. Their new national leaders have often clearly indicated their dedication to the cause of social advance in militant terms. In the West African nation of Guinea, dominated by an aggressive Marxist philosophy of social change, the attitude of the African ruling group to the illiterate animist tribes of the interior is, "They must be converted. We don't care who converts them—it can be Islam or Christianity—but their animism is an obstacle to our national social and economic development and it must be removed."

Youth especially is caught in the conflicts of social change and reconstruction which challenge traditional tribal life. Instead of gaining a larger measure of freedom from the West, they are being constantly drawn closer to it through new economic and political relationships, and thus their national revolution is, as it were, requiring them to support those forces which are challenging the whole idea of a separate African cultural and social entity. Can their distinctive African heritage be renewed, and can it endure in this new world society of which they have become a part? Can their former sense of community, and the spiritual values on which it was based, become in any way the basis of life in a world dominated by university graduates and civil service planners? Is the old attitude toward the land, toward elders, toward the family and marriage, irrevocably outmoded in the new technical society, or can some elements of these patterns be redeemed?

And if some of the traditional social patterns have to be rejected, what is to take their place? Is it possible to make changes without aggravating the social chaos, the breakdown of moral standards, and the rootlessness which are already grave problems for these countries? A young Christian in Nigeria declares that,

. . . . West Africa is today crying in loud, although sometimes mistaken, accents for a responsible, personal community arising from the democratic ordering of society demanded by an enlightened understanding and scripturally instructed conscience. It is a search for a new society, a new concept of community, and a resulting new exemplification and adjustment of social responsibilities.[2]

Is the Church in West Africa helping its youth to discover their Christian responsibility in the search for the goals of national development?

[2] Adeolu Adgebola, "Christianity Facing Religious and Ideological Forces at Work in West Africa." *The Student World*, No. 4, 1954, pp. 342–43.

Christianity is, for the young African who wants his life to be "African," in many respects the first cause of all his troubles. The Church and its missions were the ally, even the spearhead, of the Western system which so radically disrupted his own. In a recent novel, a young Nigerian writer gives us his view of the role of Christianity in undermining African social and cultural unity:

> Does the white man understand our custom . . . ? How can he when he does not even speak our tongue? But he says our customs are bad; and our own brothers who have taken up his religion also say that our customs are bad. How do you think we can fight when our own brothers have turned against us? The white man is very clever. He came quietly and peaceably with his religion. We were amused at his foolishness and allowed him to stay. Now he has won our brothers, and our clan can no longer act like one. He has put a knife on the things that held us together and we have fallen apart.[3]

Today the Church has a great responsibility to help the African rediscover himself, as a man, as an African, as a member of the human race. In the eyes of African youth Christianity has played an ambiguous role. It introduced new ideas and gave new meaning to life, shattering the unity of the old society, but it offered no new framework for community or individual life which did not seem to require them to accept completely the Western pattern of society. Christianity in West Africa has still to define its understanding of, and its responsibility to, the struggle for a new African society.

B. IN ASIA

The need to discover new goals and patterns for political and economic life is no less urgent in Asia. The situation in the Indian state of Kerala, where rival ideological groups are vying with each other in a bitter and violent conflict to determine whose philosophy and conception of social change will predominate, illustrates the problem for many areas. The antagonists in Kerala are: (1) the Communist Party, the largest political group, advocating a totalitarian revolutionary Marxist program of social change, supported mainly by landless laborers and untouchables, and representing a third of the population of thirteen and a half million people; (2) the Christian community (comprising Syrian Orthodox, Catholic, and Protestant), also constituting nearly a third of the population, which has through its Christian

---

[3] Chinua Achebe, *Things Fall Apart*. London, 1958, p. 158.

schools helped to make Kerala the most literate state in India; in political affairs it largely supports the Congress Party; (3) the Congress Party and the Praja Socialist Party, favoring democratic solutions to social problems but lacking clear-cut programs and bold leadership; (4) the Muslim and Hindu Communalist groups (e.g. the Muslim League and the Hindu Nairs) which effectively control more than a fourth of the electorate.

The Communist Party has taken the leadership in working for social change, promising to help the millions of unemployed workers and the depressed groups. The divisive attitude of the communal and caste groups has not been conducive to an effective democratic movement for social change. As a Christian study group reported in 1957: "The political mind of the people of Kerala is dominated by a deep-rooted communal outlook and by caste prejudices. This has adversely affected the growth of true democratic forces in the State."[4] The Christian community, which is large and influential, though divided, has lacked a sense of responsibility for needed change and has not been concerned with the social ills of the existing order.[5] It is not surprising therefore that the Communist Party succeeded in winning office in the elections of February 1957, supported not only by the poorer classes of the population, but also by many of the educated middle class, including Christian youth, who, desiring to work for social change, were convinced that the Communist Party was the only group which understood the urgent need for action.

During their more than two years in power, the Communists provided a highly disciplined government, but their antidemocratic doctrinaire political ideology met with active resistance, and the antireligious indoctrination in the public schools and their harsh treatment of the Christian and communal private school systems aroused militant opposition. In July 1959, the President of India intervened in the violent conflict between the Communist-controlled government and the opposition (in which Christians took a leading role), dismissing the government and calling for new elections. In the special election of February 1, 1960 a non-Communist coalition (the United Democratic Front) was returned to office though the Communist Party increased its popular support, receiving a million more votes than in 1957, or 43% of the votes cast. Although the election restored par-

[4] *The Communist Rule in Kerala and Christian Responsibility*, report of a Christian Study Conference, 1957, p. 11.
[5] *Ibid.*, p. 11.

liamentary government the fundamental question has still to be answered: can the new government find a positive answer to the old rivalries which have divided the communal groups, and can it put forward a democratic program to overcome hunger, poverty, and social injustice?

The churches in Kerala are certainly not less ethically creative than those in many other areas of rapid social change. The vast majority of Christians are members of the ancient churches that came to India in the early Christian centuries, and they are more influential in numbers than the Church in most parts of Asia. But they are divided, and they have not given attention to the social problems around them. They have tended to be another communal group rather than a force for social reconciliation and justice. Confronted with the challenge of Communism and the participation of Christian youth in the Communist Party, they expressed strong criticism of Communism, but had little to say about alternatives to it in political and social life. When aroused by Communism some church leaders went to the other extreme and issued specific directives to church members to vote for a particular party, raising serious questions about the way in which they conceived the role of the Church in political life. In the struggle to preserve the Christian schools the churches acted courageously and even sacrificially, but it is not clear they are ready to face as boldly some of the necessary issues of school reform which the changing situation demands.

We have described at length the situation in Kerala because so many of the problems confronted by the Church there are typical for many areas of Asia: the pressure for change, especially among the great masses of impoverished people; the desperate need for creative, energetic, and responsible political leadership and well organized political parties to deal with basic social needs; the challenge of religious communalism and the pull of the old cultural and ethnic loyalties which have to be reconciled with the demand for change; and the need for political education and information which enlightens the electorate on the issues of public life. All the many new and old social ideologies—communism, socialism, Western secular democratic humanism, Western "Christian" democracy, Muslim theocracy, Hindu nationalism, and a host of other powerful cultural and social movements—have something to say about the direction and nature of the social change that is required.

The churches in these situations do not yet have the means adequately to make their witness in society; and even if they had the means, they are not clear what they would say about the complex questions of social justice which face them. They are, generally speaking, unprepared for their part in the battles of rapid social change.

C. IN LATIN AMERICA

As a recent study points out, "Rapid social change is the order of the day in most Latin American countries."[6] Its economic aspects arise from a demand for higher standards of living, for better medical care, and for more educational opportunities. It has also been initiated by businessmen and investors, both foreign and national, who seek to break through the static structures of the South American economy in order to exploit natural resources and develop new industries and commerce. The constant flow of immigrants from Japan, Germany, Italy, and other European countries has brought new capital, new technical skills, and new ideas to accelerate the movement for economic and social change. The area as a whole is advancing economically, and in Brazil, Mexico, and Venezuela especially there has been spectacular industrial development; however, it has been accompanied by great social misery and disorder.

In certain regions the revolution in political life is the most significant form of change. This is particularly true of Bolivia and other countries of the Andean mountain region, where the Indians, who constitute the great majority of the population, are demanding a larger share in political life. They seek freedom from domination by the Latino group, and this involves them in a new look at their ancient customs; together these two forces have held them for centuries in conditions of peonage and poverty.

Latin America is seeking economic and political change partly in order to reduce its dependence on the United States. Its people resent the North American interpretation of the Monroe Doctrine and the political tutelage which this implies. They therefore couple national political and social reform with efforts to free themselves from control by North American capital and from interference by the United States in their internal affairs. However, lacking the indigenous capital and technical skills needed for national development, they must still look to North America and Europe for economic aid,

[6] James G. Maddox, *Technical Assistance by Religious Agencies in Latin America*. Chicago, 1956.

and this accentuates the very feeling of subservience and domination which they imagined they were in the process of wiping out.

All this change has inevitably brought with it familiar problems. The rapid industrial and commercial expansion has produced a vast movement to the cities, with the resulting slums and a growing body of disoriented, poor worker families. Social welfare and educational facilities lag far behind the need. Meanwhile the majority of rural workers continue to live in conditions of destitution.

The most striking thing about the relation of the Church to this social change in Latin America is that the change has come in the form of a secular challenge to an outdated pattern of Roman Catholic Christendom and has been marked by anticlericalism. Latin American "de-Christianization" has come about in large part because the institutional Church has not entered into the struggle for social reform; on the contrary the fight for human values has very often involved a struggle against the Church, which defended feudal structures of society. The "Christianity" of great numbers of illiterate rural people is a thin veneer of belief, mingled with local pagan customs, held with superstitious reverence. Among the majority of the intellectuals, the dominant ideological forces are European-type anticlericalism, liberalism, and positivism.

Into this situation North American evangelical missionaries brought strong individualist ethics of temperance, honesty, family responsibility, and education, while at the same time they held aloof from the wider problems of the social order. They represented very largely missions which were "non-co-operative," and this remains true even today.[7] The great tragedy of American evangelical missions on this continent is that they never really tried to discover their witness in relation to this de-Christianized cultural and social situation.[8] Professor Miguez Bonino, president of Union Theological Seminary in Buenos Aires, has written of the evangelical movement in Latin America:

How is it to intercede for a people whose preoccupations it does not

[7] In 1954 it was noted that of the ninety Protestant organizations working in Latin America as missionary agencies, with approximately 4000 missionaries, "roughly speaking, three fourths . . . are *not* cooperating. . . ." Howard W. Yoder, *The Task Ahead.* An address to the Committee on Cooperation in Latin America.

[8] Miguez Bonino, "Witness in a de-Christianized Continent," *The Student World*, Vols. I & II, 1961, pp. 96–110.

know, whose joys and sorrows it does not share, whose customs it disdains, and of whose hopes it is ignorant? The Evangelical Church has looked down upon the "sinful flesh" of humanity in Latin America, has endeavoured to rescue it from the outside, without running the risk of corruption. For that reason it has become incapable of speaking to that humanity—and at the same time ever more incapable of discerning the voice of its Lord.[8]

And a leading layman in Guatemala writes:

It is certain that our brothers from the North enabled Latin America to know peace and spiritual happiness by changing their lives, expressing the redemptive work of our Lord Jesus Christ, and preaching the Gospel. This also means change in the social field, in fact a transformation. Glory be to God! We shall never be able to forget our debt of gratitude and love. And yet it would have been possible in all those years to do more to introduce other changes in the social field. By treating these needs and outcries for justice, first as "modernism" and now as Latin American "hypersensitivity," it is easy to stigmatize them with the deadly name of foreign doctrine. And in the meantime, precious time is lost, the kingdom of darkness and misery approaches with the clarity of an apocalypse. It will become a reality in this already somber world if what should have been done for these peoples years ago is not done now. Friends and brothers from the North, it is never too late to help the South American countries.[9]

Such views are a hopeful sign. Under pressure, especially from their youth, the evangelical churches are beginning to come out of their isolation and to express their concern for national political and social renewal.[10] Christian social study groups have been formed in Brazil, Argentina, and Uruguay. In the rapidly growing Christian mass movements, especially among the Pentecostalists, there is a new sense of Christian community, and a feeling of solidarity among workers in town and city, which shows that the Gospel has not lost its power to give meaning to men's lives even in very difficult and uncertain social conditions. But the new interest in social questions has really only begun to develop.

[9] G. Villanueva, *"Nunca es tarde para ayudar a las Américas,"* *Mensajero Evangélico.* February 1961.
[10] Mauricio Lopez, "Latin American Students and their Participation in Political Life," *The Student World,* Vol. IV, 1959, p. 464.

Chapter 2

THE IRONY IN THE POSITION OF CHURCH AND MISSIONS IN RELATION TO RAPID SOCIAL CHANGE

So first let us be agreed about the level on which we are discussing this problem. It is a level whereon we are trying to consider things for what they are within themselves before going over the emotions they provoke in us; a level above blame and where all our efforts are concentrated on understanding the specific nature and gravity of the phenomenon which confronts us. . . . The situation is enough in itself without burdening it with retrospective blame. . . . We are now at a summit of painful experience and fateful disaster.

Laurens van der Post, *The Dark Eye in Africa*

We have seen that the Church today is ill-prepared to cope with the problems of rapid social change. This is a puzzling and paradoxical situation in view of the close association of the Gospel with social change in the history of the Church and missions in Africa, Asia, and Latin America. From the very beginning of the modern mission enterprise, Christians were deeply involved in social change, and it is hard to find an instance in modern mission history where the coming of the Christian evangelist and missionary did not produce social change, often at a very rapid pace.

Indeed, until practically the Second World War, most Christian workers in Africa, Asia, and Latin America regarded themselves as prime movers in the processes of "responsible emancipation," and often their greatest efforts were concentrated on changing the onerous social conditions under which people lived. The history of Christian missions is one of social reform and change. The struggle against the evil of slavery and the rehabilitation of the freed slaves in mission-sponsored colonies in East, West, and Central Africa; the movement for the rights of women and for their education in many lands; criticism and reform of pre-Christian institutions of family and marriage; the church-led campaigns against illiteracy, and the establishment of Christian schools; the fight against hunger and famine through the introduction of new skills and scientific practices in agriculture; the development of medical missions to fight disease, and the introduction of scientific hygiene: these are but a few examples of the significant action of the Church for social betterment.

I.   The Historic Connection of Christianity and Social Change

What were the underlying theological and social forces making for the early association of Christianity and social change? Three elements seem to have been at work.

First, the Gospel itself, with its unique conception of man and society, had a revolutionary impact upon pagan, tribal, and caste patterns. This has been noted even by many skeptics regarding Christian missionary work, for example, Dr. Norman Leys of Kenya, that irenic critic of most things European and Christian in East Africa:

> It is hard for people in Europe to realize how great and various are the effects of the publication of the New Testament in the language of the common speech of a people with no other literature . . . All natives of intelligence fasten on what is the central doctrine of the New Testament, if not of mission teaching, that every Christian is a child of God, a King's son, the heir to all the world, a partner by right in the equal fraternity of all Christians.[1]

[1] Norman Leys, *Kenya*. London, 1924. See chapter X "Christian Mission," pp. 233 and 239–41. At the close of the passage cited above, Leys wrote: "Many missionaries in their hearts regret that in the Magnificat thanks are given for the dethronement of princes, and that the early Church encouraged intermarriage of European and Asiatic, insisting indeed, that there was no real difference between them. In any case, missionaries say as little as possible about the doctrine of equal brotherhood. . . . It is unjust to blame them. Anyone who preached it as unreservedly as Paul did would have to leave the country. Not one European in a hundred in Africa believes that European and African Christians should behave to one another as members of the same family behave." (p. 241)

Neither the occasional timidity of the preacher nor the betrayal by European colonists of their Christian background could prevent the African from seeing the revolutionary significance of this new teaching. The missionary, through his teaching of the creative power of God over nature and over the demonic forces, brought people release from fear of evil, and freedom to experiment with new social ideas and techniques. This inevitable link between the Gospel and social change did not depend on the attitude of the missionary; he was often only the vehicle of the "involuntary emancipation" of the people among whom he worked, and frequently was hardly aware of the extent to which he was shaking the foundations of the traditional society.[2]

A second element in missions making for change was the style and pattern of Christian work. The mission station or compound was, in its day, a new form of society, a corporate structure of a kind absolutely different from any that had been previously encountered by Africans and Asians. It was a refuge for escaped slaves, for orphan children, for the independent spirits as well as the misfits of tribal society.[3] It was a state within a state, a system of law and order in situations where tribal rule had broken down and where colonial rule had not yet been realized.[4] It was under the supervision of a Western missionary whose ideas about work and discipline were the rule and whose behavior and that of his family inevitably became the pattern for all to emulate. It was controlled by a sense of order, and of the meaning of time which contrasted completely with the "native" world. Often more by accident than intent the missionaries and the Church were carriers of a new type of living and a new pattern of culture to people in these countries. Up until the Second World War the mission station continued to be the center of Christian life and work in large

[2] Professor Georges Balandier, a leading French anthropologist, writes: "Christianity played, in a large part of Central Africa, including vast stretches of French and Belgian Congo and Angola, a role of collective involuntary emancipation. It brought with monotheism a principle of unification. It imposed the example of the Messiah, who, sacrificed by the public authorities in a manner as infamous as for criminals, nevertheless triumphed over these authorities to the great joy of the faithful. It introduced all the revolutionary power which it had inside it at the time of its birth as well as the inherited hope of Jewish messianism. Our spirit must be astounded by this repetition of history after two milleniums." *Afrique Ambiguë*, Paris, 1957, p. 237 (my translation).

[3] *Cf.* Bertram Hutchinson, "Some Social Consequences of Missionary Activity among South African Bantu," *Africa*, April 1957. Vol. 27, No. 2.

[4] Roland Oliver, *The Missionary Factor in East Africa*. London, 1952, Ch. II.

areas of Africa and Asia. A visitor to a mission station in Central Africa in the early 1930s (before the Coppermines were in full operation) reports on its role as follows:

> The mission station as an island of economic activity and security is a familiar sight to the traveller in Central Africa. During a visit to one of the largest stations in Northern Rhodesia some years ago the missionary in charge pointed out to us the relation of the industrial activities of the mission to the growth of the Christian villages of the neighbourhood. Men were repairing the church roof that had collapsed during the rains; whole families were working at the brick kiln, making tiles and bricks; other labourers kept the nine-mile irrigation ditch in order, herded the cattle of the mission dairy or tended the kitchen gardens. Felling forest timber and preparing it for use in the carpentry shop and lumberyard gave employment to many. One or more buildings, related to the hospital, boys' school, girls' school, industrial school and mission residences, were always under construction, giving work to a permanent force of artisans, while the hospital, schools and missionaries' houses each required a complement of servants. The mission kept a permanent road gang to build and repair its roads; messengers, farmers and lorry drivers accounted for another score of employees. I was not surprised after spending three days in this hive of industry to learn that the mission supplied regular labour to five hundred people, representing a population of fifteen hundred or more, who resided in the two neighbouring villages. Most of these people were Christians and gained their livelihood from contact with the missions.

A third element making for change was the missionary interpretation of the social and cultural function of the Christian West in Africa and Asia. In the early period of missions, lasting until after World War I, the Gospel was practically identified, implicitly or explicitly, with the cultural and social pattern of Western Christendom. The "salvation of souls" was the main task of missions, but this involved in Africa and Asia building a "Christian" culture and a "Christian" civilization. The peoples of Africa and Asia were looked upon as underprivileged races whose lives must be changed in accordance with the best Christian ideals of the West. Writing in 1916, one of the great missionary leaders described the Christian missionary task as follows:

> In a human family a backward and defective child enjoys a special measure of care, solicitude and love of the parents. . . . may we not

2

suppose that the backward, primitive, child races of the world are of special concern to Him and that every effort to help and educate them is peculiarly well-pleasing in His sight?[5]

Looking back on this period, we are in fact startled, not by lack of concern for social change, but by the tremendous self-confidence of Western Christians in their ability to bring about the kind of change most needed in non-Christian lands. This is illustrated in Professor James S. Dennis' comprehensive two-volume study, *Christian Missions and Social Progress*, published in 1897, the first systematic attempt to explain and justify the concern of missions for the structure and development of "non-Christian society." Writing of the impetus provided by "the culture of Christianity" which would make "the coming century an era of immense and benign social progress," he defined the spirit which should motivate the Christian mission in inaugurating a new society in these lands:

Christian missions represent, . . . what may be designated in unscientific language as accelerated social evolution, or evolution under the pressure of an urgent force. . . . They grapple at close quarters with social conditions which may be regarded in the light of standards as in a measure chaotic, "without form and void." They have to contend, alone at first, and perhaps for several generations, with primitive social conditions, the confused result of age-long struggles of humanity. The spirit of order and moral regeneration has never brooded over that vast social abysm. It has never touched with its reconstructive power the elements heaped together in such a strange confusion. Christian missions enter this socially disorganized environment with its varying aspects of degeneracy, ranging from the higher civilization of the Orient to the savagery of barbarous races, and in most cases without the aid of any legal enactments engage in a moral struggle with those old traditions and immemorial customs which have long had their sway as the regnant forces of society. They deal with a religious consciousness almost painfully immature in spiritual things, so that the splendid task of a matured Christian experience as represented in missions is to take by the hand this childhood of the heart and mind, and, by the aid of the rich and effective resources of our modern environment, put it to school—lead it by the shortest path into the largeness of vision and the ripeness of culture which have come to us all too slowly and painfully. What we have sown in tears let them reap in joy. In many foreign fields missions must face conditions which are so complex, so subtle, so elaborately

[5] J. H. Oldham, *The World and the Gospel*. London, 1916, p. 135.

intertwined with the structure of society, solidified by age, and so impregnably buttressed by the public sentiment of the people, that all attempts at change or modification seem hopeless, and yet slowly and surely the change comes. It comes through the secret and majestic power of moral guidance and social transformation which seems to inhere in that Gospel which Christian missions teach.[6]

There were voices raised against this viewpoint, but generally speaking and with few exceptions, all missions accepted the assumptions, if not the exact wording, of this approach to change in the non-Christian world.[7] There was a variation only in degree between the pietist and the nonpietist, the Anglo-Saxon and the Continental European mission societies. While their concept of change seemed aimed primarily at personal evangelism, it led eventually to detribalization, the adoption of Western cultural patterns, and the breakup of the traditional culture and pattern of society.[8] But this did not mean that missions automatically acquiesced in the policy of colonial administrations or Western business and commercial interests. On the contrary, they generally recognized that their civilizing "mission" included the responsibility of upholding the highest standards of Christian civilization against all those Western forces—colonial or commercial—which preyed upon the weakness of the peoples of Africa and Asia.

[6] James S. Dennis, *Christian Missions and Social Progress: A Sociological Study of Foreign Missions*. Two volumes. Oliphant, Anderson and Ferrier (Edinburgh and London), 1897.

In 1945, John R. Mott singled out for special mention these "notable volumes" of Dr. James S. Dennis. (See his introduction to J. Merle Davis, *New Buildings on Old Foundations* [New York and London], 1945, p. viii.)

[7] There was an opposite trend to this tendency of missions to adhere to the Western pattern of civilization, especially in German missions, although this was expressed mainly after World War I, with the publication of Bruno Gutman's *Gemeindeaufbau aus dem Evangelium* (Leipzig, 1925) and *Das Dschaggaland und seine Christen* (Leipzig, 1925) which had as their thesis that the primitive structure of the *Volk* was God-given. In the Anglo-Saxon world the strongest attack on the whole Christendom idea in Missions came from Roland Allen, especially in his book, *The Spontaneous Expansion of the Church and the Causes which Hinder it* (published in 1927, but based on lectures given in 1922). For further discussion of Allen's point of view see Chapter 3. For examples of early criticism of the Christian approach to Africa the works of Mary Kingsley are interesting. See *The Life of Mary Kingsley* by Cecil Howard (London 1957).

[8] This view was proclaimed not only in the missionary circles of the Church. The famous theologian Ernst Troeltsch wrote in 1906, "Present day missions are the expansion of the religious ideas of Europe and America in close connection with the spread of the European sphere of influence." Ernst Troeltsch, *Gesammelte Schriften*, Band II, 1906, *"Die Mission in der Modernen Welt,"* pp. 779–804.

II.   *The Reaction to Western Christendom*

Despite fundamental challenges, this classical Western Christendom conception of social change in Africa and Asia has lingered long in Christian thinking.[9] The course of history in Africa, Asia, and Latin America since 1945 has, however, practically destroyed it and today there is no going back to it.

In the first place, the basic political and social situation in which the Church lives in Africa and Asia has changed. The Christendom idea was dependent on the power of the West to rule. But today independent countries have emerged and their governments are undertaking major responsibility for social and economic change based upon their own criteria of national interest. A Western Christendom approach may not have been entirely unrealistic in the India of Lord Irwin or the Africa of Lord Lugard, but it is irrelevant as a Christian strategy in the Asia of Nehru and Mao Tse-tung and in the Africa of Nkrumah and Sekou Touré.

Secondly, the changing status and diminishing role of the Western missionary enterprise, in its classical form, and the assumption of the primary responsibility for Christian advance in their countries by the national churches of Africa, Asia, and Latin America, means inevitably a change in emphasis in the Christian conception of the goals of society. The period when Western Christian social ideas could be used as the pattern for social thinking and action within the Church of Africa and Asia is over. As a study conference of the churches in the Christian Council of Ghana has said:

> Social thinking imported from abroad will no longer do. We must think creatively about our own problems and bring our own Christian conscience to bear on them. As an indigenous Church we must bring to our own government the challenge and stimulus of a Christian social conscience that rises out of our own knowledge of Christ and the experience of the guidance of his Spirit in regard to the social needs and problems of our country.[10]

[9] J. Merle Davis, *New Buildings on Old Foundations.* New York, 1945. "Among culture carriers the missionary alone aims at the spiritual transformation of native society and brings to it an organized philosophy of life, a social structure, a scheme of conduct and a moral discipline of a new faith—in short a Christian culture." p. 23.

[10] Report of Prof. K. A. Busia on the Study of the Christian Responsibility for Rapid Social Change, organized under the auspices of the Christian Council of Ghana (to be published). Some excerpts from this report appear in the article

The younger churches are interested in many problems which the Western-sponsored mission enterprise generally either could not or did not wish to take up. Moreover, many of the social and cultural transformations undertaken by missions are being challenged as evidence of Western cultural aggression conducted through the missionary movement.

Thirdly, the whole approach of a Christian civilization standing in judgment of non-Christendom has come under severe theological and historical criticism. The exploitation associated with colonial domination, the racism of the West, the ambiguous blessings of Western industrialism in the non-Western world, and the social catastrophe of the First World War shattered the illusions of most adherents of this view and radically challenged the previous identification of Christianity with a given culture. It has, however, taken a long time for the churches and missions to find an adequate alternative for the Christendom view and to work out the meaning of Christian responsibility in relation to the social change which it helped to initiate. The deepening moral dilemma of the West due to the Second World War, the new threat of nuclear war, and the preoccupation with constantly increasing standards of living has further weakened the moral confidence of Western Christianity in its own spiritual power. Meanwhile the social, cultural, economic, and political change which it helped to launch in Africa, Asia, and Latin America has increased in speed and in scope, raising new questions concerning what the Church has done and what it should now be doing in relation to social change.

The Church today thus seems to have been overtaken by the very movements of social change which it helped to initiate, and it is discovering that it needs new understanding of Christian social and cultural goals adequate for the new situation. Its bewilderment as it seeks with great difficulty to redefine its task is described by a Christian missionary at work in Central Africa, writing in 1956. His statement is typical of many:

> The churches are years out of date in their thinking, and we are all in danger of being bystanders at the birth of a new age, instead of the one midwife, having the wisdom and ability necessary to procure a safe delivery. Time is short here, and the next five to seven years may be vital, if we have as long. The old order is changing with revolutionary speed, the churches are bewildered and floundering, the

by Prof. Busia, "Sociological Evaluation of the Church in Africa," *The Student World*, Vol. LII, No. 2, 1959, pp. 134–46.

missionaries are over-burdened with the daily routine and hesitant of change either in thought forms or in methods. Indeed very few seem to be aware of the gravity of the situation.[11]

There is an ironic contrast between the situation of the Church as assessed here and that described by Prof. Dennis in 1897. The Christian enterprise, which was once sure of its role as a prime mover, and which did in fact inspire so much social change, is at present spiritually, as well as psychologically, overwhelmed by rapid developments in society, and the very Western "civilization" which formerly seemed such a sure guide for social change is today the source of a great part of its spiritual and moral confusion in these lands.

[11] Letter from the secretary of the Christian Council of Northern Rhodesia, July 1956.

Chapter 3

CHRISTIAN SOCIAL ETHICS IN THE PERIOD OF TRANSITION FROM MISSIONS TO YOUNGER CHURCH

. . . . our inquiry leads to the conclusion that all Christian social work is in a problematic condition. It is problematic in general because the power of thought to overcome brutal reality is always an obscure and difficult question; it is problematic in particular because the main historic forms of the Christian doctrine of society and of social development are today, for various reasons, impotent in face of the tasks by which they are confronted.

If the present social situation is to be controlled by Christian principles, thoughts will be necessary which have not yet been thought. . . . and which will correspond to this new situation as the older forms met the need of the social situation in earlier ages.

Ernst Troeltsch, *The Social Teaching of the Christian Churches*

A Christian social ethic based on the idea of a Western "Christendom" or "Christian culture" or "Christian civilization" was bound to become an anachronism in relation to society in Africa, Asia, and Latin America because it belonged to an age of imperialism. The identification of the Gospel with a way of life, even one which embodied certain Christian insights about man and society, inevitably leads to a kind of Christian social and cultural imperialism. Conversely, the formation of a social ethic applicable to the problems of rapid social change in the non-Western world necessarily awaited the development of the younger church in these countries, and the future growth of the universal Church. Here was the dilemma confronting the Church in the 1920s and 1930s as it began to wrestle with the challenge of rapid social change: Western Christianity could not of itself initiate the necessary radical and realistic thinking about the Christian social responsibility in relation to Africa and Asia, and the younger church, still dependent upon Western Christianity, was not yet sufficiently aware of its own spiritual danger or of the necessity to develop its own theological and biblical critique of the social situation. Nevertheless, in the period between the two world wars, groups within both Western missions and younger churches made determined efforts to cope with the changing situation in Africa and Asia. Although, measured from our standpoint, these efforts were intermittent and only partially successful, they did accomplish at least three things: (1) they awakened the younger churches and missions to the need for a more profound understanding of the relevance of the Gospel to what was transpiring in their changing world; (2) they encouraged the younger churches in their independent efforts to interpret these changes; and (3) they provoked a theological debate about the task of the Church in relation to non-Christian societies and cultures which in some measure clarified the different Christian positions. A review of these efforts of the Church to cope with the emerging social problems in this period is, therefore, essential to an understanding of the strength and weakness in the Christian interpretation of rapid social change today.

I. New Definitions of Christian Responsibility and Action for Changing Society in Africa, Asia, and Latin America

The formation of the International Missionary Council in 1920 led to the first ecumenical attempts to formulate a Christian social policy relevant to the changes in economic and social life in Africa and Asia. The date is not surprising, for it was only after the First World War that most churches in the West began to give serious attention to the human problems of industrial and economic life.

The change in missionary thinking is particularly striking. Whereas the first World Missionary Conference in Edinburgh in 1910 had said little about the social responsibility of Christians, in 1920 one of the tasks entrusted to the new International Missionary Council was:

> A study of the attitude and policy of the missionary movement in re-
> lation to the growth of industrialism in Asia and other mission fields,
> and the social problems arising therefrom.[1]

This new emphasis reflected an awakening to the fact that the missionary had not only to overthrow pagan gods, but also to deal with
the social revolution emanating from the West which was threatening
to overwhelm Africa and Asia physically and spiritually. In areas of
Africa particularly, churches and missions discovered that they were
struggling, "with only stationary or diminishing forces, against a steadily growing body of Western influences, whose operation was by no
means necessarily favourable to the growth of African Christianity."[2]

At the first international conference on "The Christian Mission in
Africa" (1926), the key topics were land, labor, race, and education,
and J. H. Oldham, a pioneer missionary thinker in this field, spoke
about "The Relation of Christian Missions to the New Forces that
are Reshaping African Life":

> If present conditions in Africa are to be successfully met, our need
> is of something radically new. To reach forward to new things will
> demand an effort. . . . We are not discharging our missionary obli-
> gation if, while present physically in Africa, we ignore these new
> forces and remain apart from them. They are a vital part of the world
> in which our Christian witness has to be borne.[3]

This approach demanded both a new understanding of the function of
the Church in the world, and also detailed information about social
and economic trends and the evaluation of these in Christian terms.

This expanding interest in the effects of social change was not confined to Africa. Churches and missions in China, Japan, and India also
discovered that they were faced with new social evils arising from the
growth of industrialism. The Y.M.C.A. and Y.W.C.A. in China played
an important part in the preparation and implementation of the Report of the Child Labour Commission of Shanghai (1924), which
criticized the conditions under which women and children were em-

---

[1] *Missions and Industrialism*, Vol. 5, Report of the Jerusalem Meeting of the
I.M.C., London, 1928. Foreword by Rev. W. Paton, p. 1.

[2] Oliver, *The Missionary Factor in East Africa*, p. 247.

[3] *The Christian Mission in Africa*. Findings of the Le Zoute Conference, ed. by
E. W. Smith, pp. 162–70.

ployed in the silk industry.[4] Christian work among industrial workers was begun in Japan, and Dr. Kagawa became a national leader in the movement for social and economic reform.[5] In India, Christian workers began to study the uprooting effect of industrial urban development, and the disintegration of traditional structures of family and village life.[6]

Attention was also given to the conditions of rural life and to land reform. Rural research was started in several parts of Asia, and rural reconstruction was promoted through technical assistance and co-operatives. Churches and missions experimented with village industries as a means to prevent the economic collapse of village life.

Although most Christian interest was focused on social problems, increasing attention was given to the rise of nationalism in Asia. This was motivated in part by the growing challenge of communism, and in part by the conflict within the Christian community itself regarding the right of people in Asia to national freedom.[7] Even though at that moment the Church was unable to reach agreement on this difficult problem, it was a place where an effort was made to listen to the voice of the awakening people of Asia.

The task of the Church and missions in society was the central theme of the 1928 Jerusalem meeting of the I.M.C., which, in sharp contrast to Edinburgh in 1910, gave great prominence to the social situations in which the missionary task was to be fulfilled. The delegates to Jerusalem were keenly aware of the difference between this and the previous World Missionary Conference. One of them, who had also been at Edinburgh, wrote immediately following the Jerusalem meeting:

When we came together in Edinburgh in 1910, the western world was relatively secure in its power to present to an Asiatic and African non-Christian world a Gospel that it felt that it had itself learned and begun to practise. In 1928 that western world has begun to see itself as the author of great materialistic and industrial forces and

[4] *Missions and Industrialism*, pp. 47–49.

[5] *Ibid.*, p. 63.

[6] *Ibid.*, p. 40–41.

[7] K. T. Paul and S. K. Datta, two Indian Christian leaders, were among those who emphasized the importance of the Christian witness in the nationalist movement. Both were members of the London Round Table Conference of 1931 to discuss independence for India. Dr. James Aggrey of Africa inspired and nourished the idea of an independent Africa intellectually and politically equal to the West.

inter-racial antagonisms which form in their uncontrolled state a menace to the world's life, and especially to the life of the spirit. It sees that its own life is thus certainly not in tune with the Gospel that it has been sending to the world; it is not even wholly sure of the full meaning of that Gospel. Therefore the western world is itself a mission field. The home base of missions is not a geographical entity at all, but is simply Christ wherever He lives in human life.[8]

This view was borne out in a portion of the Message of Jerusalem:

> We do not go to the nations called non-Christian because they are the worst of the world and they alone are in need; we go because they are a part of the world and share with us in the same human need—the need of redemption from ourselves and from sin, the need to have life complete and abundant and to be remade after this pattern of Christ-likeness.[9]

1160555

The discussion at this meeting of problems arising from economic and social change in Africa and Asia demonstrated clearly the Church's new capacity to look frankly at the harmful effects of certain aspects of Western life on peoples in the non-Western world. Attention was called to the evils of forced labor in Africa; to the exploitation of labor, especially of women and children, in Western-owned textile mills in Asia; to the responsibilities of Western capital in introducing industrial techniques in a non-technical society; to the evils of race prejudice and concepts of white superiority; to the growth of nationalism and the search for freedom from Western control.

Theologically, this social concern was based on Christian social idealism and even Utopianism. It was expressed in terms reminiscent of the Social Gospel movement in Western churches:

> . . . the Gospel of Christ contains a message, not only for the individual soul, but for the world of social organization and economic relations in which individuals live. . . .
>
> The task of the Christian Church . . . is both to carry the message of Christ to the individual soul, and to create a Christian civilization within which all human beings can grow to their full spiritual stature. . . . It is its duty to speak and work fearlessly against social and economic injustice. . . . It is its duty both by word and action to lend its support to all forces which bring nearer the establishment of

---

[8] Basil Mathews, *Roads to the City of God.* London, 1928, p. 27.
[9] *Jerusalem Meeting of the I.M.C.*, 1928. "Message on the World Mission of Christianity," quoted in Mathews, *ibid.*, p. 52.

Christ's Kingdom in the world of social relations, of industrial organization and of economic life.[10]

In a phrase often used in the statements of this meeting, the new aim of Christian social action was to "Christianize" the economic contacts of East and West and the new industrial life of the workers of the world.[11]

Although Christian social thought had been challenged by the evils of industrialism and the breakdown of old social institutions in Asia and Africa, it did not lose its optimism about the possibility of the redeemed man to achieve social progress. The Kingdom of God would come through individual conversion coupled with action by the Church for a righteous new social order. These sentiments of Jerusalem were repeated in the world missionary conference at Madras in 1937:

> As to whether we should centre upon individual conversion or upon social change to realize this Kingdom (of God), we reply that we must do both. . . . In the interest of individual conversion we must demand social change. For we see clearly that evil can be in the individual will and also in the collective will.[12]

Individual Christian leaders went even further in stating the role of missions in promoting cultural change. J. Merle Davis, the social research secretary for the I.M.C. 1930–1946, described the Christian task as follows:

> The Christian Church has the superhuman and majestic task of rationalizing, purifying, and reconstructing the disintegrating native world. The Church provides a new social grouping to satisfy the crav-

---

[10] "The Christian Mission in Relation to Industrial Problems in Asia and Africa." Statement by the International Missionary Council, published in Vol. 5 of *The Report of the Jerusalem Meeting*, 1928. *Op. cit.*, pp. 181 and 184.

[11] Basil Mathews, *op. cit.*, pp. 84–85.

[12] The World Mission of the Church, Findings and Recommendations [of the meeting] of the I.M.C., Tambaram, Madras, 1938. Report on "The Church and the Changing Social and Economic Order," p. 126. "It is not enough to say that if we change the individual we will of necessity change the social order. That is a half truth. . . . it is also a half truth to say that social change will necessarily produce individual change. We cannot sustain a new social order or bring it into being without new men. For in the ultimate analysis the whole outer structure of society rests upon human character." p. 127. Nevertheless the statement also makes it clear: "We cannot identify the Kingdom of God with a particular system, either the status quo, or any revolutionary system we desire to bring about. If any of the present panaceas offered to man were realised, even in its pure form, it would not be the Kingdom of God. The Kingdom would still judge it, for the Kingdom is the ultimate order; all else is relative."

ing for tribal solidarity and support. It creates a new fellowship and obligations based upon common beliefs and aspirations to take the place of the old brotherhood; it substitutes a new type of relationships, sanctions, and disciplines for the old; it creates a new center of authority, a new public opinion, a new self-respect, new interests and a new leadership for the old system which has been discredited; it sets up a new tribunal of moral conduct and ethical judgments and finally and most vital of all, it introduces man to a new Source of Power which energizes him and provides the strength which will enable him to meet the demands of the strange economic, social, and spiritual order that he has entered.[13]

Those who held this view assumed that they knew at least the fundamental characteristics of the "Christian society" which would encourage Christian living in Africa and Asia. This was a great presumption. They knew, and could know, little about the difficult problems of defining Christian obedience in the vast and complicated world of Africa and Asia, just as we know little today. Some spoke freely about the Christian reconstruction of society and building the Kingdom of God, when in fact the next two decades were to bring increasing tension and conflict. These men did not see what we can see from our perspective, that there was to come a period of great struggle for power and a sharp conflict between colonialism and nationalism.

II. *Missions versus Christian Social Action*

Other missionary voices argued that missions should give up altogether the attempt to define the Christian responsibility for culture and society because it was theologically uncalled for and practically unsound. One of the most eloquent members of this school of thought was the Anglican missionary, Roland Allen, whose radical views of the transcendence of Christ over culture have become popular again in our day. Allen sharply attacked the moralistic, idealistic, and "civilizing" spirit of missions. He declared that their fundamental purpose is to bring people to believe in Christ. The spiritual misery of man is not confined to civilized or uncivilized, and it is this state to which Christ speaks. The African or the Asian, whatever his social or political condition, knows this misery, and he can therefore accept salvation in Christ, as have men in every age and culture. Many Western missionaries have wrongly assumed that these peoples could not become

---

[13] Davis, *op. cit.*, p. 42.

fully Christian until they were educated and living in a so-called Christian culture. Allen argued that the social condition of those being evangelized was of no direct concern to the missionary-evangelist precisely because Christian customs must be the product of their own Christian growth and experience. He sharply challenged the view that in order to make men Christian it was necessary to ameliorate barbarous conditions:

> That is a very serious position to adopt. It subordinates Christ to conditions. Historically it is not true. Men in those conditions have become Christians, and very good Christians too, before the conditions of their life were changed. I suppose it is difficult to imagine any conditions more repugnant to all that we call Christian life than the conditions in which many slaves lived in heathen households in the Roman Empire, subject absolutely to the will of their masters; yet they became Christians and lived Christian lives in those conditions. In the mission field we need to revise our ideas of the meaning of Christian life. A Christian life is a life lived in Christ; it does not depend upon conditions. I mean that the life of a slave-girl, the concubine of a savage heathen, amidst the most cruel and barbarous surroundings, herself the instrument of the most vicious and immoral practices, may be a truly Christian life. Christ transcends all conditions.[14]

He also questioned the use of such phrases as "Christian social conditions" and "Christian civilization" in missionary writing:

> . . . . in truth we do not know what Christian civilization is. It is an ideal towards which Christians strive; it is something infinitely remote from us, and we do not know what it is in its beauty; only we know that it is in Christ and is to be attained in Him by learning of Him. That knowledge cannot be imparted to non-Christians; the only Christian civilization which we can impart directly to others is the civilization of Christian England, western civilization. But that is not Christian civilization. . . . Very often the heathen sees its iniquity more clearly than we do.[15]

However, Allen left open the possibility of Christian social service:

> It would be a totally different matter if Christians, to express their love for men, inaugurated Land Banks, introduced better seed and better agricultural methods than those previously known, established

[14] Roland Allen, *The Spontaneous Expansion of the Church*, London, 1927 (republished, 1959), pp. 111–12.
[15] *Ibid.*, p. 115.

schools for the blind or deaf, or hospitals for the sick, and taught arts and sciences in colleges. Such actions might be compared to the action of the Good Samaritan who, finding a neighbour in need, helped him.[16]

Unfortunately he did not elaborate on this; had he done so it might have altered greatly his conclusions. His way of resolving the dilemma of Christian witness in non-Christian cultures was, to say the least, facile. Can Christians "express their love for men" by teaching them arts and sciences if they have no conception of how educated and scientifically trained young Christians can live their faith in a predominantly nonliterate and nontechnical culture? Are the arts and sciences not part of Western Christian civilization? The random selection of land banks, better seed, etc., confirms the suspicion that Allen did not take seriously the impact of the Gospel on culture, man, and society. While his radical pietist theology exposed the danger of the Church allying itself with a particular culture, he refused to recognize the tremendous intellectual and theological problems confronting Christians as they sought to define their responsibility to the world society that was already overwhelming them. Moreover if Christ is not bound by conditions then he is truly Lord of the world and of the Church. What does that mean precisely in the societies and cultures of Asia and Africa? The missionary could not escape that question by claiming to concentrate on the evangelistic task, because the social and cultural situation conditions and defines that task, and is, moreover, an integral part of it.

Throughout the history of missions there has been this conflict between those who have insisted that the one and only task of the missionary was to preach the Gospel, and those who have held that Christians should be concerned about conditions in society and have consequently stressed the need for medical work, education, and technical assistance. Actually these two groups were never as far apart as they seemed and, as we have seen, even Allen in some measure combined the two views. But while in practice this difference of outlook was often not very real, it has not even yet been entirely resolved in Christian thought. It has resulted in a lag in theological thinking which has caused an unwarranted separation between evangelism and the Christian concern for society. It has meant that missions have often regarded the problems of society as only peripheral to their main

16 *Ibid.*, p. 122.

task and that the developing younger churches were nurtured on a narrow view of evangelism which still today handicaps their Christian witness.[17]

While disagreeing with Allen's reasoning, we must sympathize with his concern to avoid the identification of Christianity with Western civilization, and to ensure that the young churches would have full freedom to work out the meaning of Christianity for their own culture. His argument is often put forward today by those who feel that "the primary task of the Church in Africa and Asia is to plant the Gospel-tree and not to bring its fruits (Western civilization)."[18] But it is not so simple for those who have been reared on Christianity and Western civilization to separate them. Indeed, the worst dangers of a wrong identification are more likely to be avoided by Westerners who recognize that their Christian witness may be influenced by their cultural background than by those who maintain that they can completely divorce the two. In any case, today it is the younger churches who argue that their nations, having accepted Western political and economic patterns, cannot make these work unless they grasp the spiritual and moral foundations on which they rest. In this situation the Western Church has a responsibility to re-examine these foundations. Otherwise, it will be unable to join with the younger churches in a common effort of world social renewal.

III.   The Situation at the Close of the Inter-War Period

These efforts (1920–1939) to arrive at a Christian understanding of social change mark a decisive turning point in missionary history and indeed the beginning of new social thinking in the whole Church. They kept alive the critical function of the Church in relation to the social forces at work in Africa and Asia, especially Western economic forces. They brought to the forefront of the Church's thinking problems which had formerly been the concern of only a few pioneer think-

[17] Cf. the writings of Dr. Donald McGavran, a radical pietist who is seeking to renew the methods of pietism. His latest book, *How Churches Grow* (1960) is an illustration of this. He omits all discussion of the social and political situation in which the younger churches live. He believes that a true Christian witness in society follows inevitably upon individual conversion. He writes: "Discipling the nations in populations large and small is the surest way to social progress. We categorically reject any alleged antagonism between evangelism and social action. The reorganization of a society on Christian lines will be enormously furthered by massive accessions to the Christian Faith." p. 185.
[18] From a note by Dr. Berkhof of Holland to the author.

ers. They pointed to the need for a new understanding of the Church's task in the complex society of Africa and Asia. The social and economic research inaugurated by the I.M.C. in 1930 under Dr. Merle Davis introduced methods of study and analysis which were new to missions, and the results of which have endured to this day.

That this new approach did not have the impact hoped for has been acknowledged by missionary historians.[19] One reason is surely that it was too much in advance of the mass of Christian opinion in its emphasis on the tasks of the Church in relation to economic and social change. Another is that a much longer period would have been necessary for such pioneer study and research to make its impact on the policy and strategy of old, established mission bodies. Just as the churches in the West were slow to apply their new insights on the functions of the Church in society, so missions and younger churches in Africa and Asia came only gradually to understand the meaning of this new discovery for their work. The social research undertaken could hardly have been expected to compensate quickly for the lack of concern for social problems indicated in the report of the Commission for the Laymen's Foreign Missions Inquiry (1932), which after surveying the work of missions in China, India, Burma, and Japan, reported:[20]

> It is disappointing that with great industrial problems in the Orient confronting the missions with their challenge and opportunity, there is hardly a social worker to be found in the whole roster of missionaries trained to deal scientifically and intelligently with human beings trying to adjust themselves to a new factory environment. (p. 244).
>
> The social emphasis in the mission programme has been conspicuously absent aside from a few well directed social centers. (p. 269).

[19] "Oldham's considerable studies on Christian education in the twenties seemed to have had relatively slight effect on missionary planning and thinking. The same was true of Kenyon L. Butterfield's work which underscored the great need for Christian missions to take into account the predominant rural population of the world. Much of J. Merle Davis's extensive research, while fortunately in permanent form, appeared to have counted for little in policy guidance for missionary societies." R. Hogg, *Ecumenical Foundations*, p. 268.

[20] *Rethinking Missions, A Laymen's Inquiry After One Hundred Years.* Harper's, New York, 1932. The Commission, however, recognized that the problems of industrialism in Asia were new and complex: "The problems arising out of the development of industry are so new and intricate that there is great difficulty in developing a technique to deal with them. It is discouraging but not surprising that missionaries with a few notable exceptions remain startlingly insensitive to the social needs around them." p. 245.

Nor was what had been done during these years followed up after the war. In 1946, the I.M.C.'s study of economic and industrial problems, started in 1930, was discontinued. Individual mission societies had conducted or sponsored little social research of their own. Yet everywhere they were far behind the need in their thinking about social conditions, and a sustained effort over many years would have been required to overcome their great handicap.

We may accept the evaluation of a contemporary Christian missionary leader who said near the end of this period that the Christian message and duty in relation to the social order remained "one of the major unsolved questions of our time."[21] He believed that the reason for this was not only the lack of a theological consensus, but also the fact that the churches and missions had not yet discovered their possibilities for service and action in great areas of life. For example:

> In the great mining and factory areas it is not easy to point to outstanding efforts on the part of Christian bodies. There are notable pieces of work, such as settlements and "neighborhood houses," in Bombay and Cawnpower, in Osaka and Shanghai. . . . But even when all this is said, it is still true that in proportion to the size and gravity of the problem too little is done.[22]

On the fundamental theological issue, his judgment reflected both the hope and the uncertainty in Christian thinking at that time: "There ought, it is felt, to be a definite Christian social doctrine and social programme."

Any review of this period, just before the full force of the national revolutions of Africa and Asia burst upon the world, must lead to two conclusions: The churches had seen the growing social crisis in Africa and Asia and the dangers which threatened. But they had only begun to sense the tremendous explosion of social forces which was building up and which has now burst upon us. What Troeltsch said about the situation in the West can be applied also to the Church in its relation to society in the non-Western lands. "All Christian social work was in a problematic condition," at the moment of a great new period of testing for the Church.

[21] William Paton, *Christianity in the Eastern Conflicts*, London, 1937, p. 199.
[22] *Ibid.*, p. 198.

IV. *Christianity and Social Change in the New Missionary Situation*

It is evident that a rethinking of the role of the Church in society in Africa, Asia, and Latin America has again become necessary. Today it is often charged in Africa and Asia that Western churches and missionaries failed to challenge Western domination and were guilty of Western cultural aggression.[23] It is also said that the churches and missions are now behind the times, that they do not understand the new political and social circumstances in which they must work, and that they are a static force in a dynamic society. What exactly is our situation today?

In the past Christianity has been closely linked, even identified, with social change. Sometimes this was conscious and conspicuous; at other times it was unintentional or unexpected. It varied in breadth and depth according to circumstances and the ideas of the missionary and of the people with whom he worked. Most missionaries recognized or assumed some relationship between Christianity and social change. They would probably all have agreed in some measure with the statement of a leading European missionary scholar:

> The missionary is a revolutionary and he has to be so, for to preach and plant Christianity means to make a frontal attack on the beliefs, the customs, the apprehensions of life and the world, and by implication (because tribal religions are primarily social realities) on the social structures and bases of primitive society. The missionary enterprise need not be ashamed of this, because colonial administra-

[23] The report of discussions held during the rapid social change study in the Copperbelt of Northern Rhodesia describes African disillusionment with Western Christianity: "All of the African members stressed the point that in their first encounter with Christianity the Africans had given themselves in full confidence to the servants of the Gospel, whom they saw, often rightly, as real saints. 'The missionaries were for us as Christ,' said one. . . . Then came the years of great disillusionment, when they learned that the Church, caught in the complexities of a changing society, had great inner weaknesses, and lacked the power to offset the forces of the secular world. At the same time they began to feel that the European part of the Church was inclined to make practically unlimited adjustment to the ideologies and interests of the European community as a whole. This impression grew into a certainty when, in 1953, the Church, still led largely by missionaries, did not protest against the formation of the Federation of the Rhodesias and Nyasaland. This theme, with countless variations, was heard in many of our sessions." Van Doorn, *The Churches and Social Change in the Copperbelt of Northern Rhodesia* (mimeographed). World Council of Churches, 1959, p. 15.

tions, planters, merchants, Western penetration, etc. perform a much more severe and destructive attack. Missions, however, imply the well-considered appeal to all peoples to transplant and transfer their life-foundations into a totally different spiritual soil, and so they must be revolutionary.[24]

The same writer added, however, that most Christian workers from the West were "not good revolutionaries but blind ones."[25] They disagreed among themselves about the purpose of their work and about the methods to be used in achieving it. They were often promoting two revolutions: the prophetic revolution of justice and righteousness, of the suffering and victorious Messiah who was the salvation of all men; and the social and cultural revolution of Western values in education, social service, medical care, and welfare. These two revolutions were only partly related, and the second was inadequately expressed in relation to the goals of the first.

The era of Western missionary-sponsored social change is now practically over. This is partly a result of the very success of missions. The conceptions of man and society which they fostered have taken root in Africa and Asia, and are now being propagated, in one form or another, in the new nations. It is also related to the fact that the new demands for change have outstripped Christian programs and policies. Missions, although once identified with social change, today often tend to be looked upon as reactionary forces.

A paradoxical and dangerous situation has therefore developed. The social revolution in Africa and Asia, inspired in such large part by the Christian revelation about man, society, and history, is practically cut off from the Gospel which gave it birth, in part because of the inability of Christian movements to produce the spiritual or intellectual insights needed to nourish a new society. The question is whether the churches in the areas of change recognize their responsibility to provide spiritual leadership for the new social order? And are the Western churches beginning to look for new ways of relating themselves to the dynamic spiritual and social situation in these lands?

[24] H. Kraemer, *The Christian Message to the non-Christian World*, London, 1938, pp. 342–43.
[25] *Ibid.*, p. 343.

Chapter 4

THE SOCIAL MISSION OF THE YOUNGER CHURCH: PROMISE AND PROBLEM

The response of Christians and the churches to rapid social change cannot be put in terms of a blueprint, and it will vary from place to place in its practical expression. . . . [However] At every point, a radical rethinking of the present life, structure and forms of Christian witness is demanded. This must proceed by experiment, as Christians seek the will of their Lord amidst the dilemmas and the opportunities of rapid social change.

—Statement of the Conference on Rapid Social Change. Thessalonica, 1959

The situation of the whole Church today is radically different from that of only ten years ago because of the upsurge of the younger churches. Rapid social change in Africa, Asia, and Latin America has propelled the younger churches forward, has given them the leading role in witnessing to the Gospel in their countries. This is the decisive new fact of our situation and one which is radically altering the way in which churches around the world are approaching the problems of social change in comparison with the period before 1950.[1]

[1] It is of course wrong to attribute the formal independence of many younger churches to recent political and social developments. Many churches in Asia and Africa achieved their independence from Western missions before the present era of social change. Nevertheless the real situation, irrespective of formal independence, is that since 1940 the spiritual independence of Christians has been greatly enhanced by the changing social situation. They have been thrust out into the changing world by themselves.

In the 1930s and '40s Western churches and missions were still providing the main leadership for Christian thinking on social problems in Africa and Asia, and few national church members were expressing themselves on these questions. This was, in most respects, an inevitable, artificial, and wholly unsatisfactory situation. It was inevitable because of the lack of experience of Asians and Africans in thinking about these issues as Christians. It was artificial, especially for the Western missionaries who had somehow to think themselves into the situation and problems of African and Asian peoples. It became increasingly unsatisfactory for these peoples as the tensions grew between their countries and the West from whence the missionaries came. In such a situation, it is understandable that many Western missionaries preferred not to become involved in discussion of political and social issues with colonial governments or with their local Christian colleagues. These conditions tended inevitably to reinforce the attitude that "their proper task was a spiritual one" and that they need not be concerned with the material and social well-being of the people among whom they were working, beyond providing the politically and socially neutral welfare services associated with medicine, education, and agriculture.[2] Western leadership in the Christian Councils often discouraged a real ecumenical encounter and the expression of opinion by the great majority of Christians on the crucial problems facing their countries. There are indications that often missionaries in Africa were grateful when the situation changed and they no longer felt they were "sitting on the lid" of popular opinion in the churches.[3]

[2] A veteran missionary worker lists the factors which have prevented missions from engaging in social action. "Before intervening to protect social, economic and (more especially) political rights of native peoples with whom they are working, missionaries have to consider carefully: (1) whether, given the political and other circumstances of the area concerned, intervention may not do more harm than good to the very people they want to help, or may prejudice the possibility of carrying the Gospel there, not only by their own but by any other Christian missions; (2) whether some person can be spared from his regular missionary work to devote to the task of collecting, verifying and presenting the necessary information, the time and energy essential for making the action effective. . . . If it were not for these complications, and also the conviction on the part of some missionaries that their proper task is a spiritual one and is not concerned with social and material well-being there might have been many more examples of the kind you are seeking." (Letter of January 3, 1956).

[3] The Secretary of the Christian Council of Tanganyika indicates the situation there before the statement on Christian political responsibility issued by the Council in June 1959, following the decision of the British Government to grant independence to the country: "It has been felt for some time that the churches have

The new independence of Christians in Africa and Asia gives them the possibility for a more comprehensive, realistic, and effective response to society than in the past. And although they are often just beginning to organize themselves, there are indications that their churches are moving quickly to strengthen their witness in society.

The situation is perhaps most promising in some parts of Asia where the processes of younger church independence are further advanced than in Africa, and where there is a history of ecumenical thinking about the Christian witness in the new Asian society. Indeed, it is doubtful if the Christian concern for political and social affairs has been anywhere expressed more boldly and vividly than in the series of ecumenical study conferences held by the Asian churches 1949–1959.[4] Here they expressed with remarkable clarity their "common conviction that the Church should be a full participant in the new life of Asia."[5] These statements of Christian concern for society indicate the need for Christian action in regard to the state and political life, economic and social development, land reform, industrialization, trade unions and worker movements, population growth and family planning, the impact of technology on traditional life, and foreign economic aid and technical assistance. Moreover, they recognize that Christian thinking on these problems has only begun, that concern for a changing society has not become real for individual Asian churches, and that there is urgent need to strengthen Christian witness at the local level in relation to particular problems. But groups and individuals within the Asian churches are working hard on these problems and their creativity is having a significant impact on the whole Church.

In Africa the pace is quickening, though many churches have just begun to discover that the problems of rapid social change are their problems. At the same time they are uncovering resources of ideas and leadership which have not previously been tapped. Like the churches of Asia, those of Africa have discovered that in this encounter with

---

never made any statement on such an issue, and this silence had resulted in no small amount of misgiving and doubt on the part of the majority of nationals who are members of the churches. We have been repeatedly asked, for example, 'which side are you missionaries on' in the whole matter of political freedom and independence?" (Letter of November 12, 1959).

[4] Bangkok (1949), Lucknow (1953), Siantar (1957), Manila (1958), Kuala Lumpur (1959).

[5] *The Witness of the Churches Amidst Social Change in East Asia.* Report of the First Assembly of the East Asia Christian Conference, Kuala Lumpur, 1959.

society they need each other, and the first All-Africa Church Conference held in 1958 helped to focus attention on the need for common thinking about their ecumenical responsibility in society.

In the Middle East and in Latin America also, the churches are beginning to give more attention to the problems of changing society.[6]

All this is promising for the future. It is clear that in the next five to ten years there will be great changes in the churches' thinking and structure which should enable them to respond more effectively to new social conditions. From this standpoint we may speak confidently of a new vital ethical creativity in the younger church. In later pages we shall refer to the content of the new social thinking and point to the specific ethical contributions of the younger churches in this time of change.

There are also, however, in these churches, "inhibitors" to a more vigorous witness, which if they do not prevent, at least seriously impede, its expression. There are certain theological, institutional, and structural factors which work against spiritual and ethical renewal and which gravely hamper the Church's powers of imaginative and creative action.

I. Theological Conservatism

The most serious obstacle for the Church in meeting the challenge of social change is theological conservatism. It is not unusual for a younger church today to be confronted with a whole range of baffling social problems involving grave spiritual issues for its people, and to find itself theologically frustrated in interpreting that challenge because it is operating on the basis of theological ideas which express not the power of the Gospel in a changing world but primarily the ethos of another era or another culture. The chief need of these churches is often new insights into the meaning of the Gospel for the spiritual and moral problems of the world they know. The changing situation reveals that the old theological ethical formulations are inadequate at three points.

[6] See *The Church in Changing Africa*, Report of the All-Africa Church Conference, Nigeria, January 1958, I.M.C. (106 pp.). Also see the Report of the First Latin American Evangelical Consultation on Church and Society held in Lima, Peru, July 1961.

(1) THEY DO NOT PROVIDE THE THEOLOGICAL BASIS FOR AN ETHICAL
ANALYSIS AND CRITICISM OF SOCIAL PROBLEMS.

The Church must be concerned about rapid social change because
the Gospel is for the world, including the world of changing human
affairs. Yet very often in the past, and certainly today in the areas of
rapid social change, Christians have become involved in social questions and movements without a theological and biblical understanding
of their responsibility in society. Christians and churches suddenly find
themselves confronted with enormous social issues which they only
vaguely realize are their concern. Unexpectedly, almost unintention-
ally, they develop their Christian social action. They do not start from
explicit theological assumptions; they are not led into a concern for
society by a theology which will guide them in their exploration of the
theological-ethical dimension of human relations in a dynamic economic and political situation. On the contrary, in most cases they hit
upon it by chance. Theology is not for them an illumination of their
social situation; they become involved, and they struggle to see what
their confessional tradition has to say about their problem. Very frequently they find that, as presented to them, it has very little to say,
and they are torn between the impulse to re-examine that tradition or
to question their involvement. Increasingly they find that the Christian
understanding they have received is outdated by new theological insights. This drag of a theological tradition which is underdeveloped
in relation to the life of man in society is clearly one of the major
obstacles to the ethical creativity of the younger church today.[7] More
than anything else it explains why, in this time of immense social
upheaval, the Church is so often silent or uncertain about the fundamental task of the Christian in society. Before there can be any real
breakthrough for many churches in relation to the problems of rapid
social change, the theological basis on which the Church has to build
its ethical witness and action must be clarified. In a few places today

[7] A letter from a National Council of Churches staff member in Southeast
Asia, in June 1960, illustrates the point: "Our churches are in different stages of
awareness of their responsibility for social questions; while one or two churches
have been alive to it these last four years, one church has for the first time taken
up this subject at its synod-meeting last month."

Many reports call attention to this problem and to the need for a new theological
approach to the Christian life and mission in relation to the nation, the economic
order, and the community. See also "Social Change in an Asian Community,"
Project Paper No. 17, Department on Church and Society, WCC., Geneva,
1956. Also Emilio Castro, "Die Theologische Lage in Latein-Amerika und die
Theologie Karl Barths" in *Festschrift zum 70 Geburtstag von Karl Barth* (1956).

in the younger church there is a serious probing of theological issues underlying the Christian concern for life in a changing society which is the sign of the real Christian encounter with the world. But progress is slow.

Why is it that today rapid social change is forcing the Church to renew its thinking about society, whereas in an earlier day it was the Church which led society in these lands to break away from traditional conceptions of life? What was the Church's conception of social renewal in the early days of missions and what should be our conception of renewal in relation to the modern situation of rapid social change? In what sense is rapid social change a secular movement and what is the theological significance of this secular critique of the Church's attitude on social issues? These are examples of the theological questions which must be given attention if the Church is to discover its true witness in relation to rapid social change.

(2)   THE OLD THEOLOGICAL FORMULATIONS DO NOT HELP CHURCHES AND INDIVIDUAL CHRISTIANS TO EVALUATE THE CUSTOMARY FORMS OF COMMUNITY LIFE AND TRADITIONAL CULTURAL VALUES.

Rapid social change is both strengthening and weakening traditional African and Asian cultures. In the new nations traditional cultural patterns have acquired a new status, and to many people who know no others they appear as the natural basis for the reconstruction of society. However, most of these new nations are working toward a secular state which combines a great variety of cultural values old and new, and in which domination by traditional ideas is opposed. How do the traditional cultures adapt themselves to the new situation produced by social change? And what is the attitude of the Church to this reformulation of traditional patterns of society?

In an earlier day the Church had answers to many of these questions. But very often these are no longer helpful or convincing for Christians in the new society of Africa and Asia, who see more clearly than before their Western bias and the degree to which they were based on the Western "Christian" interpretation of the situation of these lands. Today the Church is forced to re-examine practically all its old ideas about the interpretation of the Christian message in a non-Christian world. For example, Christian studies of marriage and the family, and of other social institutions, conducted before the era of rapid social change, and usually by Westerners, have to be looked at again in light of the question, "What do Asians and Africans say about these conclusions?" That query is a challenge to all formulations of Christian responsibility, old and new, and demands a new conversation between the Western churches and those of Africa and Asia about their relation to their cultures.

Until there has been considerably more thinking on these questions, the Church will not be equipped to meet one of the basic challenges of rapid social change. Here is a topic of great importance for the younger church, both theologically and sociologically, and yet it has hardly begun to receive the necessary attention.

(3) THE OLD THEOLOGICAL FORMULATIONS ARE INADEQUATE BECAUSE THEY DO NOT PROVIDE A THEOLOGICAL-ETHICAL BASIS FOR RELATING THE SCIENTIFIC STUDY OF SOCIAL INSTITUTIONS TO THE DEVELOPMENT OF CHRISTIAN SOCIAL POLICY.

Rapid social change is forcing many churches to engage in the study of social problems, and also the study of the Church as a social institution. In this they have to work with universities, trade unions, governments, and many other professional and social groups, and theologians and social scientists are brought together in these countries, often for the first time. This confrontation raises many questions, especially in situations where secular humanism has a very powerful appeal and where scientific sociological study has come to mean free analysis and emancipation from religious obscurantism. These are crucial questions for the Church everywhere, but they are raised most urgently in the younger churches as they formulate their ideas on social questions and develop programs of action.[8] The lack of thinking on this problem, on the part of both theologians and sociologists, is a great handicap.[9]

At the moment in Asia there are only one or two centers for the systematic study of the theological-ethical issues of social change. Others are being planned, but there is great need for similar programs in Africa and Latin America. Such a combination of theological and social study must be regarded as vital, permanent work. Old theological issues remain and new ones arise; the churches' task of education

[8] For a helpful discussion of this problem see "Social Science and Christian Judgement" in the Report of the Consultation on *The Urban Community and the Urban Church*: pp. 10–19, published by The National Christian Council of India.

[9] A notable contribution is the essay by D. L. Munby, "The Importance of Technical Competence," in *Essays in Anglican Self-Criticism*, edited by David M. Paton. SCM Press, London, 1958.

and study on these questions must be seen as a long-term enterprise.

II. *The Lack of Christian Leadership for Social Change*

Creative social action by the Church in Africa and Asia depends not only on new theological insights, but very largely also on better leadership, especially in the ministry. There are many indications that the churches in all these countries are failing to keep pace with the needs of their constituencies, especially in the expanding urban and industrial populations. The 1959 International Study Conference on Christian Action in Rapid Social Change reported that one of the critical needs of the Church in Asia and Africa is "for better training of pastors in Christian social ethics related to the real problems of social change, and they for their part have a responsibility to train the laity for their evangelistic and pastoral work in society." While general educational standards are rising and more and more young people are receiving university and technical education, the number of well-trained ordained ministers remains small by comparison, with little prospect for rapid improvement. The problem is particularly acute in Africa, but it is common to all the younger churches.

The ordained pastor in most areas of rapid social change needs help if he is to provide imaginative leadership. Various studies and surveys[10] have described the frustrations of the pastoral ministry in Asia and Africa today: inadequate pay which reduces the quality and even the freedom of the ministry;[11] lack of necessary training to help educated laymen cope with the present situation; the difficulties of work in large parishes, often stretching for miles; the increasing rejection by youth who have opportunities for greater intellectual attainment and

[10] *Survey of the Training of the Ministry in Africa: Part I—East and West Africa*, by Stephen Neill, 1950; *Part II—Angola, Belgian Congo, French West Africa, French Equatorial Africa, Liberia, Mozambique, and Ruanda-Urundi*, by Drs. Bates, Baëta, Michaeli, and Sundkler, 1954; *Part III—Union of South Africa, Southern and Northern Rhodesia, and Nyasaland*, by Drs. Goodall and Nielsen, 1954. International Missionary Council, New York and London.

Also, C. W. Ranson, *The Christian Minister in India, His Vocation and Training*. London, 1946.

[11] *Changing Liberia—A Challenge to the Christian*. Report of the Rapid Social Change Study, 1959. "It is impossible for our ministers to live on the salaries which their congregations pay. . . . It is necessary for [them] to seek outside employment. . . . [this] is most often found in government. It follows that under these circumstances ministers may be reluctant to speak out on some of the more controversial problems which beset us. There is need . . . for a strong and independent ministry. . . ." p. 84.

who disparage the ministry because it is inadequately trained and because they see it as a continuation of the missionary's influence and therefore as still under white domination; the continuing burden of white supremacy in matters of church administration exercised by Western missions; the separation of the clergy from effective contact with the secular world by the isolationist theological tradition in which they have been trained. From many quarters it is reported that the ministry, indigenous and missionary, is particularly unprepared to cope with the spiritual problems of youth in an expanding intellectual society.[12] The I.M.C. report on southern Africa sums this all up:

> . . . he [the African minister] feels that the whole of society, his own Christian community included, is entering into a new situation which he does not understand. He is the leader, but in what direction is he to lead his people? He does not know the issues. He knows all the symptoms, but about the real issues of which they are symptoms, he is not clear.[13]

Social change makes it urgent that pastors have some understanding of the dynamics and structure of social institutions, and to provide this, new approaches to theological education are required. Yet, the institutions for theological education in most areas are still uncertain about the way to proceed. On the one hand, it is suggested that new subjects, especially in the field of social study, should be added to the theological curriculum.[14] On the other hand, it is said that better understanding by ministers of their role in a time of social change is not to be achieved by adding other than theological courses. Favoring this second view, two eminent Western theologians in their report on theological education in southern Africa have written:

> . . . it is not the distinctive task of the theological college to train the minister in economics, social science, psychology or a host of other subjects: the primary task of the college is to train its students in theology.[15]

and they add:

> . . . the fundamental problem (for the theological tutor) is not that

[12] *Survey of the Training of the Ministry in Africa*, Part I, p. 14.

[13] *Ibid.*, Part III, p. 32.

[14] J. Merle Davis, *New Buildings on Old Foundations* (1945). See especially Ch. XII, "The Training of the Builder."

[15] *Survey of the Training of the Ministry in Africa*, Part III, p. 41, 1954 (survey prepared by Dr. Norman Goodall and Dr. Eric Nielsen).

of introducing new and more utilitarian subjects into the curriculum; it is that of quickening in his students (and always renewing for himself) the capacity to understand theologically the real and fateful encounter between Christianity and paganism as this is lived out and fought out at the personal level. The central need is, and always will be, a thorough instruction in Biblical thinking and in the nature of the Christian message itself; but in the course of this, both the theological student and the theological tutor must be deeply engaged in the problems and tensions of the situation to which this Christian message has to be spoken.[16]

This answer appears to beg the question. How precisely is the theological student to be "deeply engaged in the problems and tensions of the situation," if in his training he concentrates solely on theological and biblical study, and is provided with no opportunity for understanding how his theological insights must be applied to society? Can theology illumine social problems when in the churches there is no understanding and no agreement on the substance of those problems? Moreover is it true that the main focus of Christian theology is to understand "the real and fateful encounter between Christianity and paganism as this is lived out and fought out at the *personal level*"? Can there be a serious encounter between the Church and the world when the pastoral and evangelistic task of the Church is defined in exclusively personal terms? It may be that a student Christian leader in India was pointing to the consequences of this approach when he declared that "he learned more real theology in the study and teaching of economics and in the SCM than in the theological college"; certainly he was justified in stating that the feeling is widespread among laymen that their ministers lack knowledge of the world.[17]

Because churches and missions have not yet solved the problem of how to train men for the ministry of the Church in the new day,

[16] *Ibid.*, p. 42. Another authority in this field writes: "It will be a major tragedy if through set, conventional and unimaginative thinking and planning the Church is unready to meet such a challenge (of moral and social upheaval). . . . We are on the threshold of an era in which dramatic change may be expected, and new and unprecedented opportunities may well confront the Church." p. 93. But he too was unwilling to propose significant departures from the theological core curriculum: ". . . in a rapidly changing society some understanding of social ethics may be regarded as almost indispensable; but where institutions have yielded too readily to the demand for the inclusion of new subjects they have often found themselves in difficulties. . . ." Ranson, *The Christian Minister in India*, p. 204.

[17] *Record of Proceedings—Conference on Theological Education in Southeast Asia.* Bangkok, 1956, p. 11.

they are having great difficulty in finding enough ministerial candidates. The 1953 survey of southern Africa reported "the [recruiting] situation seems to be almost desperate."[18] Ranson reported in his survey of theological education in India that inability to secure staff or a sufficient number of students closed a "large number of smaller institutions" in India during World War II and that "almost every institution which has continued its work had to do so with a reduced student body."[19] He did not believe this was due primarily to the dislocations caused by the war, but to the lack of interest among students in theological education because it did not seem relevant to their situation. The social mobility and economic dislocation caused by rapid social change have also undoubtedly increased the difficulty of the Church in securing recruits for the ministry.[20] But the low esteem in which educated youth hold the ministry has been a major factor.[21]

The number of ordained ministers is in general already much smaller than is required for strong leadership in the Church, and assuming that the need will increase in the future, the outlook for the future is bleak. In the years ahead in many areas the deficiency of Christian leadership will seriously cripple the ability of the Church to cope with the ever-mounting problems of social change. The Theological Education Fund for strengthening theological training in Africa, Asia, and Latin America may contribute to a re-evaluation of the content and pattern of theological study and the conception of the min-

[18] *Survey of the Training of the Ministry in Africa*, Part III, p. 33. "Where are the students for training? We met the question everywhere. . . ." p. 33.

[19] Ranson, *op. cit.*, p. 72. The last survey on theological education in China (in 1944) reported a steady decline in graduate theological school enrollment, despite the fact that the number of students in Christian colleges and universities was steadily increasing. This report noted that "the crisis in Christian leadership which confronts the non-Roman Catholic churches in China becomes glaringly evident." C. Stanley Smith, "Theological Education in China." *International Review of Missions*, July 1945, pp. 377–88.

[20] See, for example, Josef Ohrneman, "Belgian Congo: On the Threshold of Change" in *Africa is Here*, Report of the North American Assembly on African Affairs, 1952. (Africa Committee of the Division of Foreign Missions, National Council of the Churches of Christ in America). p. 47.

[21] Bishop Stephen Neill reports: "It may be that some leaders are unaware of the extent to which alienation from the Church, even contempt for it, have advanced at this age-level [adolescence]. It is no uncommon thing to hear it asserted, in my judgment falsely, that missionaries and other leaders in the Church being dependent for their salaries on the government, have lost their independent status in relation to it, are pledged to the maintenance of the *status quo*, and are hostile to the development of African freedom." *Training of the Ministry in Africa*, Part I, I.M.C., 1950.

istry which has prevailed. This is a problem which should concern the whole Church and is much too important to remain solely the responsibility of theologians and pastors. It is difficult to envisage a relevant theological training where there has been no systematic and extensive effort to think through the pattern and the content of the theological education needed to produce ministers trained for the leadership which is expected and required of them in a fast-changing society.[22]

III. Problems of Structure in the Younger Church

The effectiveness of the Church's response to social change is also greatly affected by its structure. This includes all those relations between its members that make up its institutional life, the way those relations are built up, maintained, and regulated. The structure of the Church determines to a large extent whether it will be the living community of God's people or whether it will succumb to clericalism, formalism, and conformity to class or group views. While, unfortunately, there has been little study of the structure of the Church in Africa, Asia, and Latin America in relation to social change, there is evidence of many serious structural problems which greatly hinder its creativity.

The first and only extensive study of younger church structure was undertaken by J. Merle Davis in his pioneering studies for the I.M.C. (1932–1946).[23] He was mainly concerned with the problem of "stabilising the younger churches in their environment."[24] In his view the coming of the Church in Asia, Africa, and Latin America produced not only a spiritual but also a social and economic revolution. The problem for the Church and missions was to find a structure

[22] The most recent literature on the training for the Christian ministry gives little attention to this problem. Prof. Sundkler refers only briefly to the question of training theological students for leadership on social problems in his review of the curriculum of Theological Schools in Africa (*The Christian Ministry in Africa*, Uppsala, 1960, pp. 210–30); and Mr. Yorke Allen, Jr., in his book, *A Seminary Survey*, covering Africa, Asia, and Latin America (New York, 1960), does not raise the question.

[23] His work is summarized in *The Economic Basis of the Church*, Vol. V of the *Madras Series*, I.M.C., New York, 1939.

[24] The subtitle of Davis's *New Buildings on Old Foundations* is "A Handbook on Stabilising the Younger Churches in their Environment." He did not interpret this in a static way. However, from our standpoint today his approach is dated by its assumption that stability in church and society can be achieved.

which, while bearing the marks of a true spiritual and sociological community in Christ, would also relate itself creatively and relevantly to the cultural and social environment, which was still largely non-Christian but which it was seeking to transform. In the view of Davis, churches and missions had, with a few notable exceptions, largely failed to do this. He believed the mission-founded church was too Western and too encumbered with an institutional program which could never be financed from local resources, thus necessitating continued dependence on foreign missionary support. The younger church was a David forced to fight in Saul's heavy armor of Western-style, highly institutionalized structure.[25] The lack of Christian solidarity and of people able to deal with the organizational and financial aspects of a Christian community also hindered the growth of an independent church. Perhaps most important of all was the lack of understanding in the missionary movement as well as in the younger churches of the problems of defining a church structure which would be viable in the economic and social environment in which the Church was seeking to establish itself.

Davis criticized the Church (including Western missions) for indifference to these problems, and while he could not foresee the enormous economic development which would accompany national independence, he was far ahead of his contemporaries in thinking out new approaches for the younger church in the non-Western economic setting. He was not clear regarding the points at which the Church's structure would require the economic life of the community to conform to it and the points at which the Church structure must conform to the economy. He was very confident that the Gospel must inevitably work in the direction of economic change and that the life and structure of the Church should help the new convert to better himself economically, and he stated this in very Western terms:

> Christianity further raises the economic and cultural standards of the people, through contact with the Church mission station, Christian school, college and hospital, the foreign trained native leader and through western literature. The quickening influence of the Gospel of Christ opens the eyes of people living in dirt and squalor to the dignity and cleanliness of the Christian way of life.[26]

Nevertheless he recognized that the economic situation might not al-

[25] *The Economic Basis of the Church*, Vol. 5, *Tambaram Series*, p. 88.
[26] *Ibid.*, p. 111.

ways support the higher standard of living which Christianity sought
to introduce.

> The economy of the African village, which sufficed to support the
> Bantu way of life, breaks down when asked to carry the cost of even
> the simplest amenities introduced by the Church of Christ. If the
> Church disintegrates non-Christian society and places economic bur-
> dens upon it which it is unprepared to carry, it must be ready to
> devise ways and means by which the younger Christian communities
> can meet economic needs. The alternative course is to reduce the
> overhead of the Christian way of life to a point at which the African
> can practise it on the basis of his traditional resources and economy.[27]

In relation to the social environment—the body of customary law,
the moral and religious sanctions, and the framework of social and
human relationships—Davis urged great flexibility in the structure of
the Church.

> The Church of Christ has a three-fold duty with regard to its social
> environment. The first duty is to understand it and its significance
> in the lives of the people. Second, is the necessity of transforming
> the environment by making its institutions and practices conformable
> to the Will of God and a suitable place in which the Christian life
> may be lived. Finally, we must use those forces in the environment
> that are not opposed to God's will as instruments for building His
> Church.[28]

Davis's ideas on how this was to be done were not theologically
developed and the churches he cited as examples of those which had
achieved integration with their environment have today practically as
much difficulty in coping with rapid social change as the others. He
was satisfied that the achievement of self-support would solve the
basic problem of the Church and he did not go deeply into the question of the social witness of the self-supporting church.

It is, however, a testimony to Davis's pioneering insight that the
Church is still wrestling with many of the problems to which he called
attention, and it is disturbing to see what little progress has been made
in finding solutions to them.

(1) THE INSTITUTIONALISM OF THE YOUNGER CHURCH

The Church in Africa, Asia, and Latin America is still in very con-

---

[27] *The Economic Basis of the Church*, p. 114.
[28] *Ibid.*, p. 118.

siderable measure the institutional embodiment of the Western Christian ethos. In many areas it is still tied financially to the West; many Christians are still employed in the service of the Church through funds from abroad, so that the Church gives the impression in many countries of being the last stand of the old colonial relation.[29] This, coupled with the fact that its pattern of life was formed at a time when the Western churches themselves were not very deeply involved in the problems of society, means that its structure often provides little scope for the expression of Christian concern for a changing society. Its Western-style programs of pastoral work, evangelistic witness, and service have too little reference to the developing patterns of society.

Like the older churches of the West, the younger churches are burdened financially and administratively with an institutional program whose meaning for the total Christian witness in the new situation has become increasingly difficult to define.[30] They are frequently pastor-centered churches, making little use of lay leadership for a wider outreach in the community, and in any case the laity has little idea how to make its witness on the vital issues of economic and political life. They lack a theological and sociological conception of the independence of the Church which would help them to break out of the Western forms in which they have been reared and to create something more commensurate with their service and witness as God's people in their own country. This seems to be as true of the younger churches which became independent before World War II as of those which have gained independence more recently.[31] Moreover, it is not simply a question of securing more indigenous leadership and independence, but of breaking the grip of the institutionalism which is the

[29] A recent observer of the Indian church scene writes: "Only within the Church do the vestiges of the old colonial relation remain. Only among missionaries do we find remnants of the old imperial authority. Missions are the last conspicuous reminder of the white man's burden." Grant, *God's People in India*, 1959, p. 82. However, he also says: "It comes as a shock to the visitor to discover that indigenization often seems to be mainly a missionary concern." p. 33.

[30] Today the validity of such traditional Christian services as hospitals and clinics is debated in practically every country in Asia. Often great doubt is expressed about the importance of continuing them.

[31] It is at this point that Merle Davis's definition of an independent church seems particularly inadequate today. The churches which he cited as examples of independent churches often followed a Western pattern. They have had as much difficulty in coping with social change as less "independent" churches. This is not an argument against independence. It points to the need to develop a deeper understanding of the nature of the Church.

universal problem of the Church. What is the responsibility of the Church to the nation and community and what pattern of Church life will best fulfill the calling of the Church in the new urban and rural situation in Africa and Asia? What are the functions of the Church in society and how are they to be institutionally developed at the national, regional, and congregational level? These are all questions for the younger churches (as they are for those in the Western churches) and to answer them faithfully they must break loose from old Western structural patterns and think through the essential ecclesiological issues in the light of their changing situation.

(2) RACIAL AND ETHNIC DIVISION IN THE CHURCH

In many areas of Africa, Asia, and Latin America the racial and ethnic division in society has been incorporated in the structure of the Church, weakening its evangelistic and pastoral work. In parts of Africa there are European churches where the Africans are excluded. In Asia there are churches where caste plays a big role in such issues as choosing church leaders. In Latin America, particularly in the countries of the Andes, the Indians are given a lower status by the *Latino* Christian group. The effect of this racial division on the life of the Church can be clearly seen in parts of Africa. Europeans, in many towns and cities of Central and South Africa, are gathered in churches from which Africans are excluded. The white European and African congregations in many of these cities have never met, and there is deep resentment among Africans against the "white" Church and inevitably against the whole Western missionary apparatus which has tended to be too passive about this situation. This often leads to a demand for "Africanist" churches and greater independence from missions.

"One of my greatest problems," said a young African pastor in the Copperbelt, "is that Africans outside our church say that I am only a front for the white people operating through the European missionary. They say that I am an informer, telling the white missionaries what Africans think, and in turn the white missionaries are reporting to government officers on African opinion. This is hard to refute unless I keep my distance from the missionaries. It is well known that many European Christians and some missionaries on the Copperbelt are opposed to more freedom for the African. There is little trust or understanding among white and African ministers."

The African delegates attending the All-Africa Lutheran Conference (1955) declared:

> It would greatly help the propagation of the Christian faith in Africa if missionaries in their relations with Africans showed a better example of fighting all kinds of discrimination.[32]

Today, as a result of triumphant African nationalism, this problem may be solved by the force of circumstances. Missionaries now have to accept African leadership if they are to have any possibility of working in these countries. Yet it is no credit to the Church that change had to be precipitated in this way, and it may only result in replacing one prejudice for another.[33]

The disastrous effects of continued racial division on the life of the Church are obvious. Instead of standing for reconciliation, fellowship, and a new meaning of community across ethnic lines, it is often associated with racial exclusiveness and separation. It is charged with denying its own witness in its institutional and congregational life. The situation has created suspicion of the Church, particularly in Central Africa: "Have you come to tell us more about the white gods?" cries a young African in Northern Rhodesia. "Don't tell us any more about the white gods. We have our black gods, and they are good enough for us. The white gods are only a means to soften up the African for exploitation." The Church must break away from a racialist structure if it hopes to fulfill its mission in a time when people are seeking to escape from racial exploitation and domination. Generally, however, it is making little study of this problem and it therefore has little knowledge of the situation it faces.[34]

[32] *Marangu, A Record of the All-Africa Lutheran Conference.* Lutheran World Federation, Geneva, 1955.

[33] Prof. Sundkler writes: "A recent visit to South Africa has convinced me of one thing, that relationships between African and Western leaders in the mission churches are more strained than is generally realised by Westerners. This was patent not least in some very influential Churches known to the outside world as staunch centres of liberalism and brotherhood. It is indeed later than we think.

"Let us move to the other extreme of the African continent, West Africa! In one of the oldest autonomous churches, with but very tenuous connexions with one or two 'expatriate' missions, a leading pastor told me he thought that he was regarded as pro-white and that therefore, in his dealings with missionaries, he felt that he had to give the impression of being anti-white." *The Christian Ministry in Africa.* Uppsala, 1960, pp. 184–85.

[34] Dr. Devanandan of India writes: "Because the Church in India could not define its policy in the matter of caste observances within the Church, much less enforce discipline within the life of the local congregation on the score of caste observances, we find ourselves today in the Indian Church, especially in South

(3)   THE GHETTO STRUCTURE OF THE CHURCH

Perhaps the greatest handicap for the creativity of the Church around the world, and not least in Africa, Asia, and Latin America, is the ghetto spirit of the Church and its resulting ghetto structure. In countries where Christians are a small group they frequently develop a minority complex. The Church becomes defensive, withdrawn, preoccupied with preserving what it has gained rather than moving out into the world, which is its true field of witness and service. Fortunately, many younger churches are aware of this problem. The East Asia Christian Conference meeting in Kuala Lumpur in 1959 described this ghetto life of the Church as follows:

> Instead of being concerned with Christ's redeeming mission to the whole community they (the local churches) are preoccupied with the preservation of their own life, as an exclusive community among many communal groups. This may be attributed to such factors as their economic backwardness, the predominantly non-Christian or even hostile environment, the apparent need to defend their own social, economic or political rights, or identification with a particular class or linguistic group. We need to make a study of the extent to which these and other factors tend to reduce the Christian congregation into self-centered or inward-looking communal groups. Whatever be the causes they can be overcome only by a deeper understanding of a renewed committal to the Church's mission both individually and corporately.

The East Asia statement concluded by asking for study of the sociological factors which tend to make the local congregation a self-centered and inward-looking communal group, and requested consideration also of new patterns of the ministry and of congregational life, which might help the Church to break loose from the old limiting conceptions.

At some moments in its history the Church has been, perhaps rightly, a defensive church; hard-pressed by its enemies and persecutors, it drew together in tight formation to withstand attacks upon it. That is not, basically, the situation facing the Church today. In this period of great social reconstruction, people are looking for new forms

India, confronted by various problems. This is largely due to the fact that no serious *study* of the question was undertaken. Today such *study* is urgent. . . ." "Caste, The Christian, and the Nation in India Today." *The Ecumenical Review,* April 1959. pp. 268–69.

of community and new opportunities for their children in education, in health, and economic betterment. In most countries there are still great undiscovered opportunities for the indigenous Church's witness and service in political and social life.

(4) CHRISTIAN UNITY AND SOCIAL CHANGE

An effective Christian response to social change depends also on the possibility of realizing a new measure of unity in the life and structure of the Church. Conversely, rapid social change tests the quality of that Christian unity: is it merely a "churchly unity," i.e., an ecclesiastical, formal unity, or a real and vital unity of people who are prepared to meet, think, and act together regarding the fundamental moral and spiritual problems of the changing world?

In the West the movement for unity grew in large measure from the need for a united Christian approach to the problems of modern industrial society and international affairs, and this resulted in a close connection between the renewal of the Church and the renewal of society.[35] In the "missionary areas" of the world, the movement for unity grew more specifically in relation to the need for common witness to the non-Christian world. Unity was often necessarily limited to unity for evangelism, especially because many "faith" missions did not recognize a Christian witness in society and refused to co-operate except on the basis of evangelism. This has been particularly true in Latin America, the Middle East, and Africa where mission groups which emphasize the "spiritual" concern have generally been in the majority.

These differing ways by which unity has grown have tended sometimes to produce a tension in the younger church between unity for missions and evangelism on the one side and unity for a common witness and action on the other. Is this an inevitable and permanent tension, or is it primarily a phase which will be surmounted as the churches understand better their full responsibility in working for unity?

Only those who insist on an other-worldly and individualistic interpretation of Christ and His Gospel argue that what happens to man in society is of no concern to the Church and these, happily, seem to be a diminishing race. And there is increasing agreement that one of the real tests of unity in the Church is the capacity to speak and act

[35] W. A. Visser 'tHooft, *The Pressure of our Common Calling*, 1959. See Ch. I, "How Does Unity Grow?" p. 16.

together for a responsible society. Today powerful social forces are at work, sweeping away the old narrow conceptions of unity and literally forcing the churches to relate their conception of churchly or evangelistic unity to national and social unity, forcing them to find ways of integrating the Christian concern for the spirit of man and the concern for his bodily and social welfare.

Conclusion

What conclusion can be drawn from this review of the social role of the younger church and the factors which inhibit its action? One thing is certain. Upon the younger churches rests the great responsibility for meeting the challenge of social change. The fulfillment of their responsibility requires a revolution in their life. They will have to "liberate" themselves from inhibiting influences still coming from the Church in the West. They will need to discover new patterns of witness and service relevant to the new situation of their peoples. These are not present in the structural and theological framework in which most of them now work.

These grave problems of leadership and structure make the future of the Church seem very uncertain. In fact, however, insofar as God is working through the process of rapid social change, He has already begun to show His Church what it must do to support His work.

It is amazing how the Church, which in many areas of Africa, Asia, and Latin America seemed unconcerned or passive about the problems of society, has suddenly found new life and vitality. Churches which a few years ago seemed inert and hardly aware of the social change taking place around them, with the coming of the challenge of nationalism and political independence have dramatically exhibited an astonishing new concern. But enthusiasm is no substitute for trained, qualified, and responsible leaders, or a clear conception of goals, and it will take years, and in some instances perhaps many decades, for the effects of the old understanding of the life and mission of the Church to be overcome. In this process the churches of the West can still play an important though not a decisive role, and it is to this that we must turn next.

Chapter 5

NEW TASKS
FOR THE CHURCHES
IN THE WEST

*We have presented to the world our own unsolved
problems. We have drawn all mankind within the con-
tagion of our own unrest. We have broken in ruthlessly
upon the supposed peace of the Orient without having
any peace of our own to offer in its place. We have no
finished results, or at all events, none which are worth
transmitting. . . . We have no unquestioned institutions . . . no settled economic policies . . . no finished
educational systems, no unalterable creeds.*

Edward Caldwell Moore[1]

Christians and churches in the West are deeply involved in the rapid social change of Africa, Asia, and Latin America
because through their missionary enterprise they helped to bring it
about. Having introduced a revolutionary Gospel into most of these
countries, they cannot now stand aside while their fellow Christians
struggle with their new situation. Furthermore, Western churches and
missions were deeply implicated in the social and economic changes
forced upon Africa and Asia in the period of Western domination,
and now they must share in the responsibility for finding solutions
to the tensions which embitter human relations. The nature of the
impact made by the West upon non-Western peoples through tech-

[1] Edward Caldwell Moore was Professor of Christian Morals at Harvard (1902–
1920) and President of the American Board of Commissioners for Foreign Missions (1913). The quotation is from his Dale Lectures at Oxford in 1913, later
published under the title *West and East, The Expansion of Christendom and the
Naturalization of Christianity in the Orient in the 19th Century.*

nical assistance and economic aid raises important ethical issues which the Western churches have a fundamental responsibility to study seriously. In addition to these historical and social factors, their faith compels Western Christians to be concerned about the fate of their fellow human beings. For all these reasons the Church in the West cannot be simply a spectator of rapid social change in Africa, Asia, and Latin America.

In view of their historic and present involvement, what is the specific responsibility of Western Christians and churches today in these countries? There has been relatively little discussion of this question in the Western churches in comparison with the scope of the problem, although there is a growing realization of the need for a radical reexamination of traditional conceptions of this responsibility. The attack on the missionary movement by nationalists in Africa and Asia has been unrelenting and it is forcing the churches in the West to rethink their approach to these countries. Bishop Newbigin has shown very forcibly in his recent analysis of the problem of missions that "the Missionary movement today stands in a critical situation," and that the cause of the present difficulty is not theological but is the profound change in the world situation, which makes so many of the "older ways of stating the missionary obligation . . . untenable."[2] In various ways in different parts of the world, something like the movement of decolonization in political relations has been necessary for the Western Church in its relation to the areas of rapid social change. The revolution of social change requires a revolution in Western Christian thinking about its task in Africa, Asia, and Latin America.

Gone are the days when Western churches could fulfill their whole responsibility to these lands by sending their missionaries; gone too are the days when this missionary was dealing with a static society to which he endeavored to measure out in some orderly way the consequences of faith in Christ for life in that society. As the Western colony has given way to the independent nation, so mission has given way to church, the missionary has given way to the younger church leader, and the missions council is giving way to the national council of churches.

The Western churches must continue to fulfill their responsibilities in the countries of Africa, Asia, and Latin America to a considerable extent through the missionary movement. However, the nature of

[2] Lesslie Newbigin, *One Body, One Gospel, One World*. I.M.C., 1958, pp. 8–9.

their responsibility has changed very greatly, and it is no longer theirs alone, or even primarily theirs.

Today the missionary responsibilities of the Western churches in relation to Asia, Africa, and Latin America involve new tasks in view of rapid social change:

(1) Reconciliation between peoples in the West and those of the new nations. This means helping Western countries to understand the reasons behind the hostility toward the West, and encouraging their people to examine those Western attitudes and policies which have contributed to it. It involves also reconciliation between Christians divided by social and political tensions.

(2) Support for the younger churches in their evangelistic and social witness, and exchange of ideas about the relevance of the Christian faith to changing society.

(3) New efforts to promote the social and human welfare of the peoples of Africa, Asia, and Latin America both directly as Church and indirectly through critical support of national and international assistance programs. The churches of the West must demonstrate their solidarity with the new nations by sharing in their struggles to advance the welfare of their peoples.

This list indicates how radically rapid social change has affected traditional Western conceptions of Christian responsibility in these areas.[3] These responsibilities have changed enormously as the spiritual, social, and political realities have changed. The opportunity for direct missionary service by Christian workers from the West is now increasingly limited, partly because many of the new national governments no longer permit the free entry of Western missionaries and partly because the younger church is now training its own workers to assume this task for which, due to language and other reasons, they are often better fitted. At the same time, the Western churches have a new responsibility to understand the life of the young independent nations and the life of the Church in them, a responsibility which has arisen out of their own missionary enterprise.

How well prepared are the Western churches for the task of reconciliation and the other new responsibilities which rapid social change

[3] It must be emphasized that in drawing up this list, I am speaking only of the *present* responsibilities of the Western churches. It seems to me that reconciliation has to precede Western-sponsored evangelism where the Western peoples are estranged from the peoples of Africa, Asia, and Latin America. There are theological and practical reasons for this. In the future it may be different, as it was in the past.

thrusts upon them? Like the younger churches, they are only beginning to perceive that they must find new patterns and principles of work in Africa, Asia, and Latin America. It is very difficult for most Western Christians to break the habit of thinking of these countries as primarily "mission lands," countries toward which their chief responsibility is to send missionaries. They find it hard to think of nations and churches living independently of the West.

Most Western churches still lack ways of coming to know the younger church. Their main contacts have been through the missionary movement, or perhaps in recent years increasingly through world denominational meetings or the World Council of Churches. These have been very limited and occasional contacts which have not usually provided opportunities for systematic discussion of social issues.[4] The churches of North America as yet know little about the attitude of Christians in Mexico and the Caribbean on social questions. And the Christians of Europe, whose countries were so deeply involved in the colonization of Africa and for whom the present period of rapid decolonization is a tremendous spiritual and political crisis, have as yet found few opportunities to speak together as churches with their brethren in Africa about their common Christian responsibility at this decisive moment in their political and social relations.[5] One of the most urgent tasks for the Western churches today is to discover means of coming into a real encounter with the churches of Asia, Africa, and Latin America, with whom they have so many important problems to consider.

I.   *The Western View of Rapid Social Change and the Problem of Reconciliation*

Rapid social change is in large part a revolt against the West carried on, paradoxically, in the name of such Western values as national freedom, social justice, and economic progress. How are Christians in the West to interpret this revolt spiritually and morally? How is the West to evaluate its own social institutions, culture, and values in the light of this challenge? What underlies "the massive anti-Western complex" of peoples in Africa and Asia and on what basis can a new understand-

[4] The last Lambeth Conference of the Anglican Church did raise some of these questions.

[5] Such meetings as have been held have concentrated largely on theological or evangelistic questions and have discussed social problems only incidentally.

ing be achieved? These questions involve the peoples of the West and those of Africa, Asia, and Latin America in a tense debate about their relations with each other in the modern world.

The Western churches, though deeply concerned about these problems, have not yet contributed significantly to this debate. They have made general statements about the need for good will and understanding, but with a few exceptions they have made little effort to think through the new situation. Many Christians adopt the characteristic Western ambivalent attitude regarding the areas of rapid social change: they waver constantly between a too hopeful optimism and a too despairing pessimism regarding the outcome of the present upheaval. They are thrilled and delighted that the spirit of independence and national self-realization has found expression in Africa, Asia, and Latin America, and they are deeply moved by the great social and human needs of these areas. They are confident that the path to social progress and responsible freedom for the new nations is through industrialization, education, democratic government, and the development of a sense of social responsibility sufficient to overcome the disintegrating forces in the new national communities. At the same time there is a deep pessimism about the ability of these countries to face their problems realistically, and a fear that they will stagnate in resentment toward the West for real and imagined wrongs rather than seize the creative opportunities which the new situation provides.

The Western mood of optimism-pessimism may be outlined as follows: the colonial era is over, decolonization is a fact, and the countries of Africa and Asia are rightly gaining their freedom from Western economic and political domination. However, due to historical circumstances this has all come about too rapidly and the result is social and political turmoil and disruption which favors the forces of irresponsible power. The new nations are forcing their leaders to demand complete political and economic independence, which is practically impossible for any nation today, and at the same time they expect rapid economic development. They lack not only the necessary resources and skills but also the will to work and to save. This, combined with the population explosion, tends to create a near-desperate situation in which the impatient masses will undoubtedly prefer quick authoritarian, rather than slower democratic, solutions. Some in the West believe that political and economic catastrophe might be avoided by pumping in enormous quantities of foreign aid and by other steps to promote rapid economic progress. But, generally speaking, there is slight hope in this remedy, partly because the large amounts of economic aid needed from the West have not yet appeared, and even if forthcoming, there is no guarantee that they would be used effectively, or that the social and moral basis for rapid economic development is present. There is often a feeling in the churches that the dilemma of the areas of rapid social change is basically moral and spiritual and that the present rate of social change is already too great to permit people to develop the new understanding of man in community which is needed.

Whereas in Africa and Asia there is a deep-seated conviction that the West is duty-bound to provide economic aid as a kind of moral compensation for the years of colonialist and capitalist exploitation, throughout the West there is often a tendency to deny the responsibility to give aid as long as this is construed as paying off some moral debt. A well-known American scholar and foreign policy expert and a Christian layman states this view bluntly:

> I must also reject the suggestion that our generation in the West has some sort of a cosmic guilt or obligation vis-a-vis the underdeveloped parts of the world. The fact that certain portions of the globe were developed sooner than others is one for which I, as an American of this day, cannot accept the faintest moral responsibility; nor do I see that it was particularly the fault of my American ancestors. I cannot even see that the phenomenon of colonialism was one which could be regarded as having given rise to any such state of obligation. The establishment of the colonial relationship did not represent a moral action on somebody's part; it represented a natural and inevitable response to certain demands and stimuli of the age. It was simply a stage of history. It generally took place with the agreement and connivance of people at the colonial end as well as in the mother-country. . . . Advantages, injuries and sacrifices were incurred on both sides. Today these things are largely bygones.[6]

He is further convinced that the West will inevitably be misunderstood (through little fault of its own) by the peoples who have lately discovered the advantages of modern technology and economic organization, and is therefore "faced with the task of defending a high standard of living and all the luxuries of a permissive society against the jealousies and resentments of countless millions who are just awakening to an awareness of world affairs and who would witness without pity or regret the disappearance of much that we value." What then is to be done about these feelings of people in Africa and Asia?

[6] George Kennan, *Russia, The Atom and the West*. London, 1958, p. 77.

Very little, I am afraid, over the short term, except to relax to keep our composure, to refuse to be frightened by the Communism alternative, to refrain from doing the things that make matters worse, and to let things come to rest, as in the end they must, on the sense of self-interest of the peoples concerned.[7]

In his book *Die Atombombe und die Zukunft des Menschen,* the philosopher Karl Jaspers expresses a similar opinion from a European perspective. Speaking on help to "underdeveloped" peoples he writes:

> The underdeveloped demand independence, sovereignty, and freedom in disposing of the help given to them. They want no strings attached to it. But they demand it as their right—credit, capital investments, supplies of arms and machinery, help for their hungry. When it is forthcoming, they are not thankful but suspicious of encroachments upon their independence; and if it is not forthcoming, they are indignant—it is a denial of their due, a hostile act.
>
> Of course, the underdeveloped are not all alike; this general description is unfair to each single one of them. But they have this in common: they cannot help themselves in the new technological world they are coming to know; they are familiar with the problems of hunger and overpopulation; they more or less lack the Westerners' working ethics and initiative; and they have neither experience with nor a will to domesticate political Freedom.[8]

Jaspers adds that the Western "helping countries do not present a good picture either" since their help is not disinterested and "if their expectations are not fulfilled they are still ready to try coercion."

Like Kennan he believes that the new nations must be given freedom to decide their own future. "We must wait and see how the non-western peoples develop." The main task for the West is to achieve a large measure of solidarity within itself. Unfortunately, "the western nations seem to be destroying themselves by their indecisiveness and irresponsibility." While many Western Christians would not accept every detail of this argument, a great number would agree that nationalism in Asia and Africa is destroying the basis for social renewal. They fear the success of Marxism in convincing many of the peoples of the non-technical world that they are the exploited proletariat engaged in a great "international class struggle." Often this Western attitude is complicated by a sense of guilt based on the recognition that extreme nationalism and the success of Marxism have been possible

[7] *Ibid.,* p. 116.
[8] Karl Jaspers, *The Future of Mankind,* University of Chicago Press, © 1961.

not only because the first relations between the technical and the non-technical societies were exploitative, but also because the old resentments have been sufficiently perpetuated or aggravated by attitudes of racial superiority to support the Marxist interpretation of the struggle between the West and the non-West.[9]

Until the churches in the West have developed a Christian interpretation of the social revolution in Africa and Asia and the Christian responsibility in it, they will continue to be swayed by the popular mood of doubt or indifference which discourages or paralyzes creative action. The realism of their analysis will depend very much on their willingness to meet and discuss their views together with Christians in Asia and Africa; thus far the discussion of Western responsibility has been very much of a monologue within their own circles rather than an encounter with opinion in Africa and Asia. One of the most promising aspects of the Third Assembly of the World Council of Churches in New Delhi is that it provides a much-needed opportunity for a new meeting of minds between Christian leaders in Asia and Africa and those from the West.

On what lines must they strive to reach an understanding of their common responsibility? Certain points seem to be clear.

(1) The fluctuation in Western thinking between Utopian optimism and gloomy pessimism is contrary to the Christian understanding of man and society. We know the world for what it is, as the scene of great struggles with the principalities and powers, in which the conflict with evil constantly takes new forms. The Christian hope is not for an end to all tension and misery, but that the love of Christ may be shown forth in all possible ways by care for our neighbor.

(2) The standard for determining the responsible society in Asia, Africa, and Latin America can never be a Western standard, not even a "Christian" Western standard. The fundamental meaning of the revolt of these countries is that they are as much a part of the world as is the West and that a primarily Western criterion of social order and justice can no longer guide Christian thinking.

(3) There is a solidarity of interest in the outcome of the present change in Africa and Asia which unites all people. From the Christian standpoint that solidarity rests on the brotherhood which all men have in Christ; it is supported by economic and political developments which are drawing the nations together and which make the welfare

[9] Reinhold Niebuhr, *The Irony of American History*. New York, 1956. See especially Ch. VI, "The International Class Struggle."

and integrity of all these nations matters of world concern. Is it conceivable that the West can follow the advice of Mr. Kennan and assume that after a cooling-off period the peoples of Africa and Asia will come to their senses and agree that in their own interest they must resume their co-operation with the West? This view ignores the radically new political and economic goals of the people in Africa and Asia which will inevitably create a radically new situation also in the West.

(4) Present political and economic conditions in the new nations are very much the result of Western policies. It is a documented historical fact that colonialism, whether in North Africa, Indonesia, Egypt, the Belgian Congo, Angola, Cuba, or elsewhere, involved, in a greater or lesser degree, the spirit of racial superiority and some form of domination and exploitation of weak and helpless people in the interest of the Western countries. In this measure the West bears a moral guilt,[10] even though it is mitigated in many cases by humanitarian attitudes and a real concern for the social and economic development of the countries and peoples. It is in this moral context that the West has to rethink its responsibility for building a new relationship with these peoples.

II. The Western Church and Human Need

The great practical concern of most Western Christians today as they think about the areas of rapid social change is to help meet human need, especially the need for education, employment, medical care, and food. This concern is not new in the Western churches: Western missions pioneered in meeting human needs in all these countries. Today their programs of service have received an increasingly large part of the total missionary budget and programs of interchurch aid are expanding rapidly.

The present Western Christian contribution to programs of social service through missions and other church-related agencies is enor-

[10] As the non-European members of a European study conference on Christian responsibility in Asia and Africa pointed out: "Europe's main concern in the under-developed world in the past has been to provide for her own interests. Some feel it is only right that Europe should continue to use her resources to help these peoples to develop their own economies in their own interest, as in the past they have been developed to serve European interests." *The Specific European Responsibilities in Relation to Africa and Asia.* Report from a European Ecumenical Consultation, World Council of Churches, Odense, Denmark, August 8–11, 1958, p. 5.

mous and not usually appreciated outside the Christian world. It is estimated that in 1958 approximately seventy million dollars was spent by the major Protestant missions of Europe and the U.S.A., in Africa, Asia, and Latin America, for the support of institutions of an educational, medical, or economic welfare nature. A study of the contribution of American missions in Latin America reveals that in 1952, forty percent of the missionary budget was devoted to education, health, and agricultural vocational training and improvement programs, involving 2100 full-time American workers and eight to ten million dollars. This can be compared with 664 U.S. government technical people working in Latin America in 1954 and a government technical assistance contribution of twenty-two million dollars.[11] In practically all areas of rapid social change the contribution of Western Christian missions is the largest private contribution in the field of technical assistance, second only to that of government, and has been sustained over a longer period of time than that of any other agency, private or public.

Today, in addition to their giving through denominational foreign missions, Western churches are providing increasing financial support for such national Christian aid programs as the Department of Interchurch Aid of the British Council of Churches, French CIMADE, the American Church World Service, German Hilfswerk, and similar church-sponsored aid programs in Canada, Holland, Switzerland, the Scandinavian countries, Australia, and New Zealand, all of which are steadily expanding their work in Africa, Asia, and Latin America. This giving supports a wide variety of projects directly and indirectly related to furthering economic and social development in these countries. It is estimated that individually and through their support of the World Council of Churches' Division of Interchurch Aid, the churches spend annually in this way probably another fifty million dollars. In the future this type of ecumenical aid from Western churches to churches in Africa, Asia, and Latin America is likely to become an increasingly important vehicle for Christian support of economic and social development.[12]

[11] James G. Maddox, *Technical Assistance by Religious Agencies in Latin America.* Chicago, 1956, pp. 37–38.

[12] In 1959, in their first offering for the *Brot für die Welt* campaign, the Evangelical Churches of Western Germany raised approximately nineteen million D.M. (four and a half million dollars). In the same year, the British Council of Churches' Department of Interchurch Aid received a record sum for its relief and aid program.

Individual churches and the National Council of Churches have also been strong supporters of governmental economic aid and technical assistance programs for underdeveloped countries. Their support has undoubtedly been one of the chief factors responsible for the maintenance and expansion of such aid and the ensuring that it is given with a minimum of strings attached. In their statements the Western churches have generally made it clear that the use of this aid should be determined by real need for economic and social development and must not be thrust upon any country. It must be "in the interest of helping the recipient help himself and without compromising his political independence or his self-respect." The churches have emphasized the social responsibilities of Western government, business, and industry operating in these areas in avoiding or correcting socially destructive practices. The American churches' support of the large American government aid program was clearly expressed at the Fifth World Order Study Conference convened by the Department of International Affairs of the National Council of Churches of the U.S.A. in November 1958.[13] A report on "Overseas Areas of Rapid Social Change," prepared by a commission of this conference, set forth the argument for increasing economic aid:

We believe that substantially larger sums of money should be made available through the government as well as individual and voluntary groups for economic development in the areas of rapid social change, for the purpose of helping the countries in those areas establish sound economies. We strongly believe that military and economic aid should be separated. At the present time only a minor fraction of so-called foreign aid goes for economic and technical assistance proper. We note with approval the growing recognition of the importance of such assistance on the part of the Federal government and the increased support being given. Yet the problem is of such great dimensions as to call for a much more substantial program. We could increase our support at least four times and still be allocating for this purpose less than one percent of our Gross National Product.

The message of the Conference urged Christians "to undertake themselves, and to exhort their government, to more liberal, imaginative aid."[14]

[13] *Christian Responsibility on a Changing Planet*, Report of the Fifth World Order Study Conference, National Council of Churches, U.S.A., Nov. 18–21, 1958.
[14] *Ibid.*, p. 24.

In Europe the British Council of Churches, the Synod of the Evangelical Church in Germany, the Dutch Ecumenical Council, the Swiss Churches, and the Protestant Federation of France have all urged their governments to increase support of national and international economic aid and technical assistance programs. The Central Committee of the World Council of Churches asked Christians "to make a greater response" in support of national and international economic development programs[15] and this has been followed up by the representations of the Commissions of the Churches on International Affairs to the United Nations and its specialized agencies working in the field of economic aid and technical assistance.

While churches and missions in the West have been actively promoting social change in Africa, Asia, and Latin America through their own expanding programs of social service and through support of government and international action, they are, at the same time, coming to realize that because of rapid social change their former ideas and patterns of Christian service must be revised.

Four questions particularly require attention.

(1) What is the obligation of Christian service (*diakonia*) between churches and between nations and what determines its content and the methods it uses? There is as yet little consensus among the churches on the basic theological and practical criteria which should guide churches in this regard. Many adopt a limited conception of service and demand that it must always be related and subservient to evangelism, while others insist that disinterested service is a self-sufficient way to show forth the love of Christ. Some in the West would require that Christian service be restricted to helping Christians especially where their need is great, while others emphasize the importance of service to anyone in need, including non-Christians. What is the relation between Christian service within the Church and service to those outside it? Service has often been interpreted to mean Christian philanthrophy to meet individual needs without a necessary relationship to the basic problems of justice in society. In former times also Christian service has been rendered on certain conditions, such as participation in an evangelistic program of the Church, though this is less frequent today. Increasingly in many countries of Asia and Africa, and particularly in the Middle East, only "silent" Christian

[15] *Christian Concerns in Economic and Social Development.* Statement of the Central Committee of the World Council of Churches, Nyborg, Denmark, August 1958. *Minutes,* pp. 124–25.

service is possible, with no explicit Christian witness. Is this permissible? Some Western churches confine their service primarily to their own confessional family around the world, while others emphasize the importance of service in unity. What should be the service of the Church itself and what services should be rendered by Christian groups or individuals, and what are the relations between the two? What is the relation of service to the fundamental question of international reconciliation, and how should the motivation and content of service be considered in that light?

(2) Does the content of Western Christian service correspond to the most significant human needs in the areas of rapid social change? The present pattern of Christian service, with its emphasis on schools, clinics, hospitals, and similar social welfare institutions is being subjected to scrutiny in the light of the new needs in these areas. A survey of the technical assistance of U.S. religious agencies in Latin America provides the only scientific evaluation of Christian technical assistance and service programs made in recent years.[16] It indicates that the Western churches and missions need to revise very substantially their conception of the nature of the service they render in these areas:

(a) in relation to mission schools (because of the new activity of government in stimulating education): "Most of the missionary schools are . . . . no longer in the forefront of educational developments. They are conforming to existing practices and procedures. . . . To recapture positions of leadership . . . . they must branch off from the traditional and develop new types of schools and new courses in their existing schools.

. . . . In particular, it appears that the religious agencies have not made the most of their opportunity to establish schools that constructively serve the children of lower-class families. . . . [the need is for] the teaching of vocational skills and for citizenship training in nearly all Latin American countries." (p. 104).

(b) in health: "There is . . . . a sound basis for continuing the mission institutions. At the same time, it should be recognized that few of the medical missionaries are pioneering new methods and techniques. They are practicing about the same kind of medicine as the better-trained national doctors, but with a little more emphasis on reaching poor people. . . . In practi-

---

[16] Maddox, *Technical Assistance by Religious Agencies in Latin America.*

cally all countries the major work of the medical missionaries is in curative medicine, whereas the great challenge is in the field of preventive medicine." (p. 106).

(c) in agriculture: "There is . . . . a real need for the religious agencies critically to review their programs with a view to bringing them up to date to meet conditions that have changed significantly since original patterns were established." (p. 109).

This evaluation confirms much that the Western churches and missions have themselves learned and points to the urgent need for rethinking the nature of great segments of their work. Evaluations of Christian missionary service in Asia are now being made, revealing that there also the pattern of Western-sponsored institutional Christian service is in question.[17] New forms of service are required to meet the new social problems caused by rapid industrial development. The consultation stresses hostels for urban youth, and family welfare centers.

(3) What is the relation of Christian welfare programs to the work of governments and international agencies in social welfare and development? The new role of national governments of Africa and Asia in providing for education, health, and social welfare work is a basic challenge to the traditional pattern of service of Western churches and missions. Most of their contacts with non-Christian populations have come through their schools and hospitals. The demand of the Church to continue its institutional services is weakened by the fact that in most situations the governments are paying a large part of the costs of Christian medical and educational institutions. The recent Asian consultation on service declares: "The Church can no longer think of service or of pioneering actively as something entirely divorced from state activity, and must be continually aware of the meaning and importance of political action, of the dangers inherent in it, of the advantages that can accrue, if it is properly directed."[18]

The attitude of governmental agencies on many ethical issues of education or birth control raises new difficulties for the Church.[19]

[17] See the Report of the Consultation on *New Forms of Christian Service and Participation* (for Burma, Ceylon, India, and Pakistan), Oct. 1960, published by the Committees on Interchurch Aid and Church and Society of the East Asia Christian Conference. "Christian institutions brought into being to meet a specific need, have not been flexible enough to keep pace with changing circumstances." p. 5.

[18] *Ibid.*, p. 6.

[19] "In all countries voluntary agencies have, as a result of this planning, come

Many Western missions have not yet developed principles to guide their workers in the new circumstances.

(4) What is the relation between unity and service? It is evident that often the new forms of Christian service needed in the communities of Africa and Asia can and should be provided through a common effort by Western Christians. However, most of the institutional service provided by missions is still on a denominational basis.

Service in unity is not only a question of co-operation between the churches in the West. It also requires new patterns of co-operation between the "older" and "younger" churches; and Christians in the West do not usually realize how suspect is their aid. Many younger Christians of Africa and Asia feel that aid from the Western Church is like aid from Western governments: a means to keep them under control, to influence the work of their church, and generally to increase their dependence upon Western Christians. Is it desirable to establish a high-cost institution to perform a Christian service if this means increased economic dependence upon the Western Church? Is Christian aid from the West really helping to build the local church or is it creating a class of people who obtain power through their economic connection with the West? These questions are now being discussed more openly than before in many churches in Africa and Asia.[20] Western Christians will have to give careful thought to the reactions of younger churches if they are to avoid creating new misunderstanding while acting from the best of intentions.

---

under much stricter government control. Many aspects of Christian institutions, such as the right to teach the Bible and to appoint staff, rights which are considered basic to the nature and value of these institutions, are being denied or threatened." *Ibid.*, p. 4.

[20] See, for example, the outspoken article by M. A. Z. Rolston, "The Present Conditions of U.P. Christians," *Religion and Society*, Vol. II, No. 4, 1959, pp. 40–44. The Asian Consultation on service points out that often Christian welfare institutions "have come to take so important a place in the life of the Christian comunity, that they have been used as crutches for the morale of that community, so that when circumstances or legislation removed the crutches, . . . morale was grievously weakened." *Op. cit.*, p. 5.

Part II

CHRISTIANS AND CHANGING POLITICAL LIFE

Chapter 6

THE CHRISTIAN RESPONSIBILITY FOR CHANGING POLITICAL LIFE

The movement for political independence leading to the formation of new national governments is undoubtedly the most difficult and decisive form of rapid social change for the churches. Change, particularly in Asia and Africa, means, first of all, radical political change, because the primary task confronting all the countries of these continents is the achievement of national independence followed by the building up of the political structures of a new nation-state. Moreover, as the new national governments are expected to take a large measure of responsibility for social and economic development, progress in these fields is dependent upon political unity. (It may be equally true that political order and unity often depend upon the prospects of social advance, but in most of these areas political strength and independence are the conditions. *sine qua non* for economic and social progress.) How do the churches interpret the Christian responsibility in this dynamic political situation, and what are they actually contributing to the understanding and the action necessary for a new national political order?

The response of the churches to the political struggles in Africa, Asia, and Latin America has been one of the least satisfactory aspects of the whole Christian encounter with social change. Generally speaking, missions and churches have avoided involvement in political questions; and they have generally urged their members to stay out of politics, maintaining that it is not the concern of the Church. Paradoxically, they are at the same time deeply implicated in the political situation and have been prime movers in the development of the modern nationalist movements of Africa and Asia. Christian missions provided the stimulus for movements of political change based on the ideas of progress, social justice, and freedom. Missions and churches often contributed to national development by reviving the indigenous culture and history and by helping to redeem them as a basis for national unity. Many nationalist writers comment on the fundamental contribution of missions to the spiritual, cultural, and intellectual awakening which was the starting point of contemporary movements for national liberation and development.[1]

It is a paradox that missions and churches have made their contribution to political development most often in spite of a theological outlook which considered the discussion of political affairs as foreign to the true interests of the churches. This has produced contradictions which have been reflected in their witness. In a recent study a young Christian nationalist in Africa points to the ambiguous role of the Church in relation to African nationalism:

> The Church has been only a blind instrument in the whole process of African nationalism. On the whole, missionaries in Asia and Africa have been accused, not without cause, of standing in the way of emerging nationalism. In the main, they have been staunch supporters of colonial rule so that colonial powers cannot blame the rise of African nationalism on the missionaries as a class. Our survey will, however, show that missionaries, unwittingly, have been equally helpful to the upsurging African nationalism.[2]

This failure to grasp the political consequences of Christian evange-

---

[1] A notable example is the key role of Protestant schools in the development of the Arab national movement. Writing of the influence of the Syrian Protestant College in Beirut and of its Christian students in the middle of the nineteenth century, an Arab historian declares: "When account is taken of its contribution to the diffusion of knowledge, of the impetus it gave to literature and science, and of the achievement of its graduates, it may justly be said that its influence on the Arab revival, at any rate in its earlier stage, was greater than that of any other institution." G. Antonius, *The Arab Awakening*, 1938, p. 43.

[2] Ndabaningi Sithole, *African Nationalism*, p. 51. A distinction needs to be made, however, between the attitudes of missionaries in Asia and Africa. There is a history of discussion of these questions between Asian Christians and missionaries. Throughout the history of missions there has been a struggle to preserve the transcendence of the Gospel in relation to political movements and governments. Unfortunately the manner in which this was stated must have seemed to reveal a Western bias on the part of missionaries in favor of colonialism. See *Missions and Governments*, Report of Commission VII, World Missionary Conference, 1910. Revell, New York, 1910, particularly p. 95.

lism and teaching has had tragic consequences for the "younger" church in these areas. It has produced serious confusion about the real meaning of the Christian faith. Many churches, not recognizing or admitting that they have helped to produce change in political life, have unwittingly disowned their own teaching without being aware of it. Failing to see that nationalism is in part a child of their own moral teaching and witness, the churches have indiscriminately opposed it. At the same time, the best laymen have often been attracted to the nationalist movement because of its genuine ethical and social motivation, and have even become leaders and officeholders in the new national governments. This has been particularly true in Africa, and it is difficult to imagine a more prodigal waste of the talents of the Church than that which results when years of devoted Christian teaching and nurture as represented in the lives of laymen are lost due to its inability or failure to accept responsibility for those of its members in whom it has itself created a sense of responsibility for public life. Moreover the Church has been robbing itself of the wealth of experience and ideas of its own politically active laymen who might help it to think through its attitudes to the vital issues of political life. This has happened before in church history, and indeed it repeats a pattern which is still very common in the Western churches today.

An urgent task before the Church is to help laymen active in political affairs to see their work as a Christian vocation, and to define the responsibility of the Church in politics. For most churches this will require new study of the basis of Christian political concern and the specific issues of national political development. Without it they will indeed be "blind churches." Much of the Church's opposition to certain destructive aspects of nationalism, or to ideological and social movements that seek to gain control of the nationalist movement for their own ends is ineffective because it lacks constructive ideas.

What prevents the Church in Africa, Asia, and Latin America from expressing greater interest in political life and what are the specific issues to which it must give attention if it is to fulfill this responsibility?

I. *Reasons for the Lack of Christian Involvement in Political Life*

The lack of Christian concern for political development is due to a combination of circumstances and attitudes which arise partly out of the situation of rapid change but which also represent particular interpretations of historic Christian views of the world of social and political affairs.

In the first place, the churches have often opposed involvement in politics out of a sincere desire to maintain the purity of the Gospel, to avoid identifying it with a particular political party, and to keep the Church apart from the political tensions and passions which have often divided the community. This emphasis on the transcendence of the Church and on avoiding contamination by the bitter struggles and rivalries of politics has often led to the extreme position that Christians ought to abstain completely from political life unless it conforms to a certain ideal code of behavior. This is particularly true in situations where all political parties are organized on narrow communal lines or according to religious interests; or where, because of corruption in political life, the churches conclude that they can only maintain their integrity by avoiding political temptation, and by urging their members to eschew all involvement in politics.

There are recent examples of this attitude. At the meeting of the General Assembly of the Christian Council of Nigeria in May 1960, a young Christian member of the Nigerian Federal Parliament debated with a group of Nigerian church leaders and missionaries on the Christian attitude to the bribing of voters in election campaigns. They held that it was unthinkable for a Christian to use bribery (i.e., to pay small sums or to offer free drinks and food) to influence voters: better for him to stay out of politics altogether than to stoop to such practices. The Christian politician admitted that bribery was wrong, but he insisted that he and other Christian laymen had a responsibility to take part in politics and to do what they could to improve political life, recognizing that under the circumstances this might mean compromise and perhaps even bribery. He felt that the church leaders did not appreciate the dilemmas facing the laymen. A Nigerian churchman restored perspective to the discussion by recalling that the Church itself had once won converts in Nigeria by offering schooling, food, and clothing to the children. "Was this bribery?" he asked.

The national consultation on "New Patterns of Social Witness of the Church in India," held in Nasrapur in January 1960, also called attention to this "obstacle" to more effective Christian witness in political life, namely,

the tendency among some Christians to suspect the motives and integrity of those who enter politics. This attitude is accompanied by pietism or idealism which condemn politics and is moralistic in that it sees every decision in terms of absolute right and wrong. To counter the resulting loneliness of the Christian politician and to enable Christians to belong freely to a political party despite its shortcomings, it should be clearly understood that participation in political life is also a part of the Church's ministry. To help them in making political decisions, there is need for rediscovering the implication of Christian ethics. A partial solution may be found in small groups of Christians engaged in politics developing their own fellowships and their meeting with other Christians to discuss moral dilemmas inherent in politics.[3]

A second reason for the inadequate witness of the Church on political questions is the conflict between the mission and the national church about the goals of political life. While Western missionaries have sometimes been critical of colonial policies, they have rarely advocated the abolition of colonial power. Relationships between missions and colonialist governments have varied considerably, but circumstances frequently produced close links between them, increasing the tendency for missionaries to be defensive of colonial interests and strengthening their desire to keep "politics out of the Church."[4] Recent interpretations by African and Asian writers demonstrate clearly the many ways in which the association of Christianity and Western rule has alienated thoughtful young Christians particularly. But its worst effect has been to prevent the new churches from playing their proper role in the national political movements, perhaps for fear of offending the colonial power or the mission to which they were often beholden for financial or administrative support. Out of respect for the missionary as well as because of their financial dependence upon him, younger churches often quietly accepted the situation. It was only as they grew in strength and felt the increasing pressure of the nationalist movements that they began to consider a new approach. The oft-expressed conviction that "Christian participation in the national

[3] *Report of Nasrapur Consultation—*Part I, Christian Participation in Political Life. Published in *Religion and Society* (Quarterly bulletin of the Christian Institute for the Study of Religion and Society), Vol. VII, No. 1, 1960, p. 45.

[4] "In the development of the country the Church worked as a partner with Government (and rightly so) but . . . this encouraged the attitude among missionaries that 'the government knows best' and contributed to the failure to teach the Africans the social and political implications in their condition of a following of Christ." *Where Do We Stand—A Christian Viewpoint*, p. 10. Statement approved by the Executive Committee, Christian Council, Northern Rhodesia, 1960.

struggle was not adequate" is due, in part at least, to this conservative political influence of Western missions.

In Africa, where this missionary conservatism was perhaps most pronounced and where the problem was often aggravated by color prejudice, it was an important factor in the formation of a separatist church movement as a religio-political protest against the combination of mission and colonial domination. The study of these independent churches and their contribution to nationalist political thinking in Africa is still very much an unexplored field, but several investigators confirm that in many areas of East Africa they represent a pre-political expression of nationalism: "There is in fact every evidence that African movements toward independence start with independent churches and end in a self-conscious nationalism with its total rejection of European leadership."[5] Another study compares the socio-political protest movement of the independent churches in Central Africa to the struggle of the radical religious sects of Europe and America to speak prophetically to the "establishment" churches.[6] This religious militancy was often introduced by a few "radical" missionaries from sectarian groups or from independent Negro churches in North America.

The third and probably most important reason for the weak Christian response to the political situation in Africa, Asia, and Latin America is the theological argument that political affairs per se are not the proper concern of the Church. It is argued that Christians as such have no obligations in political life because the duty of the Church is not to engage in "politics" but to preach the Gospel. Recently a Christian study leader in India has declared that "to recover the relevance of the Christian message to national life, the churches of India, as

[5] F. B. Welbourn, "The Missionary Culture" in *Essays in Anglican Self-Criticism*, ed. by David Paton. SCM Press, London, 1959, p. 68.

[6] G. Shepperson and T. Price, *Independent African*. Edinburgh, 1958. They describe the social significance of the Independent African Churches in Nyasaland: "Like the separatist churches of the European Reformation, such as the Anabaptists, or of the times of the Industrial Revolution, such as the first Wesleyans, they [the African independent churches] easily and logically became channels through which political, economic, and social grievances could be vented usually, but not always, under a religious guise; and they continually threatened to turn themselves into centres of more militant agitation that might disturb the fabric of British 'law and order.' For all the vagaries of their doctrine and their often pathetic pretentiousness, they represented the first effective stirrings in Nyasaland and Central Africa of a spirit of African independence, not of the old tribal kind of reaction to the white man's way of life but of a new kind of response to European culture along what they considered to be the lines of that culture's main elements as they saw them in their own little localities." p. 241.

churches elsewhere, have had to fight against an other-worldly, individualistic and 'purely spiritual' understanding of Christ and His Gospel which is widely prevalent."

However, as we have already noted, a revolution has taken place in theological thinking, and this viewpoint is much criticized today. Recent events have helped many Christians to see more clearly the essential spiritual and ethical issues inherent in political change. Nevertheless, the theological tradition which rejects this larger conception of Christian responsibility is not dead. Even where it has been substantially challenged, its effects are still felt. And in many situations a positive theological approach has yet to be formulated.

II. The Development of a New Christian Understanding of Political Responsibility

Despite this background of neglect, the historic connection between Christianity, human rights, social justice, nationalism, colonialism, and anticolonialism is forcing Christians in Africa, Asia, and Latin America to ask questions about their responsibility in the present situation. What is the meaning of this coming into existence of the nation and where are we as a people going? What should be the attitude of the Christian community to this new situation and the challenges it presents? What is the right pattern of relation between the Church and the nation? Above all, how can the Church make contact with the dynamic stream of political thought and life where so much is happening that affects the welfare of man?

In less dynamic times and in the framework of a Western theological approach with a narrow view of the evangelistic task, these questions may not have appeared so important. But in the context of revolutionary social and political change, they become questions of the greatest evangelistic and practical urgency which the Church in Africa, Asia, and Latin America cannot avoid. The choice before these new national churches is not whether or not to be involved, but how they can become involved in such a way as to fulfill their mission. They are free from the handicap under which foreign missions have labored in recent years, caught as they often were in the intolerable impasse between loyalty to a Western nation and a genuine desire to help people grow into a truly free and responsible society, as part of their obedience to Christ.

The Christian discussion of these questions is still very much in its

beginning. Nevertheless a new understanding of the Christian concern for political life is emerging. Recent statements of a number of
younger churches[7] reveal a growing conviction that the Christian has
to take responsibility for political life because the whole of society,
including the realm of political affairs and the state, comes under
God's rule, and finds its ultimate *raison d'être* in serving the purposes
which He has willed for it. The task of the Christian citizen is clear.
As the Indian report describes it: "God has ordained our earthly
citizenship so that in exercising it responsibly we may express our
loyalty to His law and witness to His love."[8] And the ecumenical study
conference at Thessalonica defined the political role of the Christian
more specifically as follows:

"The Christian has the duty to remind the state of two fundamental
truths: first, that the state is ordained of God for the welfare of man
and is sustained by God's law; second, that through His creation and
redemption God has made man of supreme worth and dignity, and in
view of this the state has the responsibility to protect freedom, promote justice and maintain order."[9]

This function can in most cases be fulfilled only by loyal and responsible participation in the work of government, though the "nature of that participation depends on the type of the state." Christian
responsibility in political life has actually increased in our time because of the growing influence of the state in the affairs of men and
the danger of the all-powerful state. This is especially true in the areas

[7] The statements referred to in the following pages are:
Dilemmas and Opportunities: Christian Action in Rapid Social Change, Report
of the International Study Conference held in Thessalonica, Greece. W.C.C.,
Geneva, 1959, 104 pp. Hereafter referred to as *Thessalonica Report*.
   The Role of the Christian Church in a Democratic State (The Christian Coun-
cil of Ghana). 1960. 11 pp.
   The Witness of the Churches Amidst Social Change in East Asia (Report of the
First Assembly of the East Asia Christian Conference). 1959. 19 pp.
   New Patterns of Social Witness of the Church in India (Findings of the
Nasrapur Conference in India). Published in *Religion and Society*, Vol. VII,
No. 1, April 1960 (Bangalore).
   Christian Participation in Nation-Building. Edited by P. D. Devanandan and
M. M. Thomas (Published by the National Christian Council of India). 1960.
See especially Part I—Responsible Political Life in India.
   Where Do We Stand—A Christian Viewpoint (Statement approved by the
Executive Committee of the Christian Council of Northern Rhodesia). 1960.
   The Christian Responsibility in a Changing Liberia (United Christian Fellow-
ship). Monrovia, Liberia, 1959.
[8] *Christian Participation in Nation-Building*, p. 48.
[9] *Thessalonica Report*, pp. 41–42.

of rapid social change where "the state is called to function not merely as a guardian of peace and order but as the chief organizer of human welfare and the promoter of the growing sense of national self-hood."[10]

The churches also agree that the Christian involvement in national politics is "a critical involvement and not a total one."[11] Even the most legitimate political movements expressing the most profound urge for political freedom are full of ambiguity. Christians must oppose the idolatries of political life: the worship of the nation and the suppression of cultural or ethnic groups in the cause of absolute national unity. Most current Christian statements agree that there is no political system which will guarantee the maintenance and balance of order, freedom, and justice. Responsible political life is never fully realized but only approximated. Most statements indicate that Christians should strive for democracy in the political order because it expresses the concern for man as a person while recognizing his "condition of sin and the necessities of power-politics."[12] It is based on the rule of law which embodies a realistic understanding of both the positive role of power and its inevitable abuse. However, in contrast with the Western emphasis on the role of the state in preserving freedom, order, and justice, Christians in Africa and Asia stress the idea that democracy must be dynamic: it must be able to bring about the necessary social transformation. In the words of the first Assembly of the East Asia Christian Conference:

> In Asian countries we must stress the positive functions of government in the re-ordering of economic life and the duty of Christians and other citizens to accept the authority of the state and a great measure of state imposed discipline, as a means to social progress.[13]

The churches recognize that political responsibility involves action, and that political action implies participation by Christians in parties and movements made up of people from various religious backgrounds

[10] *Thessalonica Report*, p. 42. Also *The Witness of the Churches Amidst Social Change in East Asia*, p. 7.

[11] *Thessalonica Report*, pp. 58–61.

[12] *Christian Participation in Nation-Building*, p. 46. See also *Role of the Christian Church in a Democratic State* (Ghana), p. 3. The Ghana statement observes that while we cannot give the title "Christian" to every feature of modern Western democracy, "Yet it does seem as though democracy may make possible a satisfactory relationship between Church and State, such as authoritarian forms of government find it hard to achieve."

[13] *The Witness of the Churches Amidst Social Change in East Asia*, p. 7.

and controlled by the interests of the dominant groups in them and not alone by moral purposes. Membership in such movements necessarily involves compromises and moral conflicts for Christians. Yet they should not remain aloof from such parties. The Church should not identify itself with a particular party, though it should oppose parties which favor policies inconsistent with Christian values such as anti-Semitism, totalitarianism, or discrimination on grounds of race or color.[14]

It is further agreed that in areas of rapid social change, especially where there is a multiplicity of religions, Christians should work for the development of a secular state. This is not just a strategy for Christians in a predominantly non-Christian country. It is an application of historic ideas about the separation of Church and State.[15] Secular here means not a state which promotes secularism but one which encourages religion without granting special privileges to any group, and which thus provides the only basis for religious liberty in a religiously pluralistic situation. Christians have an obligation to work for religious freedom including freedom of worship for the individual and religious community; freedom of public witness and propagation of the Gospel; and opportunity for religious institutions to acquire the material means for their existence and for their work.[16] There are no perfect constitutional guarantees of freedom and Christians must be prepared for tension and conflict between the Church and the State. At the same time, as the Christian Council of Ghana has said, "One expects the Church to show sensitiveness, not only, indeed not even most, when her own 'interests' are touched; but whenever there seems special need to come to the support of some who are exploited, or in any way denied the rights that in a developed society are felt to belong to man as man."[17]

Finally, it is agreed that the Church as Church has to do more than in the past to help its members face the ethical issues in political life.

[14] *Thessalonica Report*, pp. 48–50. All the statements cited emphasize the need for the church to avoid identifying itself with a political party, for example: "Emphatically, the Church should not identify itself with any political party, whether with the party in power, or the party in opposition, though it is loyal to the lawfully established government." (Ghana statement, p. 8) See also *Liberia Report, op. cit.*, p. 108. E.A.C.C. statement, p. 8.

[15] *Thessalonica Report*, p. 45.

[16] *Thessalonica Report*, pp. 46–47.

[17] Ghana statement, p. 7.

"The Church in most countries needs to take a new approach to politics."[18]

Only in India and Indonesia have Christians thought carefully about the nature and form of the Church's participation in political life. In India Christians have been strongly opposed to the formation of Christian political parties, but do not believe that this precludes "the Church or the Christian community lending active support to a specific programme of one political party wherever such a programme is understood to be serving the larger interests of the country."[19] However, generally the Church will exert its influence by educating its members in political matters and by helping them to participate actively in the secular democratic parties of the country. Christian citizens need information on national and local issues, they need guidance from the Church in analyzing these issues, and they need the experience of sharing in political discussion among themselves and with other religious and social groups. Only in this way can the Christian community begin to develop insights on politics which it may share with the whole nation.

To make this possible, the Indian study group proposes the establishment of a Christian Institute for Public Affairs. This is linked with the suggestion that an organized body of laymen who are in political life work with theologians and church leaders to help the Church think through problems of legislation and its position on other key political issues. They also suggest the formation of a Civic Organization of Christians to provide a national platform for mobilizing and expressing Christian opinion on important state issues and to help safeguard the fundamental rights of all Indian citizens. Citizenship and public affairs committees would be organized to encourage the study of political questions in the local congregations and to sponsor citizenship courses. They would also urge discussion and co-operation with "non-Christian leaders and groups who are likewise interested in promoting civic consciousness through citizenship education." All this work would be related to National Christian Councils as well as the regional and local Councils of Churches.

This significant new awareness of Christian responsibility in political life shows the direction of present Christian thinking about po-

[18] *Thessalonica Report*, p. 51.
[19] *Christian Participation in Nation-Building*, p. 49.

litical issues.[20] It is, however, relatively easy to set out the general Christian concern for political life; it is another and much more difficult task to define the Christian attitude to specific political problems. This involves the interpretation of contemporary political developments on which there will inevitably be differences of opinion in Christian circles. Two political problems in particular concern—and divide —Christians today: (1) the Christian attitude to the struggle between nationalism and imperialism, and (2) the role of the state in underdeveloped countries.

[20] This chapter was written before the publication of Dr. S. A. Teinonen's helpful monograph on the theology of ecumenical work in international politics entitled *Missio Politica Oecumenica*, published by the Institute for Missiology and Ecumenica, University of Helsinki, Helsinki, Finland, 1961. He writes: "The history of ecumenical conferences shows that in the past hundred years a remarkable development has taken place in the theology of the cooperation of the churches in international politics. . . . In this development the traditional (missionary) idealism has been replaced by a 'biblical realism,' which has caused great changes in anthropology and in the approach to the non-Christian religions." (p. 66). He adds, "Although there was disagreement in the churches and missions about their social and political duties in the 1920's and 1930's it is now commonly understood that in addition to the work of the Church in time and space there is a third dimension of the mission, the introduction of the Gospel to all the spheres of human life. The *missio ecclesiae*, which is a direct result of the *Missio Dei*, also includes therefore, a definite *missio politica*." p. 67.

Chapter 7

THE CHURCH AND
THE CONFLICT OF
NATIONALISM AND
COLONIALISM

*We cannot have a new vision of the Christian mission
in Asia without a Christian interpretation of Asian
nationalism.*

—M. M. Thomas, in his address to the
East Asia Christian Conference, 1959.

The decisive political event of our time is the struggle
between nationalism and Western colonialism. As Professor Pannik-
kar has so forcefully pointed out, we have come to the end of "the
Vasco da Gama era," the four hundred years of Western domination
in Africa and Asia. Great new nations have come into existence since
the end of the Second World War and the political balance of power
has been shifting from the West to the East and South. Populous
new states are clamoring to be heard in the discussion of world affairs,
challenging the predominance of the West. The movement by which
one and a quarter billion people have, since the war, changed their
form of government and by which 800 million of them have achieved
independence for the first time is a great challenge to Christian thinking at many points.

There can be little doubt that the Church has given moral support
to the movement for independence and self-determination for colonial
peoples, particularly during and following the Second World War.
One of the first ecumenical statements on postwar reconstruction
(1943) included this passage:

We believe that the Church is to proclaim that no people can claim the right to rule over another people, and that the dominating purpose of colonial administration must be to prepare colonial peoples for self-government. The Church cannot agree that colonial power be conceived as a "right" and that colonial territories should be treated as "possessions." Since each nation has a specific calling and task in God's plan, the colonial peoples are entitled to develop their national existence and to grow toward self-government. And since the colonial peoples are "brothers" for whom Christ died, since moreover many of their members belong to the Church of Christ, they cannot be conceived as objects of economic or political exploitation or as powers in the political game. The Church is, therefore, obliged to work for their emancipation through education, social advance, and political self-development.

The statement then added a sentence which expresses the relation of Christianity to national development, though this was not elaborated: "It [the Church] considers that Christian missions and the growth of the younger churches provide the true basis for the development of colonial people toward full nationhood and for collaboration on a basis of confidence and equality with the other nations."[1] These sentiments have been reaffirmed in subsequent ecumenical statements.[2]

At the same time the churches have expressed reservations about some of the methods used to gain independence and they have looked with mixed feelings upon certain manifestations of the nationalist movement.

Nationalism in many countries has been a creative force and has enabled people to win and preserve their freedom; but it displays a tendency to become an end in itself. The self-sufficient attitude of nationalism is an obstacle to international co-operation.[3]

[1] *The Church and International Reconstruction,* World Council of Churches, Geneva, 1943, p. 23.

[2] The Second Assembly of the World Council of Churches (1954) declared: "The status of hitherto dependent people has undergone radical change resulting in entirely new relationships between them and the rest of the world. The older types of colonialism and imperialism are surely dying out. . . ." And the statement added: "The legitimate right of the self-determination of peoples must be recognized. Specific assurance of independence or self-government should be given and administering authorities should take reasonable risks in speeding progress toward this goal." *The Evanston Report.* The Second Assembly of the World Council of Churches. Edited by W. A. Visser 'tHooft. Harper, New York, 1955, p. 137.

[3] *Ibid.*

This is as far as the churches have gone in their official statements, and it is now evident that they must begin an intensive examination of the conflict of nationalism and colonialism and the whole problem of responsible political emancipation. Few people foresaw, even as late as 1957, the rapid spread of the nationalist movement, particularly throughout Africa, an area which it was previously supposed would gain self-government much more gradually. Consequently, the Christian approach to this new and more aggressive state of the struggle against colonialism is not clear. There are at least three points of view within the Church which have yet to be reconciled: the antinationalist attitude which still predominates among Christians in the West; the moderate view which favors "constructive" nationalism; and the attitude of radical nationalism common among many young Christian leaders in Africa and Asia.

I.   *Christian Antinationalism*

Many Christians in the West are inclined to see the development of aggressive nationalism in Africa, Asia, and Latin America as a great threat to the world and to the welfare of the new nations themselves. This attitude is based in part on a conviction that such militant nationalism is outdated, anachronistic, and dangerous in our economically and politically interdependent world. Those who hold this view tend to look at the present political developments in Africa, Asia, and Latin America as a tragic recapitulation of the lamentable excesses of Western national history. A report of a European churches' discussion of this question sums up the sense of frustration and impatience felt by many Christians in the West:

> This [African and Asian emphasis on national independence] is happening at a time when European governments are learning to limit their formal and real independence, when they are ready to join integrated political and economic systems, and when people in Europe are realizing that the desire for self-determination can easily turn into nationalist madness.
>
> Europeans often consider it their duty to warn non-Europeans of these dangers they themselves have experienced, and are irritated by what they consider unreasonable outbursts of exaggerated nationalism. . . .
>
> European Christians regret that the newly formed governments of

Asia and Africa often seem to repeat mistakes which Europe made in the past, and that in an age when these mistakes may lead to much more dire consequences than formerly.

However it was argued that one has to be patient in an age of transition and that perhaps the nationalist mania might be explained as symptomatic of an early stage of development.[4]

The antinationalism of Western Christians also reflects their defensive attitude regarding the achievements of imperialism and colonialism. It is argued that nationalists are wildly unrealistic in their hopes and promises and unfair to the real accomplishments of the past. Dr. Max Warren, the Anglican missionary leader, has said that if imperialism is looked at "within the over-ruling Providence of God," it will be seen to have made its contribution by reducing anarchy and enlarging the idea of neighborhood for all those who came under its sway.[5] The implied conclusion is that Christians can only sanction its replacement by a system which is morally superior, and which promises at least to pursue the same principle of political development. He agrees that imperialism did exhibit demonic tendencies but believes that this aspect is usually overemphasized.[6] Many Western Christians accept this argument and therefore do not see nationalism as *ipso facto* representing moral advance: often it means a moral retrogression because it leads to the breakup of the larger political unity which colonialism achieved and also threatens government founded on the rule of law. Consequently, these Christians can support only "constructive" nationalism; for "destructive" nationalism leads to political chaos or totalitarianism, and they feel it would be irresponsible for Christians in the West to give encouragement to any tendencies in this direction. Given the disorder and the chaos which attends practically all nation-building today, this viewpoint inevitably puts a great question mark behind the whole nationalist movement.

[4] *The Specific European Responsibilities in Relation to Africa and Asia*, Report of an Ecumenical Consultation at Odense, Denmark, July 1958.

[5] Max Warren, *Caesar, the Beloved Enemy*. London, 1955, p. 27. He also says, "Imperialism would then appear to have a function as a preparation for God's goodwill for the world. At least, up till today, no other methods have been devised for so successfully keeping the peace and making progress possible."

[6] *Ibid.* Canon Warren recognizes the moral ambiguity inherent in imperialism but he qualifies his statement of that ambiguity as follows: "Because imperialism is an activity of fallen humanity, . . . it must be ambiguous in its character, like man himself. . . . Nevertheless, the Christian affirmation remains that the light has shined. The darkness surrounds but does not overcome the light." pp. 40–41.

There have, of course, been differences between the attitudes toward nationalism of the churches in the U.S.A. and Europe. A statement prepared in 1959 by a large group of American church delegates enthusiastically welcomed the enlarging dimensions of human rights especially in the lands which have won their freedom from colonial control.

> A star of major magnitude has arisen upon the horizon of international affairs within our lifetime—the rising expectations of people in every nation throughout the world for the fulfillment of human rights and fundamental freedom. . . . We, as Christians, welcome this stirring of hope, this noble aspiration in the souls of men.[7]

In contrast to this characteristic American optimism, the statements of European churches emphasize the perils of nationalism at home and abroad.[8] American Christian thinking about nationalism and colonialism has in fact had little impact on European thought because in the European view it reflects traditional American illusions about the possibilities of rapid political independence and because, correspondingly, it too readily ignores the universal problem of American economic imperialism. Although America remains "anticolonialist," the likelihood at present is that the anti-Western nationalism so prevalent in Asia, Africa, the Middle East, and Latin America will have the effect of solidifying Western antinationalism.

Clearly there is much truth in the Western critique of African and Asian nationalism, but it is difficult for Westerners to present this in a convincing way because they seem to be arguing out of self-interest, and also because their views on nationalism reflect the present Western situation which Africans and Asians do not feel is parallel to their own.[9] Christians have not yet grasped the need for that thoroughgoing criticism of their old attitudes and assumptions regarding Africa and Asia which could be the starting point for creative thinking about

[7] *Christian Responsibility on a Changing Planet*. Report of the Fifth World Order Study Conference, U.S.A., p. 46.

[8] *Cf. Christianisme et Nationalismes*. Report by Prof. J. Carbonnier to the National Synod of the Reformed Church of France at Toulouse, 1960.

[9] See Odense statement on *The Specific European Responsibilities in Relation to Africa and Asia:* "The 'nationhood' concept is not a simple echo of European influences, not a mere reaction to European rule, or a belated effort to repeat what Europe did in the past, but much more often a responsible attempt to develop human potentialities in a common effort. African and Asian 'nationalism' very often more nearly resembles the constructive features of the pioneering patriotism by means of which the American continent was developed." p. 6.

the present.[10] The Western churches have not as yet endeavored to examine and interpret the meaning of the world political revolution and the Western involvement in it, and they therefore lack the basis for a new approach to nationalism in Africa, Asia, and Latin America.

II.   Moderate "Constructive" Nationalism

The second position, that of moderate nationalism, attracts many Christians, particularly in Asia. They believe that the first position lacks historical perspective and an understanding of the dynamic spirit of the new situation, not to mention the ambiguous nature of colonialism and imperialism. They are convinced that Christians must see in the succession of nationalism to Western colonial domination evidence of God's continuing concern to establish justice and freedom for all men. They see a necessary historical-dialectical relationship between colonialism and nationalism: imperialism was necessary to establish the basis for nationalism, and nationalism was necessary to check the abuses and perversions of colonialism. Christians therefore must participate in the nationalist movement (whether in the nation-creating phase as in Africa or the nation-building phase as in Asia) because at the present historical moment it provides the only constructive hope for achieving justice, order, and progress. They believe that, contrary to the Western view, nationalism in Africa and Asia is the only way to emancipation for dependent peoples. This is its moral basis.

The theological justification for this view has been presented in an incisive analysis by Mr. M. M. Thomas, a young Indian layman, and one of the leaders of Christian political thinking in India.[11] Like the Western antinationalist, he argues that the Christian can best understand the history of national development in Asia in terms of God's

[10] *Ibid.*, p. 13: "Europeans often hurt the feelings of non-Europeans by a stubborn refusal to question many of their own traditional ideas in the light of the Christian message. They need to realise that, in the new world in which we live, many of these customary values may need revision or at least revaluation. We have in mind some of the topics which came up in our discussions, such as the rights of private property, fair profits, 'legitimate' governments and others of special concern for the relations of Europe and under-developed countries."

[11] Mr. Thomas has written two important articles on this subject: "Indian Nationalism—A Christian Interpretation," *Religion and Society*, June 1959, and "A Christian Interpretation of Nationalism in Asia," an address delivered at the First Assembly of the East Asia Christian Conference, May 1959, and published in the report of the Assembly, "Witnesses Together," edited by U Kyaw Than, Rangoon, 1959, p. 42; also published in *Background Information for Church and Society* (World Council of Churches), No. 24.

providential dealing with His people: the coming of the West was necessary to break up the static social structure and lay the basis for the political unity, personal freedom, and social development of the Asian peoples. Mr. Thomas does not say explicitly that this Western impact was divinely ordained, although he hints at this in drawing the analogy between British control over India and the Roman power under which the early Christians lived, and which St. Paul interpreted as ordained of God, "for your good." Indian nationalists like Gandhi and Nehru adopted a secular liberal interpretation of Providence which enabled them to accept the positive role of the West in bringing dynamic change to a static society and laying the foundation for social progress. However, they also came to see the demonic character of Western imperial domination, the injustice, exploitation, and corruption of Western power which were preventing India from reaping the benefits of its relationship with the West. Accordingly, India's early nationalists concluded that:

> Nationalism in India was necessary to save the creative values the West introduced into India from being destroyed by the corruptions of Western power. While the British power really produced the basis for political unity, democracy and social progress, it could not realise these goals because of the corruption of imperial power. And Indian nationalism and national freedom were necessary for the creative role of Western power to find its fulfilment. Thus Indian nationalism has saved the mission of the West in Asia. Therefore the history of Western connection and Indian nationalism is a continuous act of Divine Providence for the good of India. . . .[12]

Mr. Thomas emphasizes that this secular liberal interpretation of Divine Providence can be accepted by Christians, providing it is corrected by the biblical understanding of the ambivalence in all human change. There are demonic forces at work also in the new nationalist movement, and therefore the providential view of national development can only be accepted on two conditions:

> First, that we do not idolise the national movement as a movement of divine redemption; under God it has a creative vocation in history but it is under the judgement of sin and death even as other tools of divine providence. Second, that we relate the national progress it is called to promote, positively to the ultimate good for man in Christ,

[12] "A Christian Interpretation of Nationalism in Asia," *Background Information*, No. 24, p. 6.

namely love. . . . India's national development is to be kept under judgement in the light of the vocation of promoting ordered development in freedom and justice.[13]

While the Western-stimulated nationalist movement is not an end in itself, it is a means—a better means than the old traditional society —by which people can see the meaning of life and the possibilities of human betterment. Consequently, it is also a means for preparing people to understand the truth of the Gospel. The nationalist movement, on whatever Western ideology it is based, confronts Asian peoples with concepts and values which, even if they do not inevitably lead men to Christ, do raise the fundamental issues of man's existence. Mr. Thomas declares:

> There is one thing common to all Western values and ideologies, they do raise the right questions regarding the nature and destiny of man, world and history, in answering which Jesus Christ cannot be ignored; they therefore sharpen the issue of life in Christian terms and make a choice for or against Jesus Christ inescapable.

Those who accept this moderate nationalist view believe that the political pattern of Western democracy constitutes the main hope for responsible social change in the new nations. But it must be dynamic democracy, ready to embark on radical measures to promote economic and social welfare, measures which will undoubtedly bring the nations of Africa and Asia into conflict with the West. The success of democratic nationalism depends as much, therefore, on the intelligent understanding and co-operation of the West as on the leadership and dedication of the new nations.

III. Radical Christian Nationalism

This second position is criticized by a third view which maintains that nationalism must take a fully revolutionary position against all forms of Western political or economic influence. It is probably a minority view in the Church, and is largely held by youth. The representatives of this group are convinced that, at whatever cost, the new nations must make a decisive break with the West. They must cut all relations with the West which might endanger their newly-won independence. This means the destruction of practically all traditional eco-

13 "Indian Nationalism—A Christian Interpretation," *Religion and Society*, June 1959.

nomic and political ties. Only in this way can the new nations create quickly "the grounds of their being" as independent peoples and new communities. In this view, there is no moral reason why the peoples of Africa and Asia should not embark on this radical course, for they owe nothing to the colonialist and the imperialist West. The fact that colonialism laid the groundwork for nationalism by destroying the traditional patterns of community, making possible a new political unity, must be regarded as a fortuitous event of history. The Western powers acted only in their own interest. God may have willed the end of the old patterns of society, and colonialism may have been His instrument. But today nationalism is His instrument against the outrages of imperialism. In the interest of a new national self-respect in the former colonial areas, Western power and influence must be uprooted and rejected root and branch. This is not a question of resentment, or revenge for past wrongs; it is primarily a question of the freedom they must have to become themselves and to promote rapid economic and social development.

This view is held by some young Christian leaders in Africa and Asia, and it would be unwise and unrealistic for Christians in the West to dismiss it. It provides the dynamism for the militant nationalism prevailing in many countries. It expresses the feelings of youth who are convinced that the only means of overcoming the years of subservience and domination is dedicated, united, sacrificial action for true independence. While this inevitable disruption of the established social order may seem to the Western antinationalist like retrogression, these youth see it as the necessary first step toward ultimate national independence. "It is only by starting in this political arena," writes a young African Christian, "that we can recapture something authentic of ourselves, purge ourselves of those built-in systems, that almost made robots of us, and thus emerge as new personalities. . . . If we fail, we shall have only ourselves to blame, and that is better than to be benevolently 'guided' by colonial masters."[14]

The youth who support this attitude feel that much that passes for national independence in Africa and Asia is a fraud because it has not really shaken off the centuries-old mentality of dependence inculcated by the imperial powers. Because of this, their countries are not morally and spiritually ready to embark on a really determined campaign against all the reprehensible features of the old system. The overthrow

---

[14] Bola Ige, "Africa in the Sixties," *Federation News*, published by the World Student Christian Federation, Geneva. No. 1, January 1961.

of imperialism and colonialism is not accomplished merely by the substitution of self-rule for foreign rule: it must involve the overthrow of a whole way of life, the end of racial subjugation, economic weakness, and international impotence. Nationalism must mean a militant purging and cleansing of the old patterns of living. This is a new day, a day of almost eschatological promise. Political independence must be accompanied by social revolution, if Asia and Africa are truly to rise above their former state. As the writer quoted above remarks, "As long as we do not commit ourselves to do something that will turn us inside out, for good or ill, so long will we be neutralized." It is not surprising that Christian youth adopt this extreme position. Christianity has made them sensitive to the need for social and political renewal; at the same time the Church has generally failed to help them see the relevance of the Gospel to politics. They are frustrated by the conservatism of the Church and by their inability as Christians to participate more energetically in the revolutionary struggle. A Japanese student Christian leader describes the feelings of some Asian Christian students:

> When students realize that in the past it was not the Christians but others who took the major role in overcoming Western colonialism, that often the Christian churches and leaders take an ambiguous and uncertain attitude towards the on-going changes, very often trying to stand outside of this great tide of history, they feel humiliated.[15]

This viewpoint also helps to explain the present generation-tension within the Church on political questions. These youth feel that the Church as constituted is incapable of giving the witness which is required of it in a time of rapid political change. It is bound by the old patterns and attitudes of pro-Western thinking. It is not aware of the political awakening which is unsettling and challenging people. The Church does not see that it, as well as the world, is being tested by the "fires of history," and must be purged of those elements which keep it from expressing its message relevantly and dynamically. It is not aware of the revolutionary spiritual situation to which it is expected to speak. The Church, once a dynamic and revolutionary element in their society, has become a static institution, often even a counter-revolutionary force.

This radical nationalist attitude is a challenge to the moderate posi-

[15] Kentaro Shiozuki, "The Life and Mission of the Church in Asia." *The Student World*, 1959. Vol. LII, No. 3, p. 260.

tion with its emphasis on democratic criteria for measuring political development and its conviction that the development of Africa and Asia must parallel that of the West. The young Christian nationalists are attracted by the example of China in Asia, of Guinea and Ghana in Africa, and Egypt in the Middle East, nations which have shown by their militancy that they can gain a new measure of political parity in their struggles with nations in the West.[16]

IV. *What Should Be the Attitude of the Church?*

How should the Church evaluate these three attitudes? All include important points and their conclusions are not mutually exclusive. The most loyal Christian supporters of the civilizing function of imperialism must admit that a new era has come and that the weaknesses and mistakes of colonialism have helped to bring this about. At the same time even the most enthusiastic nationalist cannot deny that colonialism laid the foundations of the new society which he now seeks to build, and it is the paradox even of extreme nationalism that it has to affirm its unbreakable relation to the West. This is why recent Christian statements on nationalism have tended to favor the second position which recognizes this fundamental interdependence of peoples:

> There is need for the peoples of Africa, Asia and Latin America to remember that in the modern world, no nation does have or can have unlimited sovereignty in political and economic affairs and that national independence should be understood in terms of international inter-dependence.[17]

These three attitudes are also very much alike theologically. All are based on an interpretation of the Christian understanding of providence. All have in common the idea that God was using the forces of colonialism, as He is now using the anticolonialist movements, to establish His rule and to express His will for these peoples. Nevertheless the different conclusions reached raise questions about the efficacy of

[16] The political militancy of Asian and African youth coincides with the pessimism of many European and American Christian youth who feel that the European and American era has come to an end, because of its inability to speak to the new world situation, because of its own inner conflicts and divisions, and because spiritually it seemed to offer nothing to live for beyond increasing affluence. Cf. *"Europe at the End of An Era?" Federation News*, January 1961, No. 1, pp. 137–39.

[17] *Thessalonica Report*, p. 60.

this theological method. What is achieved by interpreting history as the manifestation of the will of God and the working out of His providence, if Christians arrive at such different conclusions as to what this means? Does not this in effect discredit the whole idea of a Christian interpretation of history? It may be that all three interpretations are too moralistic. There is an element of self-justification in most of this analysis, notably in the Western defense of colonialism. However, the Christian nationalists may also find too easily that God and history are on their side. All contain a kind of determinism in which all that happens is good. This hardly does justice to the divine judgment which rests upon all historical processes and which is a surer ground for Christian thinking about the action of God in history. Moreover, the very expressions, "theology of imperialism" and "theology of nationalism," suggest a tendency to absolutize particular political structures.

However, these interpretations of the relationship between colonialism and nationalism do rest upon certain realities which provide the framework within which Christians must act. As with other aspects of rapid social change, the first problem for the Church in defining the Christian duty in relation to the challenge of nationalism is to help people to face these realities. The first and most important is that nationalism has come to stay. No amount of Western neocolonialist concern for what might have been will drive it away. Condemning it will not wipe it out. It cannot be removed by Western political, economic, or military power. The clock cannot be turned back. Even in areas where the nationalist movement is least successful, there is no possibility of reverting to the *status quo ante*. Its staying power in Africa and Asia is due to its moral force—it has come in the name of emancipation and human dignity. For this reason the churches cannot stand apart from the nationalist movement; they must support it positively and responsibly. They must witness to Christ within it, because they have helped to create it, and because it is the only basis upon which a responsible society can be realized in these countries today.

The second fact which the Church must emphasize is that the nationalist upheaval has probably only begun. The colonial era brought revolutionary new conceptions of political and social order to the peoples of Africa and Asia, but the nationalist era will be many times more revolutionary in changing their lives and in recasting the balance of political power in the world. This is so because it is operating from a broader and ethically more profound concern for human welfare. It is "seeking to bring hitherto suppressed peoples into the stream of world history and to provide freedom for men and women to make the choices of human destiny," whereas the *fundamental* interest of colonialism was to increase the wealth and power of a group of relatively small Western countries. This new nationalism will inevitably change the structure and conception of world society from one which is predominantly Western to one in which Asian, African, and Latino peoples will have a very powerful voice. During the last century these countries have felt the impact of the West. In the coming century the situation will be reversed: increasingly, the West will feel their impact.

The third fact is that the political, economic, and social aims of nationalism are very largely Western and Christian in nature. Paradoxically, nationalism means more rapid Westernization than was possible under colonialism. Therefore it may be assumed that its greatest battles will be not with the West, which can have relatively little political impact on the situation, but within its own community. Given the inadequate leadership, experience, and resources, this vast political and social transformation will involve these peoples in great suffering, tension, and conflict. It is at this point that the Church, if it were properly equipped, could render its greatest service, by helping them to discriminate between good and evil in confused social circumstances, and to see meaning for the future in the chaos of the present.

The fourth fact to which the churches must call attention is that nationalism is fundamentally a spiritual revolution and that its success will depend upon the communication to a whole people of a new conception of man and society, which at present is accepted by a relatively small group. This may be accomplished through such media as a political party, the school system, and the co-operative movement. It would take decades for people to accept it voluntarily; in most cases it will probably be a "forced conversion" because there is no time for persuasion and discussion. Here the Church faces its greatest challenge. It well knows the dangers of this crusading situation: fanaticism, indifference to human freedom, opportunism, and the loss of the very sense of social justice which provoked the movement for change. Since the nationalist movement rests upon basically Christian assumptions about man, the most important task of the Church is to use every opportunity to define those assumptions and clarify their meaning. This can only be done by a church which operates positively within the nationalist movement. How far should the churches in Africa and Asia go in co-operating with the semidictatorial methods favored by some of the new regimes? How much national unity is required to cope with tribal and communal conflict, and what limits must be set to national unity in order to encourage the development of political responsibility? The answer to these and a host of other questions must be worked out on the spot by Christians of these countries. They may receive little help from the churches in the West, which have generally forgotten their own revolutionary background and identify themselves with the methods of slow evolutionary change. Christian political theory and principles, developed in the more tranquil Western political atmosphere, will not provide useful guidance in their situation. Western churches will need much more knowledge of the concrete problems facing their fellow Christians in areas of rapid social change, and will be required to do some radically new thinking on their own historic involvement in the struggle between nationalism and colonialism, before they will be able to provide valuable insight on contemporary developments.

V. *Does the Western Church and Its Missionary Movement Mirror the Colonialist Spirit?*

The Church in the West is today under heavy attack by the nationalist movement in many areas for its "complicity" in the evils of the colonial period, and for its continued refusal, in some countries, to recognize the significance of the movement for national independence. Failure to analyze and answer this attack and to define the churches' position in the new situation weakens the younger church and makes suspect the whole overseas evangelistic and missionary program.

Even where the Western Church was not directly associated with the colonial system, the radical changes in political circumstances require it to develop a new approach to questions of nationalism and nation-building. As one Western missionary scholar has said, " 'The end of Western colonialism' is indeed a colossal event that must necessarily have revolutionary consequences for all movements, institutions, interests and agencies which operated in the pre-independence days in these countries and continue to exist today."[18] The Western missionary movement has been and still is the principal link between Christians in the West and those in the countries of rapid social

[18] Hendrik Kraemer, "The Missionary Implications of the End of Western Colonialism and the Collapse of Western Christendom," *History's Lessons for Tomorrow's Mission*, World Student Christian Federation, Geneva, 1960, p. 196.

change. It has been deeply involved in political developments in these countries, even where it insisted on its nonpolitical character and its fundamental concern with evangelism. An Anglican missionary scholar has said of missions in relation to Africa, "There is not the slightest doubt that the great missionaries of the mid-nineteenth century had a profound conviction that colonial empire and Christianity were fully compatible."[19] Indeed, their understanding of this is regarded by objective scholars as evidence of their perspicacity: they saw that Western-sponsored change was inevitable, and they believed that in general it was desirable and for the good of the people. In many situations, moreover, missionary societies and individual Western missions effectively humanized the Western impact and softened colonial administrative harshness.[20] They contributed to the growth of liberating nationalist movements, frequently challenged their government's attitude on political freedom in colonial areas, and opposed giving too much power to a small minority of white colonists.[21] But generally speaking the missionary objective was not to abolish colonialism but to make the system humane and responsible, and many missionaries succumbed to the view that civilizing colonialism was "the white man's burden"; consequently they could not understand or accept the protests of the nationalist movement. Confident that their course was the right one, they only rarely supported full political freedom for colonial areas, if they discussed the question at all.[22]

For this reason the Western missionary movement, particularly in Africa and Asia, is seriously compromised in the eyes of many people. They question whether it has yet understood clearly the moral and spiritual grounds for the new political situation and the challenge to the old Western approach and whether therefore missions can help

[19] J. V. Taylor, *Christianity and Politics in Africa*, Penguin Books, London, 1957, p. 91.

[20] For a very perceptive account of the humanizing role of missions in relation to colonial rule see Dr. A. C. Kruyt, "The Influence of Western Civilisation on the Inhabitants of Poso (Central Celebes)" in *The Effect of Western Influence on Native Civilisations in the Malay Archipelago*, edited by B. Schrieke, Batavia, 1929.

[21] Cf. the Statements of the Church of Scotland and the British Council of Churches warning against disregard of African opinion in the formation of the Federation of Rhodesia and Nyasaland. The Protestant missionary concern for human rights in the former Belgian Congo, Angola, and the Union of South Africa (now the Republic of South Africa) is a glorious, and often tragic, story.

[22] Taylor, *op. cit.*, p. 92. "Missionaries . . . have too often been guilty, not of deliberately perpetuating the old conception, but of failing to give the matter any serious thought at all until it is too late."

the Church in the West to fulfill its responsibility in relation to nationalism and the whole movement for political change. They argue that the missionary movement in its Western form, in spite of the valuable contribution which it has made in the past, has been overwhelmed by change, and that the pattern for expressing the missionary concern developed in the nineteenth century and the early part of this and which reflected certain political attitudes, is clearly not relevant today and must be revised if it is not actually to harm the cause of mission.

This predicament is being discussed within the missionary movement. There are some who insist that it is only slightly affected by the end of the colonialist era, since it was mainly concerned with evangelism and service and had very little to do with the politics of that period. There are others who take the opposite position: that the missionary movement was so fundamentally linked with the system of Western domination that the end of colonialism means in fact the end of the classical missionary system of the West. One who holds this view is Professor Hendrik Kraemer of Holland, the missionary theologian and scholar. He writes: "Now it must be stated with the strongest possible emphasis that *in principle, though far from in fact, this whole* [missionary] *structure collapsed as a result of the second world war and its dramatic consequences. In this sense it is fully true that 'the era of missions has passed'—irrevocably*" (his italics). And a few sentences later he says, "Western colonialism has ended; therefore the missionary era of that period, which reflected the essential attitudes and structures of colonialism, has also ended. This is simply severe historical logic, and moreover it is a blessing in disguise, for churches and missions are thereby summoned to think and act in their own Christian categories and not in 'alien' colonial categories. This is, or at least should be, as evident as the daily rising and setting of the sun."[23] However, he emphasizes that the missionary era has ended only *in principle*, because "what *should be* rarely *is*." We are still searching for the "spiritual strategy and orientation for the new era of 'mission'." In the meantime we suffer from great paralysis and confusion.[24]

[23] Kraemer, *op. cit.*, p. 202. Professor Kraemer does not feel the need to distinguish between North American and European missions; he argues that colonialist domination took many forms and none of the Western churches and missions have escaped entirely the taint of Western association.

[24] Kraemer, *op. cit.*, p. 203.

The great need of the churches in the West today is for an adequate expression in missionary structures of their new political and social relation with the peoples and churches of Africa and Asia. Some have dropped the term "foreign" missions in favor of "ecumenical" missions, and missionaries are now often called fraternal workers, to emphasize the spirit of "partnership" between "older" and "younger" churches in a common missionary task. But these changes, desirable as they are, do not go to the heart of the matter. Many are demanding a searching Christian analysis of nationalism in Africa and Asia and of the traditional approach of Western missions to political questions. Only on this basis will the missionary movement be in a position to help the Church in the West to understand and respond creatively to the dynamic political situation in Africa and Asia.

The problem for the Western churches may be compared to that of many Western governments. Just as rapid political change has made the "colonial office" approach obsolete and required the handing over of its affairs to an office of commonwealth relations or a ministry of foreign affairs, so the Western Church must rethink its relationship with independent young churches and countries. Most Western churches lack even the means to keep their members informed of the social and political developments affecting churches in other parts of the world. These churches refuse to be dealt with any longer as an extension of the home church; their members are Christian neighbors and members of the Church Universal. These countries are no longer a mass of disorganized and helpless individuals; they are nations of people with a new sense of their unity and their possibilities as members of the whole human race.

Obviously such an analysis of the theological and historical factors linking missions and colonialism cannot leave the Western churches themselves untouched. The attitude of the missionary movement to Western political responsibility in Africa and Asia has rested on a conception of a Western Christian civilization. It must be recognized today that the moral authority of this "Christian" West is in decline. The collapse of colonialism is in large part a moral collapse. The political revolt of Africans and Asians helps the West to realize that while it may not be as bad as it is often pictured, it was never as good as it thought itself to be. Its relations with Africans and Asians were corrupted by racial arrogance, by moral hypocrisy and pride, and by the inevitable self-deceptions of too much power. The demythologizing of Western Christendom is far advanced. It is being judged according to its own standards, as interpreted by a new African and Asian "Christendom." In most situations it is a secular "Christendom" which relies for spiritual nurture on Western secular movements which are themselves based on ideals derived more or less directly from the Christian faith. The vocation of Christians in the West is not to deny the legitimacy of this new Christendom and its criticism of the West; on the contrary, they must help to strengthen its spiritual basis, at the same time realizing that Christians in Africa and Asia will, in this measure, perhaps become more, not less, sensitive to the "sins of the West."

The Church in the West can help to complete the "Christianization" of Africa and Asia by concentrating attention on the serious moral difficulties in its own society. Asia and Africa are adopting the political structures and ideologies of the West so fully and so quickly that many of the moral issues which confront Western society are already appearing in these new nations. Above all, the churches of the West must join with those of Asia, Africa, and Latin America in a search for new Christian criteria of political and social justice which will be truly universal and ecumenical, expressing the conviction of the whole "Christian" world. In this way Christians in every land will be strengthened in their struggle with the destructive tendencies of nationalism.

Chapter 8

THE CHURCH AND THE ROLE OF THE STATE IN AREAS OF RAPID SOCIAL CHANGE

Is parliamentary government the best method in all circumstances for preserving those Christian values enshrined in the word "democracy"? And is not the development of more authoritarian systems in certain circumstances a more effective means of safeguarding them? These questions are being asked in East Asian countries today. Democracy, defined as a system of government holding freedom, order, and justice in balance, can be distinguished from democracy as a parliamentary method of controlling government. But when parliamentary methods of control over the power of government are abandoned, the Christian, who knows the danger of the corruption of power, is bound to ask what other methods of checks and balances are available in alternative systems.

—From Report of the First Assembly of the East Asia Christian Conference, 1959.

For many Christians the most disquieting aspect of the new nationalism in Africa, Asia, and Latin America is the dominant role which it gives to the state and the lack of safeguards to protect the individual and the group against the abuses of state power. There is a feeling that the situation is tending toward all-powerful state control in these new nations. In a few countries like India and Malaya there has been real progress toward a viable parliamentary democracy but in many other areas it has broken down or failed to develop. In the areas where basic political institutions are still developing, where voluntary organizations like the university, the church, the trade union and business and professional societies, that ordinarily constitute the foundations of a pluralistic democracy, are very weak and are themselves often state-created and dominated, there are few checks on the power of the state. How is the Church to understand the role of the state in this situation? Have the churches a responsibility to work for the limitation of state power and, if so, how should they fulfill this responsibility?

I.   *The Need for a Strong Nation-State*

Here as in other realms of rapid social change the Church faces a quite new situation for which it has no ready answer. The demands upon the state in these countries are unique, and its role cannot be measured by traditional Christian criteria as defined in the history of the Church elsewhere. In Africa, Asia, and some parts of Latin America, a strong nation-state is practically the only hope of preserving national unity against the powerful social and ethnic forces which are working for disunity. It is clearly the only means of achieving rapid economic and social development. Even growth of democracy depends upon the initiative of the state, since the only way to establish quickly the foundation of popular citizenship is for the state to educate people into an awareness of their political responsibilities and rights in the new society. Conditions require the state to exercise great responsibility for promoting a philosophy of government and also for laying the foundations of many institutions which, according to all the classic rules of democratic government, should be independent of the state and act as a check upon its misuse of power. These countries face a serious dilemma precisely because the state must exercise great power if the hopes of their people for democracy and the transformation of society are to be realized.

There is little in the tradition or history of these countries to help them meet the real dangers inherent in this situation. A strong central government is the only form of rule most of them know from personal experience. Colonialism in most areas was autocratic rule from the top down, highly centralized and paternalistic. Efforts to organize the new nation-state are likely to reflect the methods of the previous colonial period and its principle of a totally responsible government which felt only limited obligations to those it ruled. Westerners have to bear this in mind lest their cries of alarm over the tendency toward authoritarian national government in Africa and Asia lay them open to charges of hypocrisy.

The concept of the limited state and the emphasis on the dialectic of freedom and order familiar to Christians in the West is not immediately relevant in situations of rapid national development. The great majority of the people have little understanding of the essentials of a free voluntary society nor is it of primary importance to them at present. Their main concern is to increase their opportunities for education and remunerative work and their share in the benefits of the fabulous world of science and machine productivity. Lacking the capital, the techniques, the social and economic basis for creating such new opportunities, they inevitably place their hope in a national government which will make all this possible, and hence they are prepared to support national leaders dedicated to that purpose.

The issue, therefore, is not, shall there be a strong central government with great power over economic development, the group and the individual, but rather, assuming that such a government is essential to justice and social progress, is it possible to avoid totalitarian rule? What can organizations like the Church do to help meet this danger without at the same time hindering effective state action? Is it possible for the state to aim simultaneously at all the goals desired by these countries: "national community, economic revolution, and human rights"? If it is "a question of priorities," what criteria shall be used in making choices and how shall the different values be reconciled?

It would be wrong for the Church to take the pessimistic view, common among Christians, especially in the West, that in a situation of great state power there is little chance of achieving a government answerable to the people. It would be equally mistaken to assume that a government responsible to the people will emerge automatically from the kind of political development which seems to be necessary in these regions. The truth is that rapid formation of these countries is practically without parallel in political history and requires the Church to develop a new understanding of its responsibilities in political life and to rethink its ways of working in the situation.

II. *The Meaning of Loyal and Responsible Opposition*

To illustrate the novel features involved in working for responsible state power in this situation we have only to consider the difficulty of achieving freedom for an opposition point of view.

Many observers have pointed out that much of the present insistence on a strong and united state in the new nation is an outgrowth of the emphasis on political unity in the period of the nationalist struggle against colonialism and Western domination and today the leaders in the fight for independence are heroes in the eyes of the majority of the people; opposition to them in any form is still regarded as a form of treason to national independence. In such an atmosphere the spirit of political messianism develops easily. Moreover, the danger of overemphasizing unity is heightened where these nations must continue to struggle to maintain their independence in an international situation of great tension. They are often under strong pressure from the Great Powers to take sides and they need great unity of action if they are to preserve their new independence. Thus their political thinking is colored by fear of internal dissension and aggravated by apprehension that their country will be divided anew by the international power conflicts. It is not too surprising that opposition and criticism of the state is identified with, and often really is tantamount to, insurrection and rebellion.

Moreover, what is the reality of the two-party system in lands where there has been little popular participation in parliamentary politics, where, because of illiteracy, lack of communications, etc., a relatively small group must take responsibility for most of the decisions? Is it possible to have a responsible opposition working within this elite class without creating confusion and disunity among the great mass of the people? By what criteria can the Church decide in such condition when the leaders of the state are serving the interests of the people and by what means can or should they best express their views to the state authorities?

To see the problem more clearly, the complexity of these problems can be seen by examining the situation in one of these countries. The power wielded by Mr. Nasser's government in Egypt and the seemingly contradictory policies followed internally and externally illustrate very well the difficulties of combining national unity, independence, and political freedom in the classic democratic formulation. To maintain its control of the nation, the Egyptian government deemed it necessary to put the active communists, together with the fanatical members of the Muslim Brotherhood (whose terrorism was endangering the basis of all order) into concentration camps in the Egyptian desert. All other organized opposition has been less harshly silenced. At the same time, in order to ensure the independence of the country in relation to the West and to counteract Western influence in the Middle East, it seemed necessary to bargain with the Communist countries of Eastern Europe and with the U.S.S.R. for armaments and economic aid. Furthermore, the Arab League has its headquarters in Cairo, and Egypt proclaims its desire to be the leader of the Muslim world. In such a situation the precise meaning of the Christian concern for freedom and responsible opposition is far from clear.

III.   On What Grounds Can Christians Support the One-Party State?

While recognizing that the conception of a loyal and responsible parliamentary opposition has not yet developed in some countries, can the churches support the tendency in many areas toward a one-party system? Is the only choice before the Church that between active resistance and a kind of passive acceptance of the reality of the powerful one-party state?

One-party control of many new nations in Africa and Asia arises from unusual conditions, and Christians may have to co-operate with one-party rule in certain situations. Although it is full of great dangers, even one-party rule in these circumstances can often claim to incorporate important elements of democracy, and to be in the process of establishing others. Most of these new states depend for their political strength and appeal on the assurance that they are meeting, as can no other available means, the social needs of their people. They have often won power by giving a new status to certain social groups, especially to women, and they are establishing schools and providing work opportunities for youth. They are organizing rural co-operatives in which villagers meet to discuss their needs and problems. Without ignoring the incipient or real totalitarian dangers of the situation, it is possible to accept their contention that they are more democratic than colonial administrations because they are working for their own people.

They do not claim to offer parliamentary rule in the classic sense because in the nature of their situation this cannot yet be realized. They are establishing a popular paternalistic rule by an intellectual elite group which has had the opportunity for education, and for gaining some understanding of Western liberal ideas of what the modern national state can achieve. Their rule is generally popular as long as it satisfies the deep resentment against white domination and meets the vague but nevertheless real desire for change and material welfare.

Indeed, argued in these terms there is very little which the Church can say in criticism of the one-party system because in most countries there is as yet no alternative and very little possibility of creating one very quickly. Insofar as the Church has any influence on the situation, its first responsibility in political life is to support a government whch seems to offer the possibility of effective social change and progress, even though it knows this involves great risks of oppression. The alternative is a government offering more democratic rights but sterile party strife leading to social chaos. The criteria of responsible government in these areas is not the Western democratic pattern but a state which offers the possibility of greater social advance measured by more schools, more opportunities for underprivileged social groups, more jobs, and more provision for public health. It is an unfortunate but unavoidable fact that the choice in many areas is between popular one-party national government based on promise of economic and social advance, and unpopular one-party national government which also rules by force yet represents a narrower social or economic group interest.

IV. *The Deeper Spiritual Problem of the Nation-State*

The one-party control of political life which predominates in so many nations of Africa, Asia, and Latin America and which seems likely to continue for some time, does not mean that Christians have no possibilities for promoting the growth of more responsible government. In these countries which are struggling to build the foundations of free and democratic national life there is great need for education and discussion of the meaning of citizenship, the problem of power, and responsible political life. It is one of the hopeful features that there are a number of opportunities in all these countries for the churches to help the nation by witnessing to the Christian view of political responsibility. This can be done first in the life of the Church itself. The churches in these countries in their relations with government and in their own congregational life must keep alive and develop the meaning of responsible participation in government. In most areas Christians have only begun to realize what this requires in terms of the preparation of leaders, of the education and training of the laity, and in relation even to the conception of the Church and its understanding of its function in the world. The tendency toward the one-party system is first of all a challenge to the Church to prepare itself for witness, to examine its own understanding of the nature of political order. The fact that most of these churches were born and nurtured under the one-party system of colonial rule has not usually prepared them for helping to create the conditions of democratic community. The fact that most of them lack a well-developed conception of their task in relation to the whole field of political life shows how little qualified they are to begin suddenly to admonish the state about its responsibilities. And since most of their ideas about the role of the state are borrowed from churches in the West, they have not yet convinced the national leaders that the Church is speaking to the real situation of their countries.

The social development programs of these governments also offer many possibilities for creative Christian presentation of responsible citizenship. These are often lacking in depth. While promoting the emancipation of women, and the education of youth, they offer no answer to the moral and social problems which these steps involve. They reflect the popular desire for change, but the change lacks ultimate direction and meaning. If the churches were prepared to help give meaning to such changes, they could contribute mightily to the development of a responsible society and to responsible political life as well. But this requires that they themselves explore the ways in which people can be helped to use their new citizenship in true service to the state and to the community.

Perhaps the most important area of witness is to the leaders of the new governments. Government in most of the new nations is government by intellectuals, the graduates of Western universities who because of their education and training are thrust into positions of power and leadership. Much therefore depends on the political ideas and attitudes of this group. They are almost all imbued with a Western Christian secular democratic humanist socialist tradition which has been their ideological guide in the struggle for freedom from Western domination. According to their philosophy of politics, a strong central government is not only necessary and inevitable but right and good. If the Church hopes to have any influence on the future development of government in these countries, it must understand the problems facing their leaders and recognize its pastoral responsibility to them. The report of a Christian group in India which has studied this problem points out that while the small, educated middle class is the backbone of democracy in India, their situation is not an easy one. They also are caught up in the tensions, contradictions, and conflicts between the liberal ideas to which they are intellectually committed and the traditional customs and values they follow in their personal and social life. They are insecure and uncertain how to proceed. They sense the great gap between themselves and the masses who are becoming emancipated. They are easily tempted to antidemocratic maneuvers and actions to avoid the difficulties and uncertainties of their situation, or to maintain their leadership.[1]

The Indian report declares:

> The reinforcement of democracy requires two things: it is necessary to give spiritual stability to the intelligentsia by providing their democratic ideals roots in indigenous culture. It is also essential to bridge the cultural gulf between the intelligentsia and the masses. Both these can be realised only through the democratic transformation of Indian society and culture. This, however, is a long term process. Meanwhile the stability of the leaders of Indian democracy must come from the faith that democracy accords with the true nature of man in his social life, and from the hope that by their experience of working it the people will see its value.[2]

If this is not to remain a pious hope in many areas, these people will need some introduction to the nature of the values which the responsible leader seeks to realize, as well as how these can be translated into terms meaningful for their peoples.

[1] P. D. Devanandan and M. M. Thomas (editors), *Christian Participation in Nation-Building*, pp. 23–24.
[2] *Ibid.*, p. 24.

Chapter 9

THE CHALLENGE
OF COMMUNISM

When activists in the West pray to God to liberate the peoples of the socialist countries, if we were also to pray to God to liberate the peoples under domination of capitalism we should put God in a very awkward position. [Hearty applause]. How is God to decide? If He sides with the majority of the human race and adopts a democratic attitude, He is bound to decide in favor of socialism! [Terrific applause]. But I am wandering from the subject of my report. . . .

—Report of a speech by Nikita Khrushchev, October 31, 1959

In those days (youth) I took my religion seriously and was very often to be found serving at Mass. As I grew older, however, the strict discipline of Roman Catholicism stifled me. It was not that I became any less religious but rather that I sought freedom in the worship of and communion with my God, for my God is a very personal God and can only be reached direct. I do not find the need of, in fact I resent the intervention of a third party in such a personal matter. Today I am a non-denominational Christian and a Marxist socialist and I have not found any contradiction between the two.

Kwame Nkrumah, *Autobiography*

In the areas of rapid social change several movements and ideologies are vying for leadership of the revolutionary political and social movements, and the churches must fight on many different fronts to preserve the integrity of social change which truly seeks the welfare of man. In all these countries Communism is working actively and aggressively to take control of the social revolution, and the churches have discovered, often only belatedly, that even their own members, and particularly their youth, are attracted by the power of Communism to give direction in a changing society. Indeed their members are often particularly susceptible to the appeal of Communism because of its emphasis on social justice and its concern for the needs of the poorest groups in society.

The churches have frequently discovered that they are not prepared to meet the challenge of Communism. Christian leaders in some of the new nations of Africa have even stated that they fear the coming of independence because it will mean increased Communist propaganda, especially among youth. They have made little study of Communism either as an ideology or a political movement and feel unable to answer its claims. Under these conditions their opposition very often takes the form of negative anti-Communism rather than an effort to provide an alternative answer to the problems of social change, which really responds to the urgent questions of youth.

Christians in the West often feel that the main problem in the areas of rapid social change is the threat of Communism and they tend to measure the loyalty of African, Asian, or Latin American Christians by their willingness to participate in the world-wide struggle against it. This uncertainty and even disagreement about the right Christian interpretation of the challenge of Communism severely weakens the total Christian witness.

I. The Fundamental Incompatibility Between Communism and Christianity

There is agreement, in principle, among Christians that Christianity and Communism are in fundamental opposition because of their conflicting views of man and society. In Christian conferences and Church reports it has been stated repeatedly that Communism is a scheme of redemption which pretends to have a solution not only to the problems of social organization but also to the ultimate problem of man in all his relationships. It therefore involves total ideological claims which Christians cannot accept. This has been made clear in various ecumenical statements on social questions and was reiterated in the international Christian study conference on rapid social change held in Greece in 1959: ". . . it [Marxist Communism] seeks to control the whole of culture; it fails to understand the deeper dimension of the human person; in becoming a substitute for religion and in teaching an anti-religious dogma, it leaves no place for the recognition of the judgment and mercy of God who transcends all societies. These total ideological claims in Communism Christians must reject."[1]

Christians in Communist countries have recognized this fundamental difference between the Christian and Communist view of man and society, even when they have viewed favorably the social achievements of Communism. Bishop K. H. Ting of the Episcopal Church in China has written: "In the New China the level of morality has been greatly raised. Does that mean that the question of sin has been solved? Decidedly not. The fact that man must come into a very good environment (New China) before he consciously manifests a better standard of behaviour does not at all mean that man is without sin, rather it is a demonstration that man is carrying the heavy burden of sin, which makes it impossible for him to overcome his environment."[2]

However, while Christians agree on the fundamental spiritual conflict between Christianity and Communism, there has been a great divergence of opinion, even within the same church, on how this is to be interpreted and on the proper Christian response to the challenge of Communism.

Many Christians agree that the totalitarian political and social character of Communism derives from its ideological conception of man and society; this is in conflict with the Christian interpretation not only in theory, but in practice, and for that reason the Christian cannot participate in the Communist movement. This has been stated unequivocally in a series of reports published by a group of leading Indian Christians who are keenly concerned about a more effective Christian witness in society. In a study issued in 1953 they declared: "It is our conviction that under no circumstances can a Christian be a Communist. We hold that it is not possible for anyone to remain a

---

[1] *Thessalonica Report, op. cit.,* p. 53. See also statement of the *The Church and the Disorder of Society,* statement of the First Assembly of the World Council of Churches, 1948, and *The Church in Social and Political Life,* Findings of the Eastern Asia Christian Conference, Bangkok, 1949.

[2] Bishop K. H. Ting, "Christian Theism," published in the *Nanking Theological Review,* August 1957, and translated and published in *Chinese Christian Papers,* edited by David M. Paton, June 1958. Bishop Ting also says: "If we remember that what we preach is the gospel, is Christ, something in its very nature entirely different from all ideologies, something which moves in a different orbit from any system of thought, then we shall have a clear understanding; we shall realize that all talk of a comparison of Christianity with Communism, all discussion of the differences and similarities and conflicts, is beside the point and superfluous." Nevertheless, in the following section Bishop Ting feels obliged to answer the statement of Marx that "religion is the opium of the people."

Christian and be either a Party member or a fellow traveller."[3] A statement of the Eastern Asia Christian Conference of 1949 makes it clear
why this is so: "because Communism lacks a conception of the independence of moral reality over against power, it denies the supremacy of the moral law over power politics and hence in the long run
defeats the very purpose of the social revolution."[4] These Christians
oppose Communism also because it distorts the true aim of social
and economic change. The basic problem for Christians in relation to
all economic development is, shall the nations and peoples sacrifice
everything for the sake of greater production? Christians argue that
whereas Marxism began with the desire to eliminate a threat to the
true dignity and nature of man, it has in fact only raised in a new form
the problem of man's alienation by its great emphasis on material
achievement. In this respect it repeats the errors of capitalism. That
is another reason why it is said, "Betrayal is the key word to describe
Communism."

This position has been largely reaffirmed in subsequent statements.
The Indian report on *Christian Participation in Nation-Building*
(1960) considered the possibility of Christian support for the Communist party of India, noting that it was the strongest of the Opposition parties in the Central Legislature, and concluded: "The question
has been raised whether the Communist Party of India might be developed as an effective Opposition. The principle is clear: Parties
which will put an end to the due process of law, the fundamental rights
of the human person, and the right of opposition, once they come to
power, whether they be of the right or the left, cannot be entrusted
with power; and therefore they cannot be considered a democratic
Opposition. . . . the party has so far given no evidence of a real break
with the totalitarian philosophy or of a really democratic transformation. It is not yet a party with whom our country's future can be
trusted."[5]

In 1957 in the Indian general elections the Communist Party came
to power in the state of Kerala, and a consultation of Christian leaders, meeting to examine the Christian responsibility under Communist

[3] *Communism and the Social Revolution in India, A Christian Interpretation*,
edited by P. D. Devanandan and M. M. Thomas, Y.M.C.A. Publishing House,
Calcutta, 1953, p. 74.

[4] Eastern Asia Christian Conference, Bangkok, 1949.

[5] P. D. Devanandan and M. M. Thomas (editors), *Christian Participation in
Nation-Building*, pp. 27–28.

rule in that situation, once again affirmed the dangers of the Communist doctrine of the State. The meeting concluded that "the negative aspects outweighed the positive and that the Communist rule posed a real threat to parliamentary democracy." It defined its view of the Christian attitude to the Communist government thus: "In as much as the Communists have been returned to power by constitutional means, the Communist government deserves discerning support. Mere anti-Communism without any positive approach will not be helpful in the situation. While one cannot forget the inherent dangers of Communism, the role of those who believe in democracy is that of responsible opposition. . . . As the Communist party has democratically come to power and formed the Government, it is our duty: (1) to submit to the authority of its Government and cooperate as citizens in its efforts for the protection of freedom, the maintenance of order and the promotion of justice; (2) to oppose the Government through constitutional methods and through the means of democratic parties, whenever the Government infringes on fundamental human rights; (3) to suggest to the Government through proper channels our constructive ways and means of meting out measures of justice to the people; (4) strengthen the hands of democratic parliamentary parties to act as responsible opposition in the Legislature; (5) work for the eradication of the evils within the democratic parties and help them to secure the majority of votes in the next election."[6]

A second report on the situation in Kerala, issued in 1959 after popular agitation had led to the intervention of the Central Government and the dismissal of the Communist Government, observes that the Communists were rightly deposed because of their antidemocratic spirit and their resort to a deliberate policy of encouraging class violence: "Not only by their tenets, but also by their practice in Kerala, the Communists have shown that they do not work in a truly democratic way."[7]

The report also noted that this experience should help to arouse the indifferent segments of the community to the need for dynamic social change, the lack of which has helped to bring the Communists to power. The danger is that many people will be satisfied with "a negative anti-Communism." "The task before us today is the formation of a truly democratic government which would effectively imple-

[6] *Communist Rule in Kerala and Christian Responsibility* (1957).
[7] *The Christian Responsibility in State and Society in Kerala Today* (1959).

ment a programme of progressive social change."[8] In this and in other reports the Indian Christians declare that the primary Christian responsibility is to do everything possible to strengthen social democracy. This will involve them in a constant struggle with authoritarian and antidemocratic tendencies whether they come from the party in power or the Communist Party.

II. *The Power of Communism in the Areas of Rapid Social Change*

While recognizing the incompatibility of Christianity and Communism, there are many Christians in Africa, Asia, and Latin America, especially students and youth, who insist that the Christian response must be modified or at least qualified by certain basic considerations. The statement of these considerations varies between the different areas, but in practically all countries the following points would be included:

(1) Communism is a judgment on the West and upon the lack of social concern in the churches. It has performed an important function in challenging Western imperialism in Africa and Asia, and it has also rightly criticized the Church and the missionary movement for their entanglement with Western cultural, political, and economic domination. Its sins must not be stressed so heavily that Christians forget those of Western capitalist society and colonialism. The thinking of the Church has often been too much dominated by Western-style anti-Communism. Before the Church can oppose Communism, it must engage in radical self-criticism and understand its failure to answer the needs of men struggling for a new social order. The Communist view of national revolutionary change may actually be more in line with popular hopes in Africa and Asia than the Western-style conception of gradual development often held in the Church.

(2) Christians in Africa, Asia, and Latin America, especially youth, insist that it is necessary to distinguish between the ideological pretensions of Communism and the militant action for social justice which it has produced in Russia and China. It is acknowledged in recent statements that "Many Asians, especially intellectuals and workers, are fascinated and challenged by the quicker pace of economic development in China under Communism. They would like to put economic progress as the first priority even when they are aware

[8] *The Christian Responsibility in State and Society in Kerala Today* (1959).

of the disregard of human rights involved."[9] Some Christians believe that they can distinguish between the revolutionary principles of change and the ideology of Communism. In their view this ideology does not invalidate the revolutionary interpretation of social change which Communism has shown to be necessary and possible.

(3) Given the strength of Communism in many countries and the weakness or absence of democratic political alternatives, Christians may be confronted with the need to give at least limited support to Communists. In some situations a Communist-backed party or government is the only practical medium of action for Christians who want to express their concern for political order and justice. In the political alignment in many situations, so it is argued, Communism is not the greatest evil, and the Christian has no choice but to work with them or to support reactionary political movements. It is also noted that the Communists of Africa, Asia, and Latin America are often nationalists first and Communists second, and therefore capable of distinguishing between the national interests of the country and the international interests of Soviet or Chinese power.

These considerations are very real for many young Christians who want to take part in the social revolution of their country. A young Methodist pastor and student leader in Cuba, writing in early 1961 at a time when most Christians in North America regarded the Castro regime as Communist dominated, declares: "The Cuban revolution is the most important event of this century in Latin America. . . . Colonialism is a problem not only in Africa and Asia, but also in Latin America. After a great struggle, our countries freed themselves from the domination of Spain. Now Cuba is leading the way in winning Latin American independence from another type of colonialism: the economic domination and indirect political influence of the U.S.A. . . . the fundamental difference between the Cuban revolution and other revolutions (including the Russian revolution) is that it is not the product of a definite ideology but a revolution using a common-sense strategy which has created its own ideology day by day, an ideology that corresponds to the realities of the Latin American situation. . . . the churches have not only obtained a greater measure of freedom but have had innumerable new opportunities for service and witness opened to them in the countryside, the cities, jails, hospitals and homes. Many church leaders, however, because of the close relation-

[9] *The Witness of the Churches Amidst Social Change in East Asia*, Report of the First Assembly of the East Asia Christian Conference, Kuala Lumpur, 1959. p. 7.

ship of our churches with the U.S.A. have taken a negative attitude towards the revolution and are preventing some of the Protestant churches from performing their task in this crucial hour."[10]

III.   *The Dilemma of All Christians in the Communist—Non-Communist Struggle*

Christians in the areas of rapid social change are in a great struggle to preserve both their national freedom and their social development in the present world ideological and political conflict. In relation to the cold war the new nations are involved in a struggle on two fronts: they are seeking to preserve and advance their self-identity in relation to two great ideological powers with both of which they have only limited common social and political interests. In their eyes the Western powers represent the former colonialists and imperialists who would readily reassert their spheres of influence if it were not for the threat of counterintervention by the Soviet Union. The Soviet Union is likewise struggling for power. Although it has the advantage of not having exercised colonial domination in Asia and Africa and of not having to defend old economic patterns, it would readily subvert governments and societies in order to extend its influence. Yet it is from these two world power centers that most of the economic aid and technical assistance for social development must come. To be solely dependent upon either one of them would be a national catastrophe for the countries of Africa, Asia, and Latin America. Their hope is in maintaining a precarious neutrality, thus gaining time for their own development and for greater independence of action. If either side in the great power struggle gains an advantage or presses conditions for economic assistance too far, national freedom is endangered, and the only possible reaction is to invite help from the other side. To the extent that the West refuses to accept the political and economic neutrality of the uncommitted nations, it helps to push them in the direction of Communism. It is one of the ironies of the present situation that, in their zeal to "save" nations in Africa and Asia from Communism, the Western nations frequently forget that these countries also want in some measure to be "saved" from the West; the more the

[10] Omar Diaz de Arce, "The Cuban Revolution," *Student Movement*, Great Britain, Spring 1961, pp. 9–10. Many Protestant Church leaders in Cuba who supported the revolutionary movement in its struggle against the Batista regime have now become disillusioned with the Castro government, but at the same time do not want to return to the *status quo ante*.

West tries to secure their alliance, the more these countries feel obliged to show their independence of it by accepting technical assistance, economic aid, and moral support from the Communist countries.[11] People in the West tend to regard this attitude as the result of exaggerated nationalism and supersensitivity to a Western colonialism which is now dead. In their view the precarious alliance on which effective political and military opposition to Communism depends deserves the support of all countries who desire to live in freedom. They find it difficult to understand how nations can be neutral on that essential issue. It is at this point that the peoples of the West must face the contradictions in their own profession to be the "free world" which has no other interest than to defend the cause of freedom for the new nations. The question is whether they can understand the ambiguities and contradictions of their "Western-style freedom" as seen from the standpoint of ex-colonies and peoples who have been living in subservience to the Western economic and political system. All this poses the need for a spiritual and moral critique of the Western nations in relation to the new nations in which the churches could and should play a large role. It will not involve them, in the first instance, in a critique of Communism, but in an analysis of the dangers of Western power, and the meaning of nationalism in Africa and Asia as a challenge to that power. Western power gains its moral political authority from the assumption that it is exercised in the name of Christian civilization. The churches must ask questions regarding the fundamental character and future of this Western civilization, and in doing so they can demonstrate that they share the dilemmas of the areas of rapid social change.

The Church today has the difficult obligation to maintain its spiritual freedom from political ideologies, while at the same time expressing its concern for social and political justice in a period of great disagreement about the nature of such justice, and about the best means of achieving it. It must struggle to show that "it is not the

[11] A consultation on *The Specific European Responsibilities in Relation to Africa and Asia* (meeting in Denmark, 1958) noted this: "[In some parts of Africa and Asia] Communism often appears merely as a technique of planning, as a means of transforming an agricultural society into an industrial nation, or as a response to real or alleged exploitation and corruption, so that the existence of Communist states is not always felt to be a threat; it may also appear as a balancing factor in international power politics. For this reason, European appeals to an anti-Communist solidarity are often not heeded. It is the responsibility of European Christians to base their appeals not on negative fears, legitimate as their governments' anxieties seem to be, but rather on positive hopes."

challenge of any ideology but the knowledge of the love of God in Christ for man that is the basis of the Church's social and political concern." The churches have yet to discover ways to make this real. Recent ecumenical meetings have begun to define some universal criteria for a Christian conception of freedom and justice, and these statements have served as a guide to Christians in their day-to-day struggle to realize the universality of the Church in relation to the political and social tensions which are constantly pulling it apart. However, there are churches in all countries which have yet to discover the reality of this struggle for the independence of the Church from political systems and goals. Everywhere there is pressure on the Church to take sides in the world power struggle.

The challenge is particularly real today for the churches in Western Europe and the U.S.A. At a time when Western power and security is threatened not only by the Communist world, but by the growing strength of the African, Asian, and Latin American nations, they face a fundamental spiritual dilemma. Where does their moral responsibility lie: In preserving Western political and economic power as a kind of Christian bastion from which they may hope to influence the direction of political and social development in other countries? Or in recognizing that attempts to hold on to Western political power are self-defeating, and that the Western world is inevitably in political decline with the rise to power of the new nations representing as they do the great mass of the world's people? The latter view would lead to the conclusion that the sole means of demonstrating Western Christian concern for the political future of the underdeveloped countries is through a new humility and an intense new development of the West's capacity to share the fruits of the good life with those who struggle for opportunity and self-realization. But this will require a grace of spirit which comes not from man but from God. The challenge to affluent Western society and to the churches which are so much identified with it is clearly one which they cannot meet alone, but only through an encounter with the Church in areas of rapid social change.

Part III

ECONOMIC AND
SOCIAL CHANGE

Chapter 10

CHRISTIANS AND ECONOMIC DEVELOPMENT

The great requirement for development is change; and Asia is beginning to realize it. Change is not easy. Asia has in the past been contented.

Maurice Zinkin, *Development for Free Asia*

A recent Asian consultation has stated, "Independence brought with it . . . . a renewed and heightened awareness of the economic and social backwardness of the new nations." The revolt against foreign political domination became also a revolt against ignorance, disease, poverty, and economic injustice. Today countries like China, India, Indonesia, and Nigeria are striving for economic change on a scale never seen before in human history. Their efforts to develop an economy capable of providing an adequate standard of living for their expanding populations are a challenge to the whole world and especially to the churches, which have contributed so significantly to their awakening to the possibilities of economic development. The question is whether today these churches are participating as fully as they should in this ongoing economic revolution, and whether they are able to think through the meaning of social justice in a world perspective.

I. The Background of Christian Concern

In the past the churches in these countries have given more attention to economic than to political development. Missions introduced new agricultural methods, trained people in new skills, promoted trading and small-scale industry, set up co-operatives for making and sell-ing new products, and revolutionized many areas of economic life by their experiments with the natural resources of the country and by their introduction of new foods and plants. The fruits of their eco-nomic innovations and enterprise are apparent in most countries, and verify the claim that the Church brought the first technical assistance and the first economic aid in the modern sense of those words.

There were various motives for this interest in economic life. The missionaries brought, together with their conception of man, a new conception of work, and of the right of man to share in the fruits of the earth. In situations where the traditional religious view of life stressed the illusory nature of this world, and disparaged work and wealth-seeking, evangelical Christianity, with its strong positive ethic of work and industry, produced a revolutionary new attitude to life and to the whole economic process. This has been one of the factors behind the economic revolution in many areas.

In addition to this moral and theological motivation, the missions had a practical interest in economic development. In the early days they were often self-supporting, and they organized "industrial mis-sions" in the form of plantations or small industries to support their evangelism and teaching. As the Christian community grew, the Church sometimes had to expand its economic activities to provide work for new members who were often deprived of their old employ-ment on becoming Christians.

At the same time, missions lacked any general theory of economic development, and their economic activities were always secondary to, and frequently only justified as a means to support, the work of evan-gelism. Insofar as missions thought about general economic develop-ment at all they tended to assume that it was the responsibility of the Western colonial regimes, since these countries were unable to under-take it for themselves. The Christian "ethics of empire" in relation to economic development, as expressed in the 1920s by a British mis-sionary leader, did not differ fundamentally from general colonial theory:

> As things are today, the government of backward peoples by those more advanced may be justified on two grounds. The first is that an area like tropical Africa is a storehouse of raw materials that have be-come necessary to the welfare and even the subsistence of peoples in other lands, and that only the energy and resources of the more ad-vanced peoples can make these raw products available. Vegetable oils,

rubber, hides and skins for leather, raw cotton, are essential to modern industry. Coffee, tea, cocoa, rice, sago, sugar and many other products of the tropics form part of the regular diet of western peoples. If the inhabitants of the tropics are unable to develop these resources, must not those be allowed to do so who can? Valuable products which mankind needs must not be left to rot unused nor vast areas of productive soil be left uncultivated. Humanity has its rights as well as individual peoples.[1]

Missionaries were at the same time the principal opponents of the economic injustices of the Western capitalist-colonial system. They often worked hard to see that the economic development of the colonial areas was in the true interests of the "native peoples," and missionary leaders like Dr. J. H. Oldham led the long and bitter struggle with the colonial administration and the European settlers in East Africa against forced labor and land alienation schemes unjust to the African.[2]

The international missionary movement spoke out in 1928 against certain practices and changes produced by Western industrialism in Africa and Asia.[3] It objected to the human costs of economic change, when foreign investors, public or private, disregarded the interests of the people in the "undeveloped areas" and introduced work methods which threatened their welfare and dignity. It objected also to the undermining of indigenous social institutions before these could be replaced by new forms of community.

Missionaries were also concerned about the destructive impact of materialism arising from the rapid increase of wealth. For this reason they favored economic progress through deliberate, slowly evolving, and carefully considered change realized by the adoption of the simpler techniques of the West. They were supported by eminent economic and social scholars of their day. In his address to the Jerusalem conference, Mr. R. H. Tawney said:

> The curse of some parts of the East today, as of England a century ago, is the passion for rapid economic development and the single-minded concentration on pecuniary gain by which that passion is fed, so that every form of social dislocation and individual demoralization

[1] J. H. Oldham, *Christianity and the Race Problem*, London, 1926, pp. 97–98.
[2] The story of his efforts on their behalf is well told in Oliver, *The Missionary Factor in East Africa*, pp. 250–72.
[3] *Christianity and the Growth of Industrialism in Asia, Africa and South America.* Volume V of the Report of the Jerusalem Meeting of the International Missionary Council, London, 1928, pp. 185–90.

is defended on the ground that it is essential to economic progress. But economic progress is not an end but a means; and rapid economic development in a society not prepared for it is not a blessing but a misfortune; and the naive illusion that a society becomes more prosperous if its output of commodities increases while the institutions which provide its moral stamina are undermined will deceive no one who accepts the Christian view that material wealth is to be valued insofar as, and only insofar as, it assists and enriches the life of the spirit.[4]

Ten years later at the World Conference of the International Missionary Council in Madras, the subject of economic change was once more raised. The emphasis here also was upon the threat of moral and social disruption due to rapid industrialization and economic change under capitalist auspices:

> Everywhere we see secularisation, rebellion against accepted moral sanctions, and the loss of responsibility for one's neighbour. The confusion is seen in the economic field by the introduction of an individualistic economy as over against the communal system, by the commercialization of agriculture, with its increasing dependence on an outer world economy; by the decay of arts and crafts and traditional occupations; and by a social development depending upon a competitive rather than co-operative industrialisation controlled by a minority and often involving imperialistic domination.[5]

The conference affirmed that the principal cause of the tension and social injustice in and between the nations was the "dominating social and economic order" based on competition, capitalist exploitation, racial and political discrimination, and great inequalities in wealth and income. The task of the Church in this situation was "to build an order of brotherhood where God-given resources are used to serve all mankind, where co-operation replaces competition and where social privilege gives place to justice and equal opportunity for all."[6] At this important missionary conference there was little discussion of economic development through rapid industrialization and increased production; the emphasis was rather on redistributing wealth among and

[4] *Christianity and the Growth of Industrialism in Asia, Africa and South America,* pp. 167–68.

[5] *The World Mission of the Church, Findings and Recommendations of the Meeting of the International Missionary Council,* Madras. *Op. cit.,* Section 13, "The Church and the Changing Social and Economic Order," pp. 124–25.

[6] *Ibid.,* p. 133.

within the nations.[7] Very little was said about the way this could be accomplished.

To sum up, the strategy of the Church and missions in relation to the economic problems of these lands in the period before the Second World War was based on (1) opposition to the materialist spirit and the socially disruptive effects of the rapid spread of the Western competitive industrial system; (2) efforts to better economic conditions by such measures as vocational training, rural development, self-help co-operatives and small-scale industry, where these would not disturb local social structures and customs; and (3) proposals for the redistribution of world economic resources, through co-operative efforts to overcome poverty.

Today we may be tempted to criticize these economic goals, both because they were influenced by Utopian conceptions of economic organization, and because they failed to take into account the enormous pressure building up within these countries for faster economic progress. Nevertheless, at a time when the Western initiatives were bringing great economic changes, this Christian witness drew attention to some, if not all, of the critical human problems involved.

The world economic situation today is, however, fundamentally different from that of prewar times. The independent nations of Africa, Asia, and Latin America themselves have decided as a matter of national policy to embark on a program of rapid economic development. They look for a rise in their standard of living, not primarily through a redistribution of world resources, but through radical increases in their own productive capacity, and they are determined to achieve this in the shortest possible time.

We are only beginning to look adequately and realistically at our Christian responsibility in this new situation. One reason for the delay is that the interest of missionary organizations in economic questions subsided during the war and has never revived.[8] Consequently, many churches are today out of touch with the economic realities of these

[7] *Ibid.*, p. 129. "Since economic means can purchase opportunity there can be no equality of opportunity without a redistribution of the world's economic goods. We therefore stand for a just distribution of those goods among the nations and within each nation, so that every man may have enough to promote his full growth as a child of God and not too much to stifle it."

[8] Despite the intense prewar concern with economic questions, none of the postwar world missionary meetings (Whitby, 1947; Willingen, 1952; or Accra, 1958) resumed the discussion of these topics.

new nations. They are often still hoping for gradual change at a time when the pace of change is constantly accelerating.

II.   *The Moral and Spiritual Problems of Rapid Economic Growth*

It is not easy for the Church to develop a new, positive, and creative approach to the rapid economic development demanded today by peoples in the underdeveloped countries. Not only does the great emphasis on greater wealth and income run counter to much that the churches have stood for in the past, but the present striving to rapidly increase economic wealth often only accentuates the Church's feeling that it must stress the dangers of materialism and the threat to human values inherent in the strong "worldly" desire for more goods and services. This skeptical view is not wholly unjustified. The moral and spiritual costs of economic development, especially when it is rapid, are often enormous—the breakup of old patterns of village and family life; the tension between the generations and the undermining of traditional moral and social standards; the demoralization of people in the new urban-industrial centers; the city slums—all this is part of the price of economic change. Even more upsetting for many is the threat to the religious and cultural ideas which are for them the ultimate meaning of their life. To many in Africa and Asia, economic development appears more as a menace than a hope, because it is so overwhelming in its demands and seems to be realizable only where it destroys other values. The paradox of economic development is that it must terribly uproot societies and cultures in order to introduce the new economic system which will make possible a higher standard of living. It is not surprising that people faced with choice between a higher standard of living on the one hand, and the breakup of traditional cultural and social patterns on the other, often react unexpectedly against economic change. The Asian churches have called attention to this problem:

> Secular democracy and economc progress by themselves do not satisfy the deepest longing of the individual for participation in community. They are therefore threatened by traditional community ties of culture, religion, caste, etc. which give him a sense of belonging. In this tussle the longing for community often proves stronger. Moreover democracy and economic progress are suspect as Western

cultural aggression. This situation is capable of endangering both nationhood and its economic goals.[9]

In such a situation the churches are justified in asking what conception of man and community will underlie the new patterns of economic life and the emphasis on increasing welfare. Their suspicion that this question is avoided or answered too simply is confirmed by the cavalier way in which it is treated in much contemporary discussion of how to industrialize underdeveloped countries. For example, a recent report by a group of leading Western experts sees the social and moral consequences of the development process as follows: economic development involving modern industrial organization inevitably comes into conflict with the traditional structures of preindustrial society because industrialism has "its own logic"; the result is a fundamental challenge to such "critical elements of the cultural environment as . . . . the family system, class and race, religious and ethical evaluations, legal concepts and the concept of the national State."[10] The successful fulfillment of the industrializing process may be delayed by the strength and rigidity of the preindustrial culture, *"but in the end the new culture of industrialism successfully penetrates and changes the old order."*[11] Thus the world steadily moves in the direction of a universal industrial society.

This line of argument depends on certain assumptions which demand examination. It recognizes that modern economic development requires a distinctive set of social institutions and moral values; but it assumes that these are inherent in the very structure of industrialism, and that they will inevitably and relatively easily prove their superiority or impose their authority over traditional social and cultural values. This viewpoint, very common in international technical assistance and economic aid circles, tends to reduce moral standards to the status of an industrial by-product. It is quite possible that Western industrialism does incorporate certain spiritual values, but in the light of the shaky moral and spiritual condition of Western "organization man" and the "affluent society," the confidence of these experts seems questionable. Perhaps they believe that Western industrialism is morally superior to other economic systems because of its superior technical achieve-

[9] *The Witness of the Churches Amidst Social Change in East Asia*, p. 2. Report of the First Assembly of the East Asia Christian Conference, Kuala Lumpur, 1959.

[10] "Industrialism and Industrial Man" by Kerr, Harbison, Dunlop, and Myers, *International Labor Review*, September 1960. Vol. LXXXI, No. 13, p. 241.

[11] *Ibid.*, p. 241.

ments: industrialism is right because it produces. In reply Christians must emphasize that there are other criteria than productivity by which to measure human progress and development. In contrast to such a predominantly technical approach the Church may well stress the ultimate spiritual and ethical values by which the desirability of economic development can be measured.

To what extent is it possible to resolve the dilemma produced by the undoubted need for economic growth, its threat to traditional cultural values, and the practical impossibility of introducing quickly new values which might moderate the destructive effects of a new, fast-spreading pattern of economic life? The answer seems to be, never completely. Programs of community development can ease the transition, but the kind of rapid economic development that is necessary to overcome great human misery will probably necessitate tremendous social and cultural uprooting, even where the change is carried out under the most favorable circumstances.[12] It is an illusion to think that new and attractive forms of community can be developed as rapidly as new factories and cities. There will inevitably be tension and dissatisfaction as industrialization and economic development proceed, and as people discover the harsh social and moral costs involved.

It is not enough, however, for Christians to support such rapid development as the lesser of two evils. Their task is to work for the responsible society and they must make explicit the moral basis on which economic growth should proceed. Their reservations, however, cannot lead them to oppose economic development. The moral dilemmas presented by rapid economic change cannot be used as an excuse for clinging to the *status quo*. Rather, recognizing the great dangers involved, Christians must work for responsible development; otherwise the new society may succumb to what a famous English social scholar once described as the characteristic of all industrial revo-

[12] Prof. W. Arthur Lewis speaks of this problem: "Faced with the incongruities of change, many people have wondered whether social change could not be regulated in a "balanced" way, i.e. by preventing some beliefs and institutions from changing more rapidly than others. The answer seems to be that this is impossible. A culture cannot be changed in all its myriad aspects simultaneously and in equal proportions. Some parts feel the strain more than others, and give way, pulling others with them in differing degrees. We cannot always predict what will give way first, because this varies in societies according to their history and traditions; neither can we predict what parts of the culture will be pulled along, or in what proportions. The only way to prevent unbalanced change would be to prevent all change, and this no one can do." *The Theory of Economic Growth*, London, 1955, p. 145.

lution, "the paradox of rising pecuniary incomes and deepening social misery."

In the industrial revolutions of the West, the churches helped to provide both the ethos which made the modern economic system possible and then, somewhat belatedly, the concern for social justice which resulted in the Christian challenge to the evils resulting from the new system. What is the likelihood that a similar spirit of social responsibility will accompany and guide economic development in Asia and Africa?

It is hardly likely that the churches in most parts of Africa and Asia today, smaller in influence and numbers than the churches in the West, can exercise anything like the same impact on the development of economic life in their countries. Probably the greatest contribution toward humanizing economic and social change will come, as it already has, from the secular socialist spirit which appears to be the dominating element in the dynamics of economic change in these countries. Christians must have inevitably many reservations about this spiritual and moral foundation, and they must ask whether it has the power of humanizing the economic revolution. In this situation the churches have practically unlimited opportunities to contribute their insights into the spiritual and moral problems of man and society in the midst of economic change; insights which cannot be expected from any other group in society. In this enterprise these churches have the possibility through the ecumenical movement of drawing upon the experience and ideas of churches all over the world and of the ecumenical movement itself. Yet the actual economic problems in the countries of the younger churches are so vastly different from those which confront churches elsewhere that much new thinking on their part and on the part of the whole Church is required before they can participate constructively in the new economic situation.

III. A Positive Approach to Economic Development

Church leaders in Asia are supporting economic development under certain conditions. The Asian churches expressed their approval of economic development in these terms in 1959:

> What is the Christian evaluation of the people's urge for higher standards of living and economic welfare? Many in the Church tend to dismiss this urge as materialistic. It is true that man does not live

by bread alone. But it must be affirmed strongly by the churches that economic welfare is a necessary means of the good life. It becomes materialistic when it is conceived of as the end of life. Looked at in the right perspective, the search for material security and economic justice, which is a basic drive in Asia, may become a sign of the abundant life which Christ has promised. With wrong spiritual motivation it may also become a curse.[13]

The 1959 World Council of Churches' international study conference on "Christian Action in Areas of Rapid Social Change" recognized that modern industrial and technological development provides the means for overcoming poverty and obtaining higher standards of living. In its report it affirmed the moral significance of this development:

> What, within the purpose of God, may be the significance of these higher standards of living? Economic growth takes place under God's providence and judgment and in many ways shows forth His Grace and love. Potentially it provides opportunities for the development of each person, for the enrichment of the quality of human living, and for that subduing of the earth and exercising dominion over it of which the Bible speaks.[14]

The report goes on to say: "Our ultimate aim should be a situation where there is no unnecessary poverty among nations."[15]

This positive Christian attitude to rapid economic development is based on a new awareness of the moral responsibilities of the economic situation. It is based on four ideas:

First, Christians must work for the right use of the world's resources as a part of their glorification of God and their recognition that what they have comes from the Lord of the earth. This implies putting the resources to productive use.

> In discovering and making use of the wealth of the earth and of the human mind we have some of our greatest opportunities to give Him the worship due to Him. This is as true of the exploitation of the riches of the earth as of the discovery of atomic energy or the creation of human civilisations. Men may abuse the powers they have been given, and sin makes them glorify themselves rather than God. But

[13] *Report of the First Assembly of the East Asia Christian Conference*, 1959. *Op. cit.*, p. 10.
[14] *Thessalonica Report, op. cit.*, p. 70.
[15] *Ibid.*, p. 74.

it still remains true that it is proper for man to glorify God in the use of the riches of the earth.[16]

The conclusion from this statement is that support of economic development in Africa, Asia, and Latin America is a responsibility of Christians toward God and their fellow men.[17]

Second, one of the criteria for measuring the right use of the world's resources is the "good of all men." God looks on the whole human family as one. He does not give us resources and gifts for ourselves alone but that all may be enriched and all may worship Him.[18] The consequence of this is that "no man or country, . . . has an absolute right to enjoy by themselves either the fruits of the material riches they happen to inherit, or the fruits of ability or effort. God does not draw boundaries of responsibility at national frontiers, nor can we."[19] In view of the human need in Africa, Asia, and Latin America there is need for a radical rethinking of Western economic responsibilities there. Christians in the West still have much to learn about the compulsive desire for economic development in these countries. They also have much to do in helping to shape their economic life. "Those with the greater resources and abilities have the greater obligations."[20]

Third, there can be no Christian sanction for any particular rate of economic development, and there is no inherent merit in either a gradual or a revolutionary pace. Decisions as to the desirable rate of change involve not only technical and political considerations but also moral and human values. The costs and consequences of economic change cannot always be foreseen, but every effort should be made to avoid unnecessary human costs through wise and careful planning, and the churches therefore can and must help to shape the course of economic development at every stage. The churches have often to learn that "injustice in the unequal division of the world's wealth cannot be corrected merely by protest, nor by the work of a few men. It requires patient, continuous study of the complicated facts and actions at many different levels involving individuals, business, government, voluntary groups. . . . In all these Christians have some part to play."[21]

[16] *Ibid.,* p. 72.
[17] *Ibid.,* p. 75.
[18] *Ibid.,* p. 73.
[19] *Ibid.,* p. 73.
[20] *Ibid.,* p. 74.
[21] *Ibid.,* p. 73.

Fourth, the Christian view of man warns against the illusion that economic development can provide a solution to man's deepest problems; on the contrary, it is full of new spiritual and moral dangers. The temptations of greater wealth and productivity are not a reason for opposing economic development; but their presence at all levels of economic development must be recognized. These include: irresponsible consumption, preoccupation with the means and techniques that make for an affluent society; the worship of riches; the use of increased wealth to accentuate social stratification; status seeking; drive for personal prestige and the slavery of men to the system of production due to their dependence upon it for material welfare.[22]

The question is, will the churches and their members generally accept this positive, though critical, attitude toward economic development? Christian thinking in general in Africa and Asia has been built upon the conception of static and predominantly agricultural economy, and has tended to be preoccupied with the values of the past rather than the opportunities of the present and the future. Most Western churches find it difficult and bewildering to participate in the discussion of these economic issues. They have no apparatus for studying such complex questions and for keeping abreast of the rapidly changing situation.

Some argue that while they favor economic growth in general, the important issue is the manner in which this growth will be achieved: will the emphasis on *rapid* economic development force these countries into a pattern of economic development which threatens political freedom? Here is one of the key issues to be faced in the churches.

IV. *What Kind of Economic System Should the Church Favor?*

Christians seek economic development which promotes human welfare. Should they support the Western pattern of state-regulated private enterprise capitalism? Or a completely state-controlled economy patterned after Russian communism? Or is there a third way? This is not an academic question. The end of colonialist-sponsored capitalism in Africa and Asia, the strong challenge by the new urban working class to the economic elite groups in Latin America, and the widespread desire for economic progress is forcing these countries to rethink the structure of their economic life.

[22] *Thessalonica Report*, p. 76.

The ecumenical movement has given much attention to questions of economic ideology and organization since 1937, and it has been agreed that the goal of Christians must be a responsible economic order. The meaning of this has been set forth in the statements on Social Questions of the first two Assemblies of the World Council of Churches, which favored a large measure of private enterprise but with government planning and regulation. However, these statements tended to reflect predominantly the discussion among Christians in the Western industrial countries, and the ecumenical movement has yet to define the meaning of the responsible society in areas of rapid social change. It is also unfortunate that this question has been studied only to a limited extent by Christians in Asia, and as yet not at all by churches in Africa and Latin America. The issues which confront the churches in these areas differ substantially from the economic questions of major concern in the West. The Western churches believe that they must work for an economic structure which preserves the balance of freedom, justice, and order, and in which the state has a limited role. However, as the Asian church leaders have said, "The magnitude of the social-economic development required in Asia today is so vast and pressingly urgent that it is impractical to rely primarily on private enterprise operating within the framework of the free market system."[23] They agreed that their economic development must be planned and controlled by the state, and that the government must take great initiative in starting new industries. Economic life must be so organized that rapid development will benefit the whole of society. This is the basic meaning of the phrase, "the socialistic pattern of society," which is often used in Asia to describe the pattern of economic life they seek.

It seems inevitable, therefore, that in these countries a responsible society must involve a larger measure of state control and direction of economic life than would be deemed desirable in the West, in the opinion of many Christians. Where there is no well-organized market,

[23] *The Witness of the Churches Amidst Social Change in East Asia*, p. 12. Christians in Latin America have also discussed problems of economic life in the First Evangelical Consultation on Church and Society held in Lima, Peru, July 1961. The report of the Consultation states that "Latin America is presently facing a struggle between two antithetical economic systems: capitalism and collectivism. From the Christian standpoint neither of these systems is to be considered as historically given, and as satisfying fully the aspirations of the human person. The Christian has to participate in the struggle now taking place. He must help find a new way that will overcome the deficiencies and perils of the two rival systems."

where there is often only a small and unenterprising business class with little experience in modern industrial organization, where economic development involves such fundamental social and cultural transformation, where there are great masses of illiterate and technically untrained people, and where there is very inadequate social legislation and an even less developed sense of public responsibility to protect the economically weak, the only feasible approach seems to be through state action for economic development. This does not necessarily mean that Christians should endorse government ownership and economic collectivism; it is primarily a recognition of the fact that economic development must be planned by, and carried out in the interests of, the whole nation.

Although the churches affirm that the emphasis on state control is "based primarily on practical rather than ideological considerations," in actual fact there are also ideological factors which tend to compel the governments of these countries to exercise strong control of economic life. In their history capitalism has often been associated with colonialism and is regarded as a twin evil of the era of European domination. Popular resentment against large-scale foreign enterprise often leads to insistence that the new economy be free from control by foreign capitalists. In areas where a strong and enterprising indigenous business and labor class has developed, as in Latin America and Japan, there is a little less antagonism to the private enterprise system, but throughout these areas capitalism even in its enlightened form is not generally favored by great masses of people who associate it with foreign or colonial exploitation.[24]

Thus ideological and practical considerations combine to emphasize the role of the state in economic life. The dangers for individual freedom are obvious, but it is also true that the economic conditions in which the great masses of people live do not provide the social basis for lasting freedom. As a Christian study group in India points out:

> A desperate poverty vitiates for the masses of India the very fact of freedom; and parliamentary democracy cannot be true to its whole purpose if it does not bring about rapid economic progress toward social justice.[25]

[24] Prof. de Vries describes the origins of certain criticisms of Western economic practices in his article on "Economic Imperialism," *World Justice*, Vol. II, March 1961, pp. 314–23.

[25] P. D. Devanandan and M. M. Thomas (editors), *Christian Participation in Nation-Building*, p. 6.

This well illustrates one of the dilemmas in areas of rapid social change. Democratic freedom seems threatened by the great power needed by the state to promote economic development; yet without effective state action for economic development, democracy will never gain the support of the masses.

Today it must even be asked whether the moderate, democratically conceived "socialistic pattern of society" favored by countries like India will be able to produce quickly enough the desired economic change, or whether eventually it will not be necessary to resort to more authoritarian state control. Many youth feel that in economic affairs, as in other matters, their national leaders are unable to face realities either because they are themselves from the economic elite groups or because they are still too much influenced by Western economic thinking or by their dependence on Western markets. These youth believe that the solution to their economic problems can come only through radical economic reconstruction and not by the slow evolutionary methods of semisocialistic development. In their view, the issue is not primarily one of more or less state control of economic life, since this does not of itself guarantee economic development. The fundamental question is whether there is a compelling determination, a moral and perhaps ideological zeal to eradicate the economic backwardness and mass misery and poverty which afflicts the country. Is there willingness to undertake a determined and planned campaign which enlists all the resources of the nation in a battle against these economic evils? These youth feel that all talk about freedom and democracy is hypocrisy and sham unless it can produce effective action. Many are ready to give practically unlimited power to any party, movement, or leader truly concerned about the social and economic problems of the nation.

What can the churches of Africa and Asia say and do in such a situation? The great danger is that these churches, themselves still under Western influence, may not be prepared to think as boldly as they should. As already indicated, the economic thinking of Western churches has little relevance to the problems of countries which feel they must achieve in decades what has been accomplished in the West over centuries. Their fears of regimentation and state power, their emphasis on the rights of private property, and their suspicion of ideological movements has a restraining effect upon churches in countries which feel obliged to use bold tactics and comprehensive community organization in the pursuit of a common social interest. The Church must first of all appreciate the grave dangers of inaction, of immobility, and of half measures. It must understand the hopes and the impatience of youth and the idealism of their struggle to better the conditions of their country. It must beware of stressing the dangers of state power or regimentation in such a way as to strengthen the position of those who are not prepared to take effective action. Although the Church must certainly call attention to the dangers and illusions of Utopian or inhuman ideological elements in schemes for economic development, it must at the same time acknowledge that an adequate response to the demands for change will involve new institutions and a new understanding of what economic justice means.

Chapter 11

THE CHURCHES AND RAPID URBANIZATION

This urban society [in Africa] has yet to be constructed. It needs new leaders, new values, the liberty of expression and of creativity. Until these conditions are realized the African city remains the place where numbers of men are struggling, in misery, in submission to the harsh law of work without joy, or in the futility of illusions. The social fabric remains too loose for the city dweller to find there the human warmth to which his past has accustomed him. He continues to search for it; less at home than outside; for nothing prepares him for a withdrawal which would suppose more egoism on his part and a minimum of comfort.

Georges Balandier, *Afrique Ambiguë* (p. 215)

The sheer rapidity of urban growth is one of the most astonishing and awesome aspects of the whole process of social change in Africa, Asia, and Latin America.[1] It is both the cause and effect of that change, and a measure of its depth. The city is the symbol of political, social, cultural, and moral emancipation. Under its influence the outline of the future society is being shaped, and it is the greatest threat to traditional social patterns and institutions. It is the scene of the dynamic encounter with the West and its life manifests the struggle of these young nations to discover the cultural foundations of a new social order, using the techniques of the West while preserving a non-Western ambiance. It provides the actual setting in which words

[1] Between the war years and today Jakarta, Indonesia, grew from 300,000 to almost 3 million. Calcutta increased its population by more than half a million between 1954 and 1960. Mexico City increased from one and three-quarters million in 1940 to 4,636,000 in 1960. Prof. de Vries describes the rates of growth in his book *Man in Rapid Social Change.*

like nationalism, freedom, individualism, and progress take on reality and power.[2]

But the city has the ambiguous quality characteristic of all change. It is the area of demoralizing social conditions, uprootedness, and human misery; of new wealth in contrast to mass poverty and insecurity, and consequently of new social tensions and injustice; of impersonal economic forces and an indiscriminate materialism. The new cities of Africa, Asia, and Latin America embody the two sides of rapid social change: the hopeful, dynamic, and creative, and the chaotic, inhuman, and destructive. Nowhere is the "shock" of social change so evident as in this movement of people to the large urban areas. The difficult struggle of people caught up in rapid social change to distinguish between the good and evil within it is most concrete in the urban community. Here the Church faces most urgently the need both to interpret the meaning of change and to help define the basis of a new pattern of community life. How well is it filling that responsibility?

As in so many areas of social concern, the Church and missions were pioneers in calling attention to the problems of urban life in Africa, Asia, and Latin America. They inspired the first urban social work, and Christian colleges undertook the earliest sociological study of urban social conditions. Some of the first books on urban social problems were written by Christian workers.[3] Christian social workers have been instrumental in improving the conditions of workers in urban industrial areas.[4] Even non-Christian scholars testify to the role of Christian social service in stimulating other religions to examine their attitude to the needs of man in society.[5] Government urban social work has often been patterned on Christian ideas and institutions.

Despite this early interest, recent Christian concern for the social problems of the rapidly growing urban areas of Africa, Asia, and Latin

[2] For the relation between the development of the new towns and the general national social and political development, see for example: *The Social Implications of Industrialization and Urbanization: Five Studies in Asia*, UNESCO, 1956. Thomas Hodgkin, *Nationalism in Africa*, 1956, chapter on The New Towns. Michael Banton, *West African City*, 1957.

[3] Three noteworthy examples: C. W. Ranson, *A City in Transition, Studies in the Social Life of Madras*, 1938. Ray E. Phillips, *The Bantu in the City*, 1939 (Johannesburg). J. M. Davis, *Modern Industry and the African*, 1933 (Copperbelt).

[4] This was true especially for the mining industry in South Africa and some industrial centers in Asia.

[5] S. Natarajan, *A Century of Social Reform in India*, 1960. "Social service as distinguished from social reform, is a new feature of Indian life, which we owe chiefly to the example of Christian missions."

America seems, even to Christian leaders, peripheral and slight, compared with the opportunities for action and service; the churches appear to be out of touch with the contemporary urban scene, and they are not responding to the dynamic challenge of the changing urban situation.[6] This is the conclusion reached in recent Christian studies, which explain the situation, at least in part, by the strong rural orientation of the Church and missionary movement in these lands. For example, from India it is reported:

> The Christian response [surveyed in the Indian study] is obviously very inadequate as an expression of the Church's responsibility to urban society in India. The Indian Church is, on the whole, rurally oriented. Perhaps understandably so. Even Christian congregations in urban areas are transplanted rural congregations seeking to preserve rural ways of life in the city environment. Where they have become urban they have too easily conformed to the pattern of atomisation of life and ceased to be centres of renewal of urban community.[7]

An official church study group in Liberia declares that the growing urban problem there is a challenge to the traditional conception of Christian missions:

> The missions have contributed richly to many phases of Liberian life. However the work of missions is least evident in urban and industrial areas. It is indeed odd that where there is the greatest concentration of population there is also the least concentration of missionary effort. . . . in Monrovia, where the population has more than doubled within the last fifteen years, only two missionary installations have been added within that period. . . . In order to understand this comparative lack of concern for the urban areas on the part of missions,

[6] The statement of a Seminar on Industrialization and Urbanization for Mission Board Executives and Professors of Missions in the U.S.A. convened by the Center for the Study of the Christian World Mission (University of Chicago) concludes: "Many of the members were left with the impression, as voiced by one of them, that modern industrial society is radically reshaping human personality and life in directions opposite to that transformation intended by the Gospel, and that consequently most of our mission program and methods appear to be utterly theoretical, and irrelevant. This realization makes us humble and penitent, and it moves us to a searching revaluation of the aims and methods of the mission now employed in the ministry of reconciliation in Jesus Christ which God has committed unto us." From the mimeographed report of the Seminar: "Christian Responsibility in the Emerging World Situation: The Population Explosion, Industrialization, and World Mission." The Federated Theological Faculty, University of Chicago, March 1959.

[7] P. D. Devanandan and M. M. Thomas, editors, *Community Development in India's Industrial Urban Areas*, 1958, p. 128.

it is necessary to consider the traditional role of the missionary in Liberia. There seems to be a feeling that the deeper one goes into the bush, the nearer one comes to the area of greatest need and the more valuable service one can render. Accordingly in the mission field the missionaries who work in the hinterland have achieved a superior status to those who work on the coast. . . . The hinterland movement of missions continues, in fact it is so pronounced as to indicate that as the people move from east to west the missions are moving from west to east. We suggest that the service to our brothers in the interior is needed and important. We feel, however, that this has taken place at the expense of coming to grips with new and emerging problems of the areas of concentration of population. The jungles which nature has created are formidable, and to conquer them for civilization is a noble endeavour. We point out, however, that the jungles which man has created in his teeming and seething cities with their tremendous human problems offer a challenge to service second to none.[8]

From Northern Rhodesia, an area of so much pioneer Christian study of urban problems, it is reported that the impact of urban life has proved to be more complicated and far-reaching than the Church and missions realized:

The Church [in the Copperbelt] is at present the Church of a part of the Western layer of society and of a part of the rural layer. If it is to become the Church of the "in-between," a new approach and a real spiritual struggle are required. The upper-Western and under-rural layers of society are more or less certain to diminish in strength and importance.[9]

Pastors have to be well trained, first theologically, but also sociologically, to work fruitfully in such a complicated situation. Men with such training are still lacking on the Copperbelt. Practically all the Christians on the Copperbelt come from the rural areas, so that church attendance has depended up until now on the strength of mission work in these areas. Conversions on the Copperbelt are few. . . . A new approach to the work is demanded.[10]

Ironically, this rural emphasis has often been justified on the grounds that the Western missionary movement was, by its origin, naturally urban-centered, and that to overcome this handicap it was

---

[8] *Changing Liberia, A Challenge to the Christian*, 1959, pp. 84–85.
[9] Van Doorn, *The Churches and Social Change in the Copperbelt of Northern Rhodesia*, 1959, p. 54.
[10] *Ibid.*, pp. 66–67.

necessary to give special attention to rural areas. Dr. Merle Davis held this point of view. He wrote in 1946: "The typical mission church is a city church, its pastor a city trained man, and its schools are based on the model of city schools."[11] Accordingly he placed primary emphasis on the need to develop the rural church, apparently assuming that traditional Christian work in the city seemed to call for only slight alteration.[12] He was writing before the great postwar rush to the city had begun and before the development of the nationalist movements which demonstrated the social and political significance of the cities.[13] Perhaps one of the underlying reasons for the neglect of urban developments has been the rural conservatism of the Church and the old suspicion of urban-centered life. There has at times been a strong "rural romanticism" in Christian thinking which distrusts the artificial and material character of the great city in contrast to the family and tradition-centered quality of rural and village community. The Church is now discovering its lack of involvement in urban society in many countries and is making a belated effort to do justice to the task of the Church in both city and village.

However, Christian thinking, like all thinking about urban life in Africa, Asia, and Latin America today, is almost paralyzed by the sheer dimension of the human need in the city. By comparison, the opportunities for voluntary service and self-help programs in the rural and village areas seem very attractive. Experts point out that despite some examples of improvement, the difficulty of finding any general solution to the problem of these teeming cities must be recognized. "With the threat of still worse conditions to come, the pressure for effective action in the congested metropolitan areas is still mounting."[14] There is no clear evidence that general betterment is realizable. As the Indian churches' study of urban problems reveals: "In the matter of housing, one cannot yet visualize a time when a minimum

[11] Davis, *New Buildings on Old Foundations*, p. 35. See also p. 259.

[12] In this book, which summarized his 15-year social research program for the I.M.C., Davis gives slight attention to the problems of urban society, concluding that "a vital and steadily growing city church will continue to be basic to the future of the Christian movement." *Ibid.*, p. 266.

[13] The neglect of the urban problem by the Church also marked Christian thinking in the West in the postwar years. Only in recent times have the special needs of the "inner city" been looked at carefully and realistically by the Western churches.

[14] Catherine Bauer, "The Pattern of Urban and Economic Development: Social Implications." *Annals of the American Academy of Political and Social Science*, May 1956, p. 62.

tolerable standard will ever be attained in our cities. A national study of 1953–54 discovered that one-fourth of the houses investigated had plinths and walls and roofs of mud; 44% had only one room. . . . The considered opinion of the national planning Commission is that as matters stand the congestion which exists in urban areas is likely further to increase."[15] It is one of the parodoxes of rapid social change that the great urban areas, which are the source of so much social transformation, have generated new social problems which impair their role as the centers of national development.

It is not possible here to deal with all the questions which the Church must face in relation to rapid urbanization. Four points of particular concern indicate the great range of issues involved: (1) Cultural conflict and social disintegration; (2) Urban moral and family welfare; (3) Problems of youth; (4) Social justice in urban life.

The extent to which the Church can influence thought or action in relation to any of these problems varies greatly from place to place. In some countries it could have an enormous influence. In all areas it has practically endless opportunities to demonstrate the meaning of the Gospel in relation to the search for the new social institutions and new human relationships required by urban life.

I. Cultural Conflict and Social Disintegration

The fundamental human and spiritual problem produced by rapid urbanization in Africa, Asia, and Latin America, is the violent cultural and moral uprooting of people. In Africa and Asia the move to the cities does not take place within the framework of one civilization, but involves "a leap across the great divide" which separates traditional culture from that of the West. The new city dwellers often come from rural areas where urban influence has not yet deeply penetrated; the vast majority are immersed in a strange new society before they have had any possibility of understanding its cultural and moral basis. The result can only be cultural disintegration and conflict within the individual and between cultural groups.[16]

Thus the city comes to stand both for freedom and personal development and for human degradation and a cheapening of life. In the name of new values and new ideals, the city gradually destroys the basis of all values. Lacking standards of social behavior for the new

---

[15] *Community Development in India's Industrial Urban Areas*, pp. 105–6.
[16] W. A. Visser 'tHooft, *Christianity, Race and South African People*, 1952, p. 8.

situation, people often succumb to a purely materialistic culture, produced by the erosion of the old connections between society and religion. Ranson described this process in his study of the Indian City:

> No intelligent and disinterested observer of Indian city life can fail
> to notice the ambiguity and confusion of contemporary social
> thought. This is to some extent the reflection of a confusion which is
> universal, but it is intensified by a marked failure to appreciate and
> to grapple with the fundamental incompatibility between the old so-
> cial tradition and the new social idealism. There is a widespread flight
> from religion. The "catholicity" of the Neo-Hindu movement, with
> its assertion that all religions are equally true, is in many quarters
> giving place to the skepticism which boldly affirms that all religions
> are equally false. This is not an illogical development.[17]

However, traditional religion and culture often persist through a
process of compartmentalization by which the urban dweller struggles
to hold fast to the old communal and social securities while at the
same time endeavoring to fulfill his obligations in the new civic life.
The result is a spurious sense of community and a great tension within
the individual and various social groups concerning the values they are
to uphold and their fundamental social loyalties. An observer in India
describes this contradiction in the life of the city:

> . . . the large number of human beings and their privilege of moving
> about within the city and in the same sports, gives the false impres-
> sion that all are on a par. [But] taboo functions to sort people and
> to separate them from one another, maintaining the ancient status
> system . . . The superficial observer sees a mass of humanity in the
> city bazaar and thinks the principles of liberty, equality and fraternity
> have migrated here from France. But let him spend a day observing
> from a distance, the rituals at a pipal tree, surrounded by its taboo
> system, sorting and separating people from each other.[18]

[17] C. W. Ranson, *A City in Transition*, p. 264.
[18] The power of primitive religions in the city is described by the same writer:
"Our city is a mosaic of tiny interdependent groups, each surrounded by psy-
chological and social barriers, one of which is taboo. If those barriers yield, allowing individuals to escape into other groups, or allowing disintegrating factors
and forces to intrude into the group to destroy its solidity, the situation of the
mid-India urbanite becomes precarious in the absence of formal social legislation. Taboo helps to buttress the dykes. Taboo provides a religio-magical
power that back-fires against anyone who dares to pull the trigger of non-
conformity. Taboo does not love, woo, forgive and restore the norm-breaker;
it demolishes him. . . . Taboo therefore reinforces the overall social order,

In personal life the individual has struggled to hold these two worlds together with little help. The extent to which this problem preoccupies contemporary African thought is illustrated by its constant recurrence as a theme in the work of young African writers.[19] A Nigerian poetess writes:

Here we stand,
infants overblown,
poised between two civilizations,
finding the balance irksome
itching for something to happen,
to tip us one way or the other
groping in the dark for a helping hand,
and finding none.
I'm tired, O my God,
I'm tired.
I'm tired of standing in the middle way
but where can I go?[20]

Today nationalism and independence, with their emphasis on the revival of indigenous cultural patterns, have actually heightened the tension. There is now a great desire to purge the colonial-style urban cultural patterns and to remove Western forms and ideas. As the Christian study group on urban problems in India pointed out, this involves a critical evaluation of both traditional customs and the law structure:

Today positive law has been enacted to take the place of custom in many areas of social life. But many of the laws have been criticized as Western importations made without sufficient knowledge of the indigenous conditions which they seek to change or control and as enacted without sufficient public opinion to support them.[21]

The Church is not particularly well prepared to aid in thinking

---

and preserves the social fraction against the levelling processes of urban life. . . . in our mid-India city [it] operates to preserve the social group against the individualistic tendencies of urbanism." Dr. Henry H. Presler, "Primitive Religions in the City—Taboo." *India Cultures Quarterly.* First Quarter 1961. Vol. 19, No. 1.

[19] Recent novels by African writers which deal with this theme are Mongo Beti, *Le pauvre Christ de Bomba* (1956); Chinua Achebe, *No Longer at Ease* (1960); T. M. Aluko, *One Man, One Wife*; perhaps most important of all, Peter Abrahams, *A Wreath for Udomo* (1956).

[20] Mabel Imoukhuede. The lines are taken from *Federation News,* World Student Christian Federation, January 1961, p. 122.

[21] *Community Development in India's Industrial Urban Areas,* p. 60.

through the fundamental issues involved in cultural and communal integration. It has discovered that this cultural conflict also exists within itself and that it has much thinking to do about the ways in which the Western and the non-Western elements are combined in its own institutional and cultural life. The fact that the former have often been dominant, handicaps the Church in its attempts to aid individuals or groups who are struggling with this problem in the larger social setting.

There are two points of view within the Church concerning the way in which this problem should be resolved. The first emphasizes the importance of a positive Christian approach to traditional culture and the need to overcome Christian aversion to indigenous forms. The second point of view, while welcoming this endeavor, emphasizes that the Scriptures provide the basis for determining what is permissible for a Christian.

> The problems multiply when we try to think through the application of old customs and rules in the urban area. . . . In considering the ethical implications, we must emphasize the necessity of choosing, not the way of adjustment and integration, but that on which the signposts are in accord with the fundamental principles of the Decalogue.[22]

The question, however, has hardly arisen for most urban churches. Middle-class economic and social values dominate in most urban situations, and the great majority of urban churches have tended to identify themselves with these values. They have therefore little in common with the great mass of newly-arrived workers and peasants who come to the city looking for new securities and a new sense of community. This may explain why the various "sect" groups have frequently shown more capacity to understand and speak the language of the newcomer who is beginning to face in his own personal and family life the tensions of social change.[23]

[22] Van Doorn, *op. cit.*, p. 83.

[23] In Latin America it is reported that the sectarian groups are spreading in the city because they are concerned about and understand the moral and spiritual problems of cultural displacement: "These [Pentecostal] movements are establishing in the urban situation a religious society which is helping to meet the need that the 'displaced persons' from the villages have for a face-to-face society. In the men's meetings in the church . . . the participants may on occasion join together in prayer for their wives and families, or may hold a Pentecostal-type prayer session in which each puts his arm around the man next to him and prays aloud for him. This type of thing, and their projects of economic support of

II.   *Urban Moral and Family Welfare*

No aspect of urban social change has such dramatic and far-reaching consequences as the changing pattern of marriage and family life. This change is due to the different functions which marriage and family perform in the tribal or traditional society of Africa and Asia and in modern urban industrial life. It is also due to the development of the new conceptions of the meaning of marriage and the status of women introduced by Christian missions.[24]

It is difficult to imagine two more different structures of human relationship than the traditional African or Asian joint-family pattern and the pattern of "one man, one wife." The former involves complex and detailed marriage and family responsibilities which go far beyond those of the parent-child unit that is the basic pattern of the West. Conversely, the conjugal or unitary family involves a radically new definition of the mutual responsibilities of husband and wife, of their relationships to their children, and of the place of women in the home and in society.

It is not surprising that the transition from the customary marriage pattern to one conforming to the new conception of family relations and the economic and social demands of urban life has been incomplete, with the result that today the greater number of urban marriages are apparently contracted outside of either traditional or civil law. This situation is viewed with grave concern by many churches and Christian Councils throughout Africa and Asia.[25]

---

work in which all may participate, serve to build up an intimate fellowship. People are thus given a sense of belonging in a new group, which helps compensate for the displacement that many of them have undergone with respect to their traditional social environment." W. Wonderly, "Urbanization and the Challenge of Latin America in Transition." *Practical Anthropology*, September–October, 1960.

[24] See Devanandan and Thomas (editors), *The Changing Pattern of Family in India* (1960). For Latin America, see O. Lewis, *Five Families, infra.* For Africa see Michael Banton, *West African City, A Study of Tribal Life in Freetown* (1957), and T. Baker and M. Bird, "Urbanization and the Position of Women" in *The Sociological Review* (Special number on Urbanism in West Africa), July 1959, pp. 99–112.

[25] A recent resolution of the Christian Council of Nigeria is illustrative: "Having in mind that marriage under the Marriage Ordinance is not generally acceptable, as is seen from the few that use it, and that customary law marriage is rapidly becoming unsuitable as the social conditions in which it came into existence are disrupted, and that many young couples, especially in cosmopolitan townships finding no suitable form of marriage open to them, are living together

A speaker at a Christian study conference in West Africa in 1951 pointed to the gravity of the situation:

> Married life . . . does not appear to be in a happy position and though the picture is gloomy, the facts must be faced. The basic relationship upon which the family is founded is insecure, . . . the state of pre-marital relations between men and women, and the evident standards within marriages are clear enough to compel us to see the problem of marriage and married life as one of the biggest facing the nation. We have to lift married life to a new level of morality. . . . Traditional standards have broken down. . . . The Church is providing new and higher standards. Few have accepted these standards and fewer still endeavour to keep them.[26]

The Church is deeply involved in this situation because it has in the past condemned the traditional marriage pattern and has been largely responsible for the introduction of Western forms. Even today some Western theologians speak strongly against any compromise with non-Christian marriage customs.[27] But a growing body of Christian opin-

---

without being legally married: This Council asks the Federal Government to appoint a Commission to consider the necessity of a Marriage Law for Nigeria suited to an independent nation and to the changed social and economic conditions now prevailing in the country. The Christian Council recognises that any such law would have to recognise several types of marriage, but respectfully requests that one type should provide for a monogamous form of marriage." *Report of the Twelfth Meeting of the Christian Council of Nigeria, May 12–20, 1960.* While the Nigerian proposal outlines the pattern for monogamous relationship it offers no comment on the nature of the other patterns to be given legal sanction.

[26] Dr. K. A. Busia, "Married Life and the Family," *The Church in the Town.* Report of the conference on this subject sponsored by the Christian Council of the Gold Coast, 1951, p. 29. See also Ione Acquah, "Moral Welfare," in the same report.

[27] Prof. Roland de Pury, a well-known Swiss theologian, writes as follows about the African custom of "bride-price" or "bride-wealth": "Marriage as practised in Africa today, is a real form of exploitation of the young by the old. I even wonder if that is not the main reason why Africa is so backward in the social evolution of the world. For a society in which the young are sacrificed to the old, instead of the old giving themselves to the young, is condemned to remain static. It is the Christian message which, by directing human history towards the Kingdom of God, has readjusted the situation and started the movement in favour of the new generation, thus starting the evolution of culture and civilization. The system of the bride-price as practised in Africa today, is only the symptom of a society which has not yet turned its face to the future [under the influence of Christianity]." He also says: "When a system is bad it must not be maintained on the pretext that it used to be better, or that God may improve it in the future, or that it exists in other continents. It must be *abolished.* . . . It is obvious that the system cannot be adjusted bit by bit, it must be blown up all at once. The Church must take a collective, unanimous decision that henceforth it will

ion recognizes the real dilemmas which confront people, including church members, who are under pressure from both the old and the new cultures in which they live. In many countries the churches and missions have developed pastoral and educational services such as the Christian Home and Family Life movements which provide courses in homemaking aimed primarily at strengthening the quality of Christian family relationships. But there have been few careful investigations of the basic tensions and conflicts or of the marriage patterns appropriate for countries undergoing rapid social change. The conclusions of the detailed study of African marriage (1953) sponsored by the I.M.C. and the International African Institute have been formulated as follows:

> In every section of the population victims of changing circumstances are left without adequate support, and irresponsible individuals find it possible to escape control, entering on unions which can hardly be expected to develop into stable households and assured family life. The wiser observers . . . . agree that something must be done; but it has still to be ascertained what would be both widely effective and generally acceptable. . . .[28]

The same report points out that there is need for some means of bridging the gap between traditional marriage and the Christian ideal.

> . . . . it is apparent that there is need for some method of getting married, appropriate to the new conditions of living on earned money and being free to move about as employment demands, yet not demanding a spiritual profession which the parties concerned may not be prepared seriously to make. Between custom and the new religion there has appeared a gap.[29]

The report makes clear that this confronts the Church with a great dilemma:

---

ask every Christian family to give up drawing any material advantage whatsoever from the marriage of its children, but to try on the contrary to help them to start their new home, otherwise the Church will refuse to consecrate the marriage. Why should this not be possible?" Roland de Pury, "The Bride Price System and God's Covenant With His People," *Laity*, World Council of Churches, May 1959, pp. 20 and 24. This article is a translation of some portions of Prof. de Pury's book *"Les Eglises d'Afrique entre l'Evangile et la Coutume"* (1958). Prof. de Pury has been professor of theology for the last two years in the theological college of the Cameroons.

[28] Thomas Price, *African Marriage*, I.M.C. Research Pamphlets, No. 1. London, 1954, p. 21.

[29] *Ibid.*, p. 26.

Is it practicable for the state to provide two statutory systems of marriage, one for pagans and one for Christians; or would this in itself, undermine the stability of the more rigid and demanding form?[30]

According to a recent survey of the changing family pattern in India, a similar tension between "the traditional and the individualistic ideal is present in almost every family situation."[31] The resurgence of traditional cultural and religious ideas has added to this tension,[32] and in this struggle the Christian community is rethinking its position:

> The Christian community, influenced by the modern western missionary movement, tended to adopt western culture uncritically in the past. However, now there is an awareness of the deficiencies in western culture and a realization of the values in the Indian tradition. As a result, a process of cultural synthesis is beginning to take place in the Christian community. If the Christian family is able to adjust itself and to overcome some of the stresses and strains of this process of acculturation, it will be in a better position to help other communities in the same process.[33]

The nature of this cultural synthesis is not described. However, the report does point out that the Christian family idea has now penetrated throughout Indian society and has served to strengthen and enrich family life in the nation.

The conclusion of these several surveys is that rapid social change, especially through urbanization and nationalism, has raised questions regarding the family and marriage for which there is no clear answer. "Most of these questions will have to wait to be resolved by high-level conferences at which agreed conclusions can emerge and be laid down with authority. Meanwhile individual field workers have to do each what he can in conditions as they are."[34] The Africa survey was completed in 1953 and the high-level conferences have yet to be held. Quite possibly the delay is due to an uncertainty in mission circles about their competence, and a new awareness that while in the past the study of these matters was largely the work of Western Christian

[30] *Ibid.*, p. 54.
[31] P. D. Devanandan and M. M. Thomas (editors), *Christian Participation in Nation-Building*, p. 173.
[32] See Devanandan and Thomas, *The Changing Pattern of Family in India* (1960), on the marriage and family ideas of renascent Hinduism, pp. 96–111.
[33] *Christian Participation in Nation-Building*, p. 198.
[34] Price, *op. cit.*, p. 55.

specialists,[35] any new approaches must reflect primarily African and Asian Christian opinion.

Christian conferences on family marriage problems have been held in Africa, Asia, and Latin America in recent years by the World Council of Churches' Department on Cooperation of Men and Women in Church and Society and by the International Missionary Council's Home and Family Life Movement.[36] These meetings have shown that Christian women especially are eager for the Church to display a greater understanding of the problems of marriage and family life and also that its policies and practices should not condone customs affecting women which are contrary to Christian teaching. In one meeting there was strong objection to the indulgent attitude in the Church to bride-price, polygamy, and the treatment of widows. This same meeting proposed service projects to help those who are the victims of old customs and attitudes toward women. Speaking of the pioneering role of these Christian women in Africa, an ecumenical leader writes: "Nothing stops them, neither the weight of tradition nor their elders' lack of understanding, nor the need of constantly inventing a new style of life to suit unprecedented situations. They are rarely helped by the men, who are themselves too occupied with their own evolution. They are on the march with bewildering speed like all Africa. Their obedience, or their disobedience, concerns not only Africa, but the whole Church."[37]

Nevertheless, she adds, the question remains whether these efforts at change promoted by Christians are not so largely "inspired purely by western concepts of marriage" as to make unlikely that they can "become the rule in countries where Christians are only a minority amongst Moslems and Animists. Are the social structures of the West the only ones possible in the twentieth century? Are they the only ones a Christian can accept? Will the groups of church women cam-

[35] It has been noted that the Survey of African Marriage reflected very largely Western opinion and drew very little on African Christian thinking about this question. (See De Vries, *op. cit.*, chapter on Family Relations.)

[36] See, for example, *Consultations in Africa*, a report on two Christian conferences to discuss the theme: "Men and Women in Africa Today," and "The Service of Women in the Church." The first was held in connection with the All-Africa Church Conference, January 1958. The second was a congress of Christian Women in the Cameroons, February 1958. The report is published by the Department on the Cooperation of Men and Women in Church and Society, World Council of Churches, 1958.

[37] M. Barot, "African Women—Through the Eyes of a European Woman," *Laity* (A Bulletin of the World Council of Churches), May 1959, p. 14.

paign in favour of the Convention [on marriage] proposed by the United Nations? Or will the churches seek to put forward some more African type of legislation which is also compatible with Christian standards?"[38]

III. *Youth in the Urban Setting*

The problems of youth in a time of rapid urbanization are of grave concern for the Church. Every report speaks with alarm of the effect of urban uprootedness and the disintegration of the family on youth. Certain issues are common to all these areas. In many of the growing cities of Africa there are large numbers of "free" youth, "young people under eighteen years of age who are not living with an organized family or responsible adults."[39] The churches in Liberia describe this problem as follows:

> These youth come to Monrovia, or are sent by their parents to earn money, or to avail themselves of the better educational opportunities afforded here. They sometimes come to escape the obligations and responsibilities of their native villages. Without regard to the reason for their coming, they do not have proper help and guidance after they arrive. They come from the village, where there was strict discipline, to the city where there is none. The city offers films (which are largely westerns), comic magazines, night clubs and bars. . . . The law relating to the sale of alcohol to minors is not enforced.[40]

The report from Liberia also mentions the lack of recreation for youth in the city:

> We have little planned recreation for our youth. . . . The Y.M.C.A. has the only recreation program for children, and this does not provide for out-of-school youth. There is practically no recreational activity for girls. We need to urge on our officials the importance of establishing public play grounds and recreational areas. As the urban areas grow this need can only be met at high cost. We should set aside some space while there is yet time.[41]

Perhaps the greatest range of problems in these new nations is associated with the growing demand for education. Various reports call

[38] *Ibid.*, p. 11.
[39] *Changing Liberia, A Challenge to the Christian*, pp. 44–45.
[40] *Ibid.*, p. 45.
[41] *Ibid.*

attention to some of the problems faced by young people from the village and rural areas who move to the city in search of educational opportunities: lack of adequate financial support, and the resulting tendency toward a kind of "boy nomadism" as they seek help from relatives and friends;[42] the housing problem for adolescent school-boys who often live in crowded rooms or in the kitchens of relatives or guardians;[43] and the breakdown of moral standards which such conditions produce. The projected rapid expansion of schools in these countries will greatly aggravate this situation as more youth are drawn to the city.

For many children no schooling at all is available. The conclusion of the Ashby Commission on Higher Education in Nigeria concerning the challenge this presents to the nation and the world could be applied to many areas of Africa:

> Millions of the people who will live in this Nigeria of 1980 are already born. Under the present educational system more than half of them will never go to school. Like people elsewhere their talents will vary from dullness to genius. Somehow, before 1980, as many talented children as possible must be discovered and educated if this vision of [a new] Nigeria is to be turned into reality. This is a stupendous undertaking. It will cost large sums of money. The Nigerian people will have to forego other things they want so that every available penny is invested in education. Even this will not be enough. Countries outside Nigeria will have to be enlisted to help with men and money. Nigerian education must for a time become an international enterprise.[44]

In all these countries the great need is for technical education. The Copperbelt study declares:

> The most important problem in boys education . . . and perhaps the greatest social problem on the Copperbelt—is the inadequate provision for technical education. Here the question of social righteousness must be raised. In a country where technical development is so central in the minds and activities of the people, the rising generations must have full opportunity to get a technical education. . . .[45]

Even where this is available, it is sometimes denied African youth on

---

[42] Van Doorn, *op. cit.*, p. 71.

[43] *Ibid.*, p. 72.

[44] Sir Eric Ashby, "Investment in Education in Nigeria," *Progress*, Vol. 48., No. 268, March 1961, p. 66.

[45] Van Doorn, *op. cit.*, p. 76.

the grounds of race. The Copperbelt report notes that in 1958 the Federal Rhodesian Minister of Education opposed technical education for Africans in the two advanced institutes for technical training on the grounds that "the time is not ripe to open them to Africans." That policy is still followed today.[46] This is only one example of the social injustice against which youth is demanding that the churches speak out.[47]

In Asia educated youth have great difficulty in finding work. This appears to be due in part to the "white collar" emphasis in their education, to the disinclination of some to take jobs involving manual work, and in part also to the failure of the economy to develop rapidly enough to provide sufficient new jobs.

But the gravest dilemma of youth in all these countries lies in their need to interpret the rapid changes in their society. Most of them become enthusiastic nationalists and eager supporters of economic development. But as the frustrations and difficulties of securing rapid change mount, they become disillusioned, and tend to fall victims to many different movements, some reactionary, some totalitarian. The struggle of youth to find itself in the midst of the various currents of changing urban life is one of the most tragic aspects of the present situation.

The churches are beginning to see that they have failed to keep up with the changing problems of youth. The All-Africa Church Conference in 1958 pointed out that "an examination of the youth situation in Africa today, no matter how cursory, reveals how imperative it is for the Church to redouble and strengthen her services to youth. Everywhere in Africa young people are poised between two civilizations, between two worlds, unable to see their place clearly and lacking any definite standards of life and thought."[48] The same statement points out that the traditional methods and attitudes are inadequate for the present time, and calls for new efforts in leadership training, the raising of the standards of Church youth and Sunday school pro-

[46] *Ibid.*, p. 76.
[47] I was present in a Northern Rhodesia city on a Sunday evening in 1957 when the African Methodist youth and the European Methodist youth met together for the first time in the home of the missionary pastor of the Methodist Church for Africans. The youth vowed together that they would never again meet separately, but the reaction of the European church to joint meetings proved to be too strong and only intermittent meetings have since been held.
[48] "The Church and Youth," in *The Church in Changing Africa*, Report of the All-Africa Church Conference, January 1958, p. 30.

grams, and the strengthening of ecumenical planning and activity in this field.[49]

The success of the Leadership Training program which the World Student Christian Federation has been carrying out in Latin America for the past ten years and is now beginning in Africa, points the way to similar efforts for Christian youth. However, it is not yet apparent that the churches around the world are ready to meet the cost of such a program in terms of money and trained personnel. Moreover, the experience of the W.S.C.F. has shown effective leadership training depends upon previous study and analysis of what is happening to youth in these areas; the basic need in the churches is for more serious thinking about the nature of the problems youth now face.

IV. Social Injustice in Urban Life

Great inequality in conditions of housing, education, and community services is one of the chief characteristics of the urban situation in all the new nations and gives rise to a great sense of social injustice within these communities. Sometimes this inequality originated in colonial patterns of enforced communal segregation and involved huge differentials between conditions in the European and the Asian or African towns. Today it is more often due to the movement to the cities of thousands of unskilled peasants who are unable to pay for the necessary municipal services or housing and for whom the city often can provide little help.[50] Unemployed and generally unemployable, they struggle against poverty and social misery in the *favelas*, the

[49] *The Church in Changing Africa*, pp. 30–32. In contrast to this statement by the African churches, the East Asia Christian Conference meeting in 1959 said nothing significant about the Church's response to the challenge of youth.

[50] Oscar Lewis, writing about urban conditions in Mexico, describes a practically universal problem: "With the rapidly rising population and urbanization the crowding and slum conditions in the large cities are actually getting worse. Of the 5.2 million dwellings reported in the Mexican census of 1950, 60 percent had only one room and 25 percent two rooms; 70 percent of all houses were made of adobe, wood poles and rods, or rubble, and only 18 percent of brick and masonry. Only 17 percent had private, piped water. In Mexico City conditions are no better. The city is made more beautiful each year for U.S. tourists by building new fountains, planting flowers along the principal streets, building new hygienic markets and driving the beggars and vendors off the streets. But nearly 2 million Mexicans, or about one half of the city's population, live in slumlike housing settlements known as *vecindades*, suffering from a chronic water shortage and lacking elementary sanitary facilities." *Five Families: Mexican Case Studies in the Culture of Poverty*, 1959, p. 10.

bidonvilles, or slums in every major city in Africa, Asia, and Latin America. The expectation of social stability and order is a pure illusion in situations where a large segment of the urban community lives in such great physical distress while another enjoys the benefits of highly-developed Western-style life.

This urban poverty and misery is of such dimensions as to challenge practically all traditional conceptions of remedial help and social action, and it is necessary to think anew about the meaning of the Christian concern for social justice in these situations. What does it mean to work for social righteousness in situations which seem to offer so little hope for general improvement even in the long run?

There has been as yet extremely little substantial Christian study of this question, and consequently such Christian action as has been undertaken has been piecemeal, drawing mainly upon old Western strategies which seem to have very little relevance in the new situation. The great danger is that just because the problem of urban social justice is so great it may paralyze the will of communities to do what they can. In order that the Church may help develop within the urban community a sense of responsibility for the conditions of life of all its members, three types of action are needed:

(1) *Christian Investigation of Urban Social Conditions.* Without continuing Christian study of these questions, the Christian community cannot be actively and intelligently involved in this immense struggle for urban social order and justice. There is need of more information about urban living conditions and the social effects of urban poverty and slums, especially upon children and youth. Municipal governments are often unprepared or unwilling to study the problem, while national governments are too preoccupied with the question of general economic development. The churches can help to call attention to the human problems of overcrowding and disorder through surveys and consultations. However, a report from Asia points out that "most urban congregations are unaware of their responsibility to the larger [urban] society. The great majority are ingrown communities, concerned primarily, if not exclusively, with their own problems. Even where they are conscious of a wider responsibility, pastors and lay people are uncertain where to begin, . . . Local congregations need the advice and help of the whole Church."[51]

[51] *Community Development in India's Industrial Urban Areas*, p. 130. Urban studies are now being considered by Christian groups in Rio de Janeiro, Kingston, Jamaica, and in Chile.

Urban social survey is a new field of endeavor for the Church in these lands. Very often these efforts suffer from lack of resources and expert sociological guidance. A realistic effort requires much thought and planning at the local, national, and world levels. Generally, the churches need not survey the problems themselves, but can make use of material collected by other agencies and even stimulate these agencies to a wider conception of their responsibility. In some areas governments conduct surveys but do not publish all the findings for fear of political repercussions. University or other private research bodies which undertake investigations often avoid discussion of the moral and social implications lest this seem to detract from the technical quality of their work. The churches could do much to supplement the work of other bodies in helping the urban community to see the needs of all its people realistically and with compassion.

(2) *Action for Urban Social Justice.*   Reports from many areas indicate that often action only awaits a recognition by the Christian community of its responsibility to act. This applies especially to the development of a democratic urban social structure. In many situations, especially in Africa, where social injustice is based on racial discrimination, the churches could have exercised a key influence. In the Copperbelt towns of Northern Rhodesia it is stated that the old barriers between the African and European communities will only give way when there is a new awareness of the demands of justice in community life. The special task of the Church is described thus:

> A multi-racial society, in which a just balance of the interests, rights and duties of all is achieved, does not evolve from within the society itself. . . . If justice is to be established in the relationships between the component parts of a nation, a struggle for righteousness is unavoidable, and a willingness to sacrifice non-essential elements in their culture is demanded of all groups. Only spiritual power can bring this about.[52]

One of the difficult points of discussion for many churches in South Africa is whether the urbanized African has a moral right to the greater civic privileges within the urban community which the World Council of Churches' Consultation in Johannesburg in 1959 suggested he should have.[53]

[52] Van Doorn, *op. cit.*, p. 100.

[53] The statement of the World Council of Churches' Consultation with member churches in South Africa, Johannesburg, December 7–17, 1960, includes the following points: "It is our conviction that the right to own land

In many areas of Africa Western churches could remind Western firms and government officials of their obligation to encourage a morally responsible community and challenge remnants of what the Liberia report calls "the plantation psychology," often evident in the segregated housing and the communal living of the Westerners in these areas.

In some areas of Africa there is a strong feeling among Africans that the whole structure of society has been such as to maintain the inequality of the African and keep him the servant of the white boss.[54] In Asia also, urban social democracy demands Christian action against segregated housing, which has continued to follow the pattern of colonial times:

> The special European origin of our cities has given them a distinctive geographical pattern based on segregation according to function. They were all planned with large areas set aside for the almost exclusive use of spacious, uncongested and un-Indian living by the European rulers. . . . Senior Indian officers, both of government and business firms, now live in the segregated areas built by the senior European officers for themselves. This makes for great inequality in living conditions in the city. . . . In considering this heritage of our cities, we must certainly ask whether the continuance of it is in accord with the ideals of Indian democracy.[55]

The political and social future of the nations in areas of rapid social change will depend very much on the structure and spirit of life in the great cities. Concern for the rights of people within the urban areas, regardless of their race, color, or creed, is undoubtedly part and parcel of the total Christian concern for responsible citizenship and in accord with the Christian attitude to mankind as children of the one God.

(3) *Christian Social Service.* The churches and missions have fostered a great variety of social services, though the quality and extent

---

wherever he is domiciled, and to participate in the government of his country, is part of the dignity of the adult man, and for this reason a policy which permanently denies to Non-White people the right of collaboration in the government of the country of which they are citizens cannot be justified." "The Consultation urges, with due appreciation of what has already been done in the provision of homes for Non-White peoples, that there should be a greater security of tenure, and that residential areas be planned with an eye to the economic and cultural levels of the inhabitants."

[54] Wilson, *Social Change in Central Africa*, 1946.
[55] *Community Development in India's Industrial Urban Areas*, pp. 7–8.

of these has varied radically from place to place. Today this social work is being restudied in the light of the needs of rapidly growing urban communities and new thinking about the social responsibility of the churches. It is widely agreed that voluntary social work programs are still needed, particularly in the urban areas, and that every Christian congregation ought to be engaged in community service. However, it is noted that this work needs to become a vital part of the ministry of the local church in Africa and Asia and not remain foreign-sponsored.[56]

Many Christian social and educational services and institutions were developed in an era when government welfare programs were unknown or underdeveloped.

In today's world where governments are rapidly expanding their social welfare services, there is need for "continuing re-appraisal of each Christian institution and its usefulness in relation to the nation."[57] New types of voluntary service are needed to meet the urgent social and human needs of the growing cities: youth hostels, leadership training for urban community work, the stimulation of housing co-operatives, and education for workers, as well as the expansion of certain types of older social services.[58] Christians can also make a significant contribution by challenging from a Christian perspective "the developing social work methods and techniques, which tend to be manipulative in character and to usurp to themselves a disproportionate importance."[59]

Perhaps most important of all, Christians must rethink the relation of social work to social justice, especially in view of the government efforts to establish a welfare state. The paternalistic and individualistic sentiment often characteristic of social work in the past must give way to a broader conception of social responsibility in which the needs and the rights of all members of the community are considered.[60]

[56] A consultation in India declares: "Our social work programme is very unstable as it depends wholly on overseas initiative and support. We do not know of any Church in the United Provinces that has a social work programme. This indicates that the present foreign-supported programmes do not arise out of the life of the local Church and do not therefore reflect our social conscience." Findings of the Consultation on the Social, Economic and Political Problems of the Christian Community of the United Provinces. *Religion and Society*, December 1959, pp. 45–71.
[57] *Christian Participation in Nation-Building*, pp. 216–17.
[58] M. Takenaka, *New Forms of Christian Service and Participation*, pp. 20–25.
[59] M. Takenaka, *Reconciliation and Renewal in Japan*, New York, 1957, p. 30.
[60] *Ibid.*, p. 31.

Chapter 12

THE ETHICAL AND
SPIRITUAL PROBLEMS
OF WORK AND WORKERS

*During the Ramadan (Muslim month of fasting), all
work is held up. Just at the very moment when we are
doing our utmost to increase production. How can we
resign ourselves to seeing it brought to a standstill? . . .
I contest that religion can impose such a decree. It is
inconceivable that it should ever be an obstacle to the
well-being of the Muslims, an element of stagnation in
their progress. The Prophet himself broke the fast to
overcome his enemies. We also have an enemy to overcome: poverty. By the voice of His Prophet, God is
calling us to be stronger in order to overcome our
enemy. . . .*

—Speech of President Habib Bourguiba
of the Republic of Tunisia, February 1960

Economic development and rapid industrialization
presage the swift growth of the industrial worker class in Africa, Asia,
and Latin America. What is the Christian responsibility toward this
key social group and how well are the churches meeting it? There is
a growing interest in this question although present study and action
are still extremely limited in comparison to the immense challenge
that is posed.[1]

Thirty or forty years ago the churches were giving relatively greater
attention to the problems of workers than they are today. The action

[1] See the *Report on the First Asian Conference on Industrial Evangelism*,
Manila, June 2–13, 1959; also the Report of the Consultation on Urban Life in
Africa, organized by the All-Africa Church Conference, held in Nairobi, March
1961.

of Christian leaders against forced labor in Kenya,[2] the Belgian Congo,[3] and Angola,[4] the Christian concern for the conditions of exploited industrial and plantation labor in China, Japan, India, and other areas of Asia,[5] and studies of the I.M.C.'s Department of Social and Economic Research,[6] revealed a practical, if underdeveloped, interest on the part of churches and missions in the problems of workers. The Jerusalem meeting of the International Missionary Council in 1928 was remarkable for its concern with the issues of expanding industrialism in Africa and Asia, especially its harmful effect on nonindustrial peoples. Mr. H. A. Grimshaw of the International Labour Office, speaking at the Jerusalem meeting about the impact of capitalist industrialism on the peoples of Africa and Asia, pointed to the need for greater efforts by churches and missionaries to protect workers from the almost inevitable dangers of exploitation.[7]

During the war interest declined, and in recent years it has had to be awakened almost anew. The reason for this diminished concern seems to have been the failure to provide some means to follow-up study of these questions and, perhaps more important, the gradual decline of the social gospel movement which had furnished much of the theological stimulus for the earlier interest.

[2] The work of J. H. Oldham on this problem in Kenya has been mentioned earlier (Ch. 10).

[3] Missionaries of the American Presbyterian Mission (South) made effective protests to the Katanga Company in the Belgian Congo—see R. L. Buell, *The Native Problem in Africa*, New York, 1928, Vol. 2, pp. 415 ff. Missionaries of the Baptist and "Regions Beyond" missions in the Belgian Congo were active in making known the abuses in the collection of rubber under the regime of Leopold I.

[4] "A Commission under Dr. E. Alsworthy Ross was sent from America to study and report on labour conditions in Portuguese Africa in the 1920's. The presentation of their report provoked great resentment in Portugal and African Christians suffered as a result. Leaders who had given evidence to the Commission were deported and the Protestant missions were held responsible for the share they were supposed to have had in the Commission." I am indebted to Miss Bertha D. Gibson, the former private secretary to Dr. J. H. Oldham, for this information.

[5] The Preliminary Paper prepared by William Paton on "Christianity and the Growth of Industrialism in Asia and Africa" for the Jerusalem Conference of 1928 describes the concern of churches and missions in Asia with harmful labor conditions. This is published in *Missions and Industrialism*, Vol. 5 of the Jerusalem Meeting Report. The study of industrial conditions in India, undertaken for the National Christian Council of India by Miss M. Cecile Matheson (*Indian Industry*, London, 1930), was an effort to open up this problem.

[6] J. Merle Davis, *Modern Industry and the African*, London, 1933.

[7] H. A. Grimshaw, "Industrial Revolution Among Primitive Peoples," *Missions and Industrialism*, pp. 155–56.

Renewed Christian attention to industrial workers has been provoked by the new social problems, different from those of the prewar period, which have been created by rapid industrialization.[8]

In most of Africa and Asia industrialization is no longer Western-directed and -sponsored; and private capitalism, both Western and indigenous, has lost much of its power. Economic development is now dependent on the initiative of national governments. Not only has the pace of industrialization been greatly accelerated, but it is usually accompanied by the welfare state philosophy and very much concerned with the rights of workers. The rate of economic expansion, the extent of government control of the labor movement, and perhaps most important of all, the capacity of the community to mitigate the cultural and social upheaval of economic change—these are the factors which most directly affect the welfare of the industrial worker today.

The Church in Africa and Asia has yet to develop in detail its interpretation of this new industrial situation, and its meaning for man and society. The available reports suggest certain issues which should be of particular concern to Christians: (1) the meaning of work in the new technological situation; (2) social justice for workers; (3) the development of trade unions; (4) the conditions of migrant workers.

I.   The Meaning of Work in a Time of Rapid Technological Change

The cultural and social clash induced by the new wave of industrialization in Africa and Asia inevitably raises a number of questions about the difference in the meaning of work in a non-technical and in a technical society, and the moral and spiritual problems of people who must make the rapid transition from one to the other. Where there is a fundamental conflict between these two concepts of work, by what criteria is it to be decided that one should be sacrificed to the other? Assuming that governments must strive for rapid industrial growth, what are the social and moral assumptions about work on which such development depends, and how are these to develop in the different cultural conditions? These are urgent questions in Africa and Asia. Many reports speak about the moral and spiritual confusion of people who are encountering for the first time the technological system and the radically new ideas about the world which it brings with it. It is now seen more clearly that the dehumanization and de-

[8] *Report on the First Asian Consultation on Industrial Evangelism,* pp. 1–3.

personalization of rapid industrialization are a "challenge to the Christian conscience."[9]

The Asian churches have recognized the great difficulties experienced by people coming from rural areas in making the transition from the old to the new patterns of work:

> The nature of work in these modern factories is entirely different from work in the farm and in the small cottage industry. Technology increases the possibility of work becoming monotonous, fragmented and apparently less creative. The factory system also engenders impersonal relationships between employers and employees and even among employees themselves. This is partly the reason for the feeling of loneliness and isolation which drives the worker back to his village periodically. Also modern industrial work requires a form of training outside the family in technical institutions. It requires a new type of discipline, with the labourer working in coordination with thousands of other workers. . . . The place of living and work is separated. . . . Technological development also sets man in a new cycle of time. He is free from natural time, but ruled by mechanical time. . . . Thus while the transition from rural to industrial patterns of life creates the opportunity for growth for independent selfhood, it produces at the same time new forms of destructive pressure upon personality marked by loneliness in the city, new forms of bondage in organized industrial life, meaninglessness due to the mechanical drudgery of the new setting, and lack of creativity in work.[10]

The conflict between traditional attitudes to work and those demanded in a developing industrial society is also apparent in Africa. The *African Labour Survey* of the I.L.O. shows that:

> . . . with the changes in technology involved in the economic transformation of Africa which is at present taking place, the African worker is in many cases being called upon to alter fundamentally his pattern of living and habits of thought which were appropriate to his traditional environment, in order to fit into an industrialized society; side by side with the traditional economy, the most modern techniques have been introduced in certain sectors of employment without the intermediate technological stages of progress which have facilitated adjustment in a number of other communities. The gap between the two ways of life necessarily involves a great strain on the

[9] *Thessalonica Report, op. cit.,* p. 19.
[10] *The Witness of the Churches Amidst Social Change in East Asia, op. cit.,* p. 17.

capacity of adaptation of the workers involved and must be regarded as providing a fundamental explanation of the position in regard to the output of many African workers.[11]

In the continuing and intensified spiritual and social struggle of African and Asian workers to find themselves in the new industrial pattern of work, the Church must witness to the Christian concern for the dignity of man. This witness is especially important at a time when government and industry are inclined to determine policy primarily on the basis of increasing productivity.[12] Some churches and missions have begun to search for ways to fulfill this responsibility, but these are still very scattered experiments, and it is too early to say in what measure they have even discovered what they have to do.[13]

The basic difficulty is that the churches have yet to work out their criteria for evaluating the situation posed by the juxtaposition of a technological society and cultures which stand for conflicting attitudes to work and society. Most Christians are agreed that, in spite of the spiritual dangers it involves, especially the temptation of technological man to regard himself as "a self-sufficient creator," they should take a positive attitude toward technology:

> We should not conclude that technology should be abandoned, but that Christians must strive to create the fundamental spirit and the varied conditions of social, economic and political organization, so that technology can contribute to the full dignity and freedom of the human being.[14]

But how are these necessary spiritual and sociological conditions to

[11] *African Labour Survey*, International Labour Office, Geneva, 1958, p. 16.

[12] The *African Labour Survey* states: "There can be no doubt that the African is ill-adapted by any conditioning he has received through his economic and cultural background for assimilation as an effective element in a wage economy on the European pattern." pp. 141–42.

[13] Various churches and missions are experimenting with "industrial missions." The East Asia Christian Conference, through its Committee on the Laity, has been publishing a Church Labor Letter to promote interest in Christian witness in an industrial society. The Church Missionary Society, in co-operation with the Anglican Church of West Africa, undertook a survey of the possibilities of Christian work in relation to industrial and plantation labor in Nigeria. (P. P. Bloy, *Aspects of the Growth of Industrial, Urban and Agricultural Life in Nigeria,* Church Missionary Society, London, 1959, 58 pp., mimeographed.) The aim of all these efforts is to get away from the purely revivalist conception of industrial evangelism. Yet they all suffer from a substantial vagueness about the nature of industrial evangelism in relation to social change, e.g., the Bloy report, Section III, "The Church's Approach in the New Nigerian Society."

[14] *Thessalonica Report, op. cit.,* p. 19.

emerge in cultural and social contexts which have so little in common with the presuppositions underlying the technological and industrial pattern of life? The negative attitude of Gandhi and of the reformed Hinduism which he led, to large-scale industrialization, and their fear of too much technology, suggests that in India there is still a fundamental conflict between the national plans for industrialization and the traditional cultural values of that country.[15]

In Islam the conflict with economic and technological modernization may be due primarily to the interference of certain Muslim fasting habits with the demands of organized industrial production, but perhaps also to basic differences in the attitude to work.[16]

The attitude of a group of Ceylonese Buddhist laymen illustrates a common ambivalence in Asian culture with regard to Western techniques.[17] On the one hand, technology is regarded as fundamentally important in improving man's material welfare.[18] But this is interpreted in relation to a dualistic view of life which ends in disparagement of the technical in relation to the spiritual. People gain real happiness through the spirit:

. . . . personal progress takes place in the inner world, and is independent of advancing technology and the changes in external circumstances which it brings about. True human progress consists in increase of aesthetic, intellectual and spiritual experience and satisfaction.[19]

According to them, the problem is to keep the modern preoccupation with technology from overwhelming the spiritual realm as it already has in the West.[20] Christians would rightly complain that such in-

[15] P. D. Devanandan and M. M. Thomas (editors), *Christian Participation in Nation-Building*, pp. 257–58.

[16] See the article by Robert J. Muller, "Society and Islam in Tunisia," *Background Information*, November 1960, p. 24.

[17] *The Revolt in the Temple*, Sinha Publications, Colombo, 1953, 700 pp. The origin of this interesting publication is obscure. It is attributed to a group of Buddhist laymen in Ceylon who seek to interpret Buddhism in relation to contemporary social and political life.

[18] *Ibid.*, p. 509.

[19] *Ibid.*

[20] "The nations of the West are all 'sick societies,' disintegrating under the impact of an advancing technology that destroys the patterns of familial and communal living, cuts off man from contact with Nature, deprives him of opportunities for spontaneously creative activity, imposes upon his organism the clock-work rhythm of machines and makes him think of the world and his fellows in mechanist terms which are basically inappropriate to life and personality." *Ibid.*, p. 529.

terpretations are based on a wrong separation between the material and the spiritual, and they would argue that technology is a gift to God to be used to His praise and glory.

In Asia and Africa there is a tendency to disparage manual labor, and education is looked upon as an escape from working with one's hands. Western colonialists and capitalists have often contributed to this outlook by their attitude to the masses of African and Asian workers and by linking manual labor with racial inferiority.[21] Viewed from Asia and Africa, the Western attitude seemed to be that those who did hard physical work were socially inferior and could be exploited. It is undoubtedly part of the moral appeal of Communism for workers that it challenges this pattern of an intellectual or social elite which does not have to toil. It is reported that in China the intellectuals and administrators are forced to spend time working with the masses of peasants and industrial workers in order that they may develop a correct ethic of work! National economic development inevitably requires the breakup of "parasitic" social classes, both traditional and contemporary, who live off the sweat of somebody else's brow; the basic question is whether the churches have the capacity to bring the revolutionary power of the Gospel to bear on this new equalitarian work situation, or whether they have become too closely associated with the well-off members of society or with well-off nations to understand the ethical issue at stake. As the international Christian conference on rapid social change pointed out:

> Perhaps the most bitter fact in the world is that it is divided between those with white skins in relatively rich countries and a much larger number of men who have coloured skins and who are desperately poor. . . . The Christian Church is largely made up of white people in the rich countries. In the world today the gap between these groups is not growing smaller, and in some respects it is clearly growing wider. The rich white "Christian" West is not as sensitive to this offense to God as the facts demand, while poor coloured countries suspect that the riches of the West have been increased by exploitation of themselves.[22]

Can a meaning of work be developed in relation to traditional African and Asian cultures which will also be adequate for a technologi-

[21] The work ethics which developed in the colonialist situation are well described in J. M. van der Kroef, *Indonesia in the Modern World*, Bandung, 1954, pp. 155–56. See also Eric Williams, *Capitalism and Slavery*, Chapel Hill, 1944.
[22] *Thessalonica Report, op. cit.*, p. 72.

cal system? Or does the technological system demand a new social structure? If the concepts of work and industry developed from indigenous culture are not capable of challenging the "leviathan" character of the technological drive, what means can be found to prevent the destruction of fundamental human values in the constantly accelerating industrializing process?[23] Methods of evangelism which are not conceived in reference to these questions will not meet the deep spiritual needs of industrial workers in these countries.

II. *Social Justice for Workers*

There is a close connection between the meaning of work and the demand for social justice in industrial life in the rapidly developing countries. If workers are to accept rapid industrialization, it must be accompanied by a spirit of social justice, and hence the development of a welfare state in these countries has been one of the essential conditions for securing the co-operation of workers. Deprived of his traditional family and social securities, the worker is dependent on urban industrial society for his welfare. His role in the new industrial system is generally weak and he suffers from many social handicaps. There is increasing recognition that one of the tasks of the Church in the future is to define the meaning of a just and responsible society in this situation. The problems which demand attention can be mentioned only briefly here.

One is the growing inequality in the distribution of wealth and income between different social groups in rapidly industrializing countries. Even in the welfare-planning states of Asia it is reported that the effect of industrialization has been to accentuate this disparity. "Not only does wealth tend to be concentrated in the hands of a few people, but political power also tends to be concentrated in the hands of industrialists, unless proper checks are enforced."[24]

[23] See R. S. Bilheimer, *Ethical Problems of Economic Aid and Technical Assistance*, study published in the series *Project Papers*, World Council of Churches, June 1957. Dr. Bilheimer poses the basic question: "How the present [technological] process can be continued in Asia, that is, how the spiritual and cultural presuppositions which are required to make technology work can be developed in terms which are truly indigenous to Asia. The impending tragedy, already discernible, is, at root, that in the interests of human justice a technological means is employed which founders for want of a spiritual power and value. The shape of ultimate victory is also apparent: the triumph which consists in the fact that the spirit of man in Asia, having faced the temptations of the technological age, can control and use it in its own terms for the true well-being of humanity." p. 20.

[24] *Community Development in India's Industrial Urban Areas*, p. 27.

Another issue is that of wages and working conditions. In many countries minimum wage laws are hopelessly inadequate and even these are generally poorly enforced. Working conditions are a threat to human welfare. Little attention is given to the problems of worker housing and family welfare. In Africa particularly, wages and housing often follow the old pattern employed for male migratory labor, and are completely inadequate to maintain the worker and his family in the urban situation. The result is great distress among women and children and great instability in urban society.

A major source of social injustice among workers, particularly in Africa, is racial discrimination in the conditions of employment. While this will undoubtedly diminish with African independence, it is still a serious cause of worker unrest in many areas. It is also one of the chief complaints against foreign business and industry. The African Labour Survey of the I.L.O. (1958) notes that the whole process by which Africans learn and accept new patterns of work in a number of African countries has been seriously disturbed by racial discrimination which limits the advance of Africans and restricts their contact with whites who have the technical experience and knowledge they need.[25] In one of the few instances where churches have publicized the facts about such discrimination, it has helped to bring about a change in policy.[26]

Another problem is the use by the state of unemployed and unskilled labor, especially youth, in work brigades. This sometimes involves "involuntary recruitment" of workers for the construction of bridges, roads, and other public works, requiring great quantities of untrained manpower. The conditions under which this human investment in national development is given or taken by the state raises ethical issues which have not yet been carefully considered in the churches, and the urgency of this question may grow as countries seek in this way a solution to the shortage of capital.[27]

[25] *African Labour Survey*, pp. 16 and 532.
[26] The Liberia Christian group asks regarding the exclusive white managerial policy in the rubber plantations: "Isn't it possible to begin to consider some able Liberians for training and for managerial posts? Aren't there some Liberians . . . who have the potentialities of becoming good Division Managers?" (*Changing Liberia: A Challenge to the Christian, op. cit.*, p. 33) It is reported that following the publication of this report a major rubber company of Liberia decided to alter its policy and introduce Liberians into the managerial echelons and thus into the managerial residential estates.
[27] Some Christian Councils in Africa have raised the question of "labor brigades" but arrived at no decision. There is a strong feeling in some missionary circles

The factors which combine to produce these and many other forms of social injustice need hardly be recounted here. The headlong rush for economic growth; the ignorance of the new industrial worker about the operation of the money economy, his inadequate understanding of labor laws and the absence of machinery to enforce them, his dependence on those with capital, the lack of effective trade unions, the pressure of large numbers of unskilled and unemployed workers for the available jobs—all these work to maintain laborers in a weak economic position. The churches could supplement the efforts of government, trade unions, universities, and other groups by studying the economic situation of urban industrial workers and by helping to define the relative responsibilities for working conditions of employers, the state, and the trade unions.[28] The Church's possibility of influencing working conditions varies from situation to situation, but in some areas it could carry great weight. The report of the Christian study group in Liberia is indicative of the new awareness of Christian responsibility in this field:

> It is the opinion of your committee that the Church has an obligation to use its influence to bring about improvements in the wages of labor and in general working conditions. We feel this to be especially true in this case, because the great number of people involved do not have the knowledge or the technique for making their just grievances known. The church can speak out against inequities in our society, and call attention to the fact that we cannot build and maintain a prosperous Liberia unless we provide those who toil with a more equitable share of our national production. We can promote the cause of vocational education in order that our workers can increase their skills. We can speak to our elected representatives urging passage of legislation which would not only improve wages and conditions of employment but would also make it possible for them to gain the knowledge and skills which would enable them to earn more.[29]

that such measures are to be opposed as government reigmentation of labor. The 1961 International Labour Conference included this question in its agenda. See Report of the Director General of the I.L.O. Part I: Labour Relations, Geneva, 1961, pp. 53–56.

[28] One example is S. Jayakor, *Rural Sweepers in the City*, Student Research Monograph published by Department on Social Research, Leonard Theological College, editor H. Presler, 1952.

[29] *Changing Liberia*, p. 43.

III.   *The Churches and the Development of Trade Unions*

Justice for the industrial worker in the West has depended on the development of the organized labor movement. The workers of Africa and Asia, generally speaking, lack such organization, and where trade unions have been formed they lack trained leadership and often suffer from domination by government or interference from company unions. The education, organization, and preparation of workers for an effective role in nation-building through the trade union movement very few governments and political movements are prepared to undertake. It involves a theory of the labor movement in relation to social, economic, and political development. The development of a stable, responsible, organized labor movement presupposes years of planning and worker education.

The churches have played a large role in the growth of the organized labor movement in many countries of the West, and if they were prepared, they could promote the effective organization of workers in those countries where Christians are a minority group. The Church recognizes that the trade union can be an important influence working for democracy and social responsibility within the community as a whole as well as within industry. It can provide opportunities for worker participation in democratic leadership and for education regarding the national economic situation.[30]

Unfortunately the churches in Africa and Asia cannot borrow directly from the experiences of Western churches, because the problems of union development are often very different. But Western churches could help more than they have in the past by providing persons with specialized knowledge of the structure of the labor movement, and to help the churches understand the role of the trade union in national life.

The specific problems of trade union development in African and Asian countries are well known: trade union instability; the lack of understanding among workers of the nature and purpose of trade unions; the lack of leadership among the workers and the need to draw upon political or other groups for leadership, creating a tendency toward control from the top down rather than from the bottom up; the dependence on government initiative and encouragement in starting unions, leading to intervention in the union life and even to control

---

[30] *Christian Participation in Nation-Building*, p. 195.

of its policies; the tendency of trade unions to be captured by political or ideological movements seeking to use workers for their own purposes. The practice of forming separate trade unions for different racial groups creates grave difficulties in some parts of Africa. Another problem is the formation of an elite group of organized workers in certain basic industries while large numbers of workers in small and medium-size industries remain unorganized.[31]

The churches have not been completely silent on these questions. In many areas Christians have worked for better human relations in industry and for more understanding of the social conditions of workers.[32] They have also encouraged responsible trade union development. The Evangelical Labour Academy, organized by the Enshu Christian Church in Hammamatsu, Japan, is an example of what can be done. This was conceived as a Christian service to help industrial workers to understand their status, role, and function in contemporary Japanese society. The pastor of the church which sponsored this Labour Academy explains why it was started:

> In the true sense of the term [the organized labor movement] came into being only after Japan's defeat in the last war. It was initiated by the Allied Occupation Forces. . . . It is not something which the workers, of their own will and initiative, struggled to achieve. Furthermore, low wages and poverty coupled with the financial burden of a series of strikes to better conditions, has made it impossible for labour unions to find resources for training and educating their members. As a result the greatest weakness of organized labour in Japan today is in the educational aspect of its task.[33]

To help meet this need the Enshu Christian Church set up the Labour Academy, which has met twice a week for six months every year since 1955. A similar academy was started in Tokyo in 1956 and a third in Otsu in 1957. The course offered in these academies provides education on the theory of trade unionism, labor law, and prob-

[31] See K. Watanabe, "The Problems of Small and Medium Enterprises," *The Common Christian Responsibility Toward Rapid Social Change in Japan. Op. cit.*, pp. 27 and 49.
[32] See Eiichi Isomura, "Problems of Poverty," *The Common Christian Responsibility Toward Rapid Social Change in Japan.* Published by National Christian Council of Japan, Tokyo, 1959, pp. 14–23. Also the publications of the Industrial Evangelism Committee of the United Church of Christ in Japan (Kyodan) on problems of the Japanese labour movement.
[33] Rev. Y. Matsumoto, "Enshu Evangelical Labour Academy," *Background Information*, No. 21, December 1958, W.C.C., Geneva, pp. 27–30.

lems of industrial relations. Because of this work, reports the pastor, "our parish is well thought of by the citizens of Hammamatsu as a going concern which has something to offer to the well-being of the citizenry at large."

The Mindolo ecumenical study and conference center in the Copperbelt of Northern Rhodesia is holding conferences for workers and employers to discuss common problems of industrial relations in the mining industry. Race relations seminars for mine managers and trade union leaders are being held there for the first time in 1961.[34]

Thus churches are discovering that they can render a valuable service in helping the worker and in bettering human relations in industry. Such efforts need to be extended and buttressed by more Christian study of the moral contribution which the trade union movement can make to responsible nation-building.[35]

IV.   *The Problems of the Migrant Worker*

A large proportion of the industrial labor in these new nations will probably continue for some time to be migratory. This weakens the labor movement, and makes for instability in family and community life. It is an outcome of three factors: seasonal labor demands, especially in the large plantations; the policy in some areas of Africa, and especially in the mining industry, of encouraging only male workers to come to the urban area; and the tendency of many workers to regard their departure from their traditional environment and their venture into industrial urban life as only temporary.

The moral and social problems associated with the migrant labor pattern are well known: the disruption and eventually the disintegration of the traditional economic and social life in the village, the failure to develop a stable urban community, and a high turnover in industrial labor.[36] The opinion of experts is that the migrant system,

[34] These seminars were led by the Rev. Daisuke Kitagawa, Secretary for Racial and Ethnic Relations of the World Council of Churches.

[35] The *Proceedings of the First Asian Conference on Industrial Evangelism,* Manila, 1958, p. 268, indicates the projects which are under consideration in many churches of Asia. These reports show that very frequently the efforts to reach the industrial workers involve a radically new orientation for the Church, e.g., "The first effort of this project [of Industrial Evangelism] has been to educate the different churches in Kampur [India] to the need of a concerted and united drive in this field." M. A. Z. Rolston, p. 67.

[36] These social problems have been discussed in numerous surveys, e.g., *African Labour Survey,* pp. 127-37.

which both disrupts old communities and prevents the creation of stable new ones, should be abandoned wherever possible. As Prof. Monica Wilson said in her report to a study conference on rapid social change, organized by the churches of South Africa:

> The presence of large numbers of migrants means that the town is like one with an army camp attached to it. The country people regard the towns as corrupt, and themselves as respectable citizens, but urban householders see a threat to their family life and discipline in the flood of unattached men—and now also girls—who come in from the country and who are free from home controls. . . . When a large body of people is constantly moving from country to town and back as well as between town and town, and job and job, the ordinary controls exercised by kinsmen and neighbours diminish in strength. It is so easy for a man—or woman—to disappear and evade responsibility. . . . For the women [left] in the country there are no advantages. . . . They are lonely. They are poor. They are left to bring up the children and look after the old and ailing, to cultivate the fields and keep the home going.[37]

Even those who defend the migratory labor system in the mines of South Africa agree that it cannot be justified on sociological grounds.[38]

> It is . . . the moral duty of the [mining] industry rapidly but with foresight and cognizance of realities to increase the proportion of permanent workers settled with their families. . . . No authority that claims to be just, humane or Christian should limit or discourage such a development.[39]

The churches in some areas have been the most persistent opponents of the whole system, and they have often carried a major share of the welfare and social work activities in the migrant labor compounds. But today the growing demand for industrialization and for more justice in labor relations presents opportunities for new and creative solutions to this old problem, and the churches have as yet not developed a policy or strategy for dealing with it. However, the statement from the South African Consultation convened by the World Council of Churches with its member churches in the Union has again

[37] Prof. Monica Wilson, "Effects of Industrialization and Economic Development" (mimeographed), December 1959, p. 4.

[38] See "Migrant Mine Labour in the Union of South Africa" (mimeographed), December 1960, p. 1.

[39] *Ibid.*, p. 10.

called attention to the problem and asked the Government to act to correct the evil effects of the system:

> We call attention once again to the disintegrating effects of migrant labour on African life. No stable society is possible unless the cardinal importance of family life is recognized, and, from the Christian standpoint, it is imperative that the integrity of the family be safeguarded.[40]
>
> The Consultation urges the appointment by the Government of a representative commission to examine the migrant labour system, for the Church is painfully aware of the harmful effects of this system on the family life of the Africans. The Church sees it as a special responsibility to advocate a normal family life for the Africans who spend considerable periods of time, or live permanently, in White areas.[41]

[40] *Statement from the South African Consultation,* convened by the World Council of Churches at Johannesburg. December 1960, p. 3.

[41] *Ibid.,* p. 5.

Chapter 13

THE CHURCHES AND RURAL CHANGE

The integrated village society [in Indonesia] crumbled under the influence of urban culture. In the latter half of the 19th century and all through the 20th century rural disorganization becomes more pronounced. With it the cities grew, for those for whom a traditional communal environment proved no longer satisfactory went to seek a new existence in the towns. The result was the gradual growth of a city mob, often living on the brink of economic disaster, cut off from the protective confines of the village and gradually exhibiting all the phenomena of a mass society. The dislocation of village society under pressure from the city has taken on an almost universal economic character: it has immensely augmented the problems of a dual economy, in which the village as a precapitalist society is in conflict with the methods of a fullblown financial capitalism centered in the cities.

J. M. van der Kroef, *Indonesia in the Modern World*

In the countries of rapid change traditional rural and village life has been completely disrupted by the impact of urban society. The disintegration of the rural areas has driven people into the cities, and the attraction of higher incomes and urban freedom has hastened rural decline. In most areas national economic development necessitates the reorganization of the agricultural sector in order to feed the increasing population and to provide a better living for those on the land. This in turn requires further migration to the cities since in many countries the land is overcrowded. In this process traditional social values are often sacrificed to economic demands, intensifying rural dislocation. Today there is a search for new patterns of rural life to replace those which are crumbling. But on what lines shall rural economic and social development take place? What is the concern of the churches in the development of these new patterns?

This is not the first time that the churches have faced these questions of rural life. In the past they have given more attention to rural and village life than to other social questions. Missionary technical assistance in agricultural and rural development has been second in importance only to work in education and medicine.[1] Christian missions working in societies which were predominantly agricultural early became aware of rural poverty, overcrowding of the land, peasant indebtedness, the evils of tenant farming, the decline of village industry, and the impact of urbanization. They struggled to overcome illiteracy and other handicaps of rural life through programs of education and training for rural development. In 1908 in Brazil the first agricultural mission school was started,[2] and in the following years Christian agricultural institutes and training centers were developed throughout Asia and Africa. In 1914 the Y.M.C.A. in India established a department of rural work and in 1916 opened a Central Co-operative Bank to provide credit for rural areas through village co-operatives.[3] This program was later expanded by the addition of rural welfare centers to campaign for literacy and village economic uplift. In Korea, and in China also there were outstanding Christian enterprises in rural development and agricultural research, in which churches, missions, Y.M.C.A., and Y.W.C.A. all played an important part.

Missions in rural areas were not discussed at the First International Missionary Conference in Edinburgh in 1910, but were given primary attention at the Jerusalem Meeting of the I.M.C. in 1928. This interest was inspired by the work of Dr. K. L. Butterfield, a Christian layman who emphasized the need for a more dynamic missionary approach to rural society in Africa, Asia, and Latin America. He wrote:

> The rural folk should be mobilized on behalf of world progress. . . .
> It is absurd to think of a world-development formula that omits the
> rural people from its scope. . . . If for any reason they are not mak-

---

[1] For an account of the development of agricultural missionary work see *The Christian Mission in Relation to Rural Problems*, Vol. VI of the Report of the Jerusalem Meeting of the I.M.C., 1928.

[2] *Ibid.*, p. 67.

[3] *Ibid.*, pp. 83–84.

ing the contribution they should, so much the more reason for paying attention to these potential reserves in the campaign for a better world. Probably for the remainder of this century at least, half the world's population will be rural folk. Are they or are they not to make their full contribution to the Christianizing of the world? . . . The restlessness of rural populations, as indicated in modern agrarian movements, is indicative of the presence of problems that should be worked out from the Christian point of view.[4]

On the basis of his suggestions churches and missions in China and India concentrated on developing "comprehensive rural reconstruction units," combining work in the home, the church, the school, the hospital, and the credit bank to achieve a better rural society. These units worked with groups of contiguous villages. In both China and India they made substantial efforts to develop village and cottage industries.[5]

Since that time agricultural missionary work has continually expanded. The Rural Missions Cooperating Committee of the Division of Foreign Missions (National Council of Churches, U.S.A.) and Agricultural Missions, Inc. have been the most active promoters of this work. Since 1954 the latter has held twenty-seven conferences on rural work policy and procedure in different parts of Africa, Asia, and Latin America. The purpose of these meetings was "alerting people to present day needs and opportunities, sharing of experience and assaying the results of efforts made during the years."[6]

I. The Christian Contribution to Rural Development Today

How is the significant contribution which churches have made to rural and agricultural development in the past to be continued today in the new situation facing Church and nation? One urgent need is for a conception of rural work related to the social conditions of rapid change. The Christian concern for rural society has either been expressed in extremely idealistic and Utopian terms[7] or has concentrated

[4] *The Christian Mission in Relation to Rural Problems*, p. 12.
[5] *Ibid.*, p. 197.
[6] Letter from Dr. Ira Moomaw, Director of Agricultural Missions, Inc., August 18, 1958.
[7] The aims of rural missions, as defined at the Jerusalem meeting of the I.M.C. (1928), remains the only world ecumenical statement of Christian rural objective and is in fact still reflected in contemporary statements of many rural mission programs: "The rural work in mission fields is an organic part of the service demanded of the Church everywhere—East and West—to lead in the effort to

on the very practical problems of rural development.[8] It has lacked a profound Christian understanding and interpretation of the upheaval in rural society. This has become all the more pressing in view of the new efforts of the state to cope with rural problems, and especially the rapid growth of national community development projects, which have taken over the methods and the idealism of Christian work, but which are tempted to put their emphasis solely on the material benefits of change. As the Indian Christian study on social change has pointed out:

(The many Christian) establishments for rural service have contributed to the formulation of the (present) approach to village development plans. More recently the Community Projects have taken up the task within the national plan, giving it greater urgency and a broader basis. It is necessary to add, however, that their emphasis on material targets—necessary as it is—has led to a certain neglect in defining clearly the goals towards which the changes in social structure are to be directed and their correlation with material objectives. This may be due to the fact that at the national level, the differences be-

---

build a rural civilization that shall be Christian to the core. This effort looks toward the development of an intelligent, literate and efficient rural population, well organized and well led, who shall share the economic, the political and the social emancipation, as well as the continued advancement of the masses of men, who shall participate fully in world affairs, and shall be moved and inspired by the Christian spirit." *Missions and Rural Problems, op. cit.*, pp. 287–88. The aims of community development are listed as follows:

"(1) The development of Christian character, Christian fellowship and Christian service.
(2) Healthful living in a healthy environment.
(3) The effective cultivation of the physical resources necessary for the food supply and the sound economic development of people in villages and in the open country.
(4) The improvement of family life through a knowledge of such home activities as the care of children, food, sleeping facilities, sanitation and all that centres about the life of women and children.
(5) A social attitude towards neighbours which makes possible sincere co-operation despite obstacles of religion, nationality, race, colour or language.
(6) The constant re-creation of personality—physical, mental and spiritual—which may be gained not only from a sound use of leisure time but from an appreciation of the beautiful, the good, and the inspiring nature and in humanity." p. 290.

The Meeting of the International Missionary Council in Madras in 1938 largely affirmed the definition of rural missions worked out at Jerusalem. See *The World Mission of the Church*, pp. 173–76.

[8] See, for example, the interesting description of village development in Egypt; Galdas and Finney, *Village Reborn* (The Committee on World Literacy and Christian Literature, 1958).

tween the different approaches to rural development remain unresolved. Perhaps unanimity of approach would be premature at this stage, but already the broad lines of a national plan are emerging. Christian social agencies, in the light of their long experience of village reconstruction work, can make a contribution to the evolution of it, a contribution which may be humble but not insignificant.[9]

This suggests that Christian rural work must rethink its function, examining the theological, political, sociological, and practical issues involved. Though strong in practical assistance projects, missions and churches have often slighted basic issues of rural social order and justice. Admittedly it was difficult in the past for Western missionaries to dwell too much on questions with political implications, but today there is little reason for the churches not to show their concern in this area.

II. *Social Change and Social Justice in Rural Life*

Christian descriptions of the rural problem of Africa and Asia generally show little concern with the tragic breakup of the old structures. It may be that churches and missions never fully appreciated the disruptive effect of the new urban society on rural life because they were themselves often engaged in a devastating attack on traditional rural society.[10]

As Prof. de Vries has stated, the life and witness of the missionary movement in Africa and Asia in the nineteenth and twentieth centuries has been with few exceptions an extension of the pattern of Christian rural life in Europe and the United States.[11] Today the development of the younger church makes possible a new policy and line of action. This is likely to develop slowly, and meanwhile the situation in the rural areas is becoming steadily more precarious. The social and cultural disruption will be accentuated in the future by the need for further radical economic change in order to support the rapidly growing population. The new nations are struggling with great difficulty to cope with agrarian problems and the whole structure of rural life is being changed. The question in most countries is, can a pattern of efficient rural economic development be found which will retain some

[9] P. D. Devanandan and M. M. Thomas (editors), *Christian Participation in Nation-Building*, p. 179.
[10] Van der Kroef, *op. cit.*, p. 189.
[11] De Vries, *op. cit.* (Ch. X–Rural Change)

semblance of traditional social and cultural life, or is the village social system already doomed because it is unable to support the renewal of rural society?

In the Western Region of Nigeria the government is launching a revolutionary land development scheme aimed at the reconstruction of the agrarian pattern and more efficient use of the land. It has borrowed the pattern of the Israeli farming collectives or co-operatives (*kibbutz*) and Israeli advisors have been working in Nigeria to set up the program. It involves the enlistment of youth for several years' training in new farm institutes, after which they will be located on co-operative farms. During the first five years of training and work, they will be subsidized by the government on the condition that they spend a further definite period in the farm settlement. The government plans were considered at a meeting of the Christian Council of Nigeria (1960) which recognized the radical changes in rural life which they implied:

> Very great interest was expressed in the Western regional Government's wide-reaching scheme of Farm Institutes and Farm Settlements, which calls for a revolution in family life and village society, and the creation of groups of educated farmers, not farming family land, but in cooperative settlements. This calls for an awareness by the churches of the social and moral problems that are likely to arise in their development, and a readiness to meet them.[12]

But the churches of Nigeria are as yet unprepared to say what those problems are or to advise their members how they can prepare to cope with them.

> The creation of these Institutes and Settlements constitutes a great challenge, and a great opportunity of witness to Christ and of evangelism, and the Council urges its member-churches in the areas concerned to seize the opportunity, and, by working together, to ensure that pastoral care is given in these Institutes and Settlements.[13]

[12] Minutes of the Conference of the Christian Council of Nigeria, 1960, *op. cit.* It is one of the ironies of social change that while both the traditional and Western conceptions of private property are thus being fundamentally challenged in the new Nigerian agricultural system, the opening paragraph of the Council's statement on urban life states: "The Council draws attention to the main tasks of an agricultural missionary, to win the village farmer to Christ, and to build up a strong rural community around the Church. It suggests to all its member-churches that they give a lead in teaching Christian stewardship of land and property, beginning very practically with the improvement of all church and school compounds and buildings, and church members compounds and houses. . . ."

[13] *Ibid.*

The Council also "expressed its concern that attention should be given to suitable training for the girls who would become the wives of these young cooperative farmers."

The latest proposals for Indian national rural development and land reform present an equally serious challenge to the Church there. The land reform undertaken in the past has now to be reviewed in the light of India's need for increased agricultural production. Moreover, since the land is already overcrowded, there is a limit to further subdivision, and the problem of the landless laborer remains. The government proposes to increase farming efficiency and overcome the effects of land division through co-operative joint farming. This scheme would benefit both landowners and landless labor because "land will be pooled for cultivation, the farmers continuing to retain their property rights, getting a share from the net produce in proportion to their land. Further, those who actually work on the land, whether they own the land or not, will get a share in proportion to the work put in by them on the joint farm."[14]

This plan has led to a nation-wide debate. Christian groups have not yet expressed their opinion, although there has been some discussion of the proposal. On the one hand, Christians approve of the idea of land co-operatives as a voluntary method of solving the agrarian problem; on the other hand, they fear that if the voluntary method of forming these co-operatives proves unsuccessful, the government may be tempted to use coercion to achieve its goal. Nevertheless, it is recognized that Christians could make a unique contribution to the co-operative program since they understand the moral and social assumptions on which such co-operation depends and could, through participation in such a scheme, "become involved more closely than ever in the life and welfare of their fellow-men."[15]

In Japan also the churches are confronted with changes in rural life. The radical postwar land reform and reliance on the voluntary development of the co-operative movement has not solved the problem of overcrowded land and underpaid farm labor. This question has been considered in the churches and the United Church of Japan has stated that,

Farmers, who by means of excessive toil supply the basic needs of society, as persons handicapped economically are placed in circum-

[14] *Christian Participation in Nation-Building*, p. 76.
[15] *Ibid.*, p. 83.

stances where they must put up with an unfavourable social status. The state must formulate a radically new policy for the sake of the renovation of agriculture as a backward industry. We must rightly evaluate the social significance of the cooperative movement and strive to strengthen its development in order to protect the life of worker and farmer.[16]

In the Philippines the problems of rural life have been highlighted by the development during the war of a peasant resistance movement which has since continued as a militant political movement for agrarian social justice. Though demoralized by the internal struggle for power between Communists and non-Communists and by the failure to secure needed reforms, the Huks continues in certain areas as a protest movement, leaderless and bewildered, and exploited by other political and ideological factions which are ready to use the grievances of the rural masses for their own ends.[17] No church has yet come to terms with the realities of peasant needs. The Roman Catholic Church is seeking to develop a "Federation of Free Farmers" on familiar Catholic rural reconstruction lines. The Protestant churches are dominated by the "Protestant ethic," which leads their rural members to strive for individual progress and economic advance. However, the largest non-Roman Church in the Huk area of Central Luzon, the "Iglesia ni Cristo," is a strong force in the peasant movement.

> Most of its members come from the poorer class. Once converted to the faith, they seem to become hardworking people and learn the practice of Christian stewardship. Their church is well supported. They have a closely knit organization, and in a sense their church membership may be considered a membership in a peasant union. Politically this Church is a power courted by every politician. In their public religious meetings they are given every protection by the government.[18]

A Filipino Church leader who has worked in this rural area concludes that Evangelical Christians have to discover two important aspects of the Christian faith before they can transform the Church into the Living Body of Christ in this situation.

[16] "The Christian's Guide for Social Action." *The Ecumenical Review*, Vol. XII, January 1960, p. 265.
[17] F. P. Galang, "The Huk Movement in the Philippines—Its Significance for Grass-Roots Christianity," *Background Information*, March 1960, No. 24, pp. 18–22.
[18] *Ibid.*, p. 21.

Firstly, they must discover the vital relationship of worship and Christian nurture to the daily activities of individuals, families, and communities. Secondly, they must discover the significance of the dispersed or scattered [diaspora] Church in order for them to understand that they have a ministry to fulfil in the workaday world. This is not just a "social implication of the Gospel." It is a vital part of our high calling, of our Christian vocation.[19]

The writer adds that through keener awareness of the political issues and the social problems, the churches could help the peasant movements to fulfill their true prophetic mission.

The familiar problems of rural social and political justice are now extremely urgent in Africa, Asia, and Latin America, and churches in these countries can no longer postpone discussing them. It is disturbing that churches confronted by the enormous injustice of land alienation in many parts of Africa, land tenure problems in Asia, or the exploitation of landless peasants in South America, have so rarely expressed their opposition to these conditions or encouraged their members who were working against such evils.[20]

[19] F. P. Galang, *op. cit.*, p. 21.

[20] No Protestant church has issued a statement on land reform in these countries which compares in vigor and in searching examination of the issues with the trenchant pastoral instruction "Purchased Peoples" of the Roman Catholic Bishop of Umtali (Southern Rhodesia). He deals with the whole complex of social and political problems afflicting Central African life today and on the subject of Land Hunger he says: "Although it is frequently stated that the Land Apportionment Act was introduced to protect the African and to prevent his being rendered completely landless, there must surely exist in many minds doubts about the honesty of acquiring so much land so easily from a primitive and unsuspecting people. . . . [although there is some moral justification for European ownership] Can you in conscience blame the African, if ekeing out a tenuous existence from poor soil in an overcrowded Reserve, he is swayed by subversive propaganda, when close beside him there lie hundreds of thousands of acres of fertile soil which he may not cultivate nor occupy nor graze, because although it lies unused and unattended, it belongs to some individual or group of individuals who perhaps do not even live in the country, but who hold the land in the hope of profit from speculation?" pp. 27–28.

Part IV

CONCLUSION

Chapter 14

THE CHURCH AND
THE SEARCH FOR
THE MORAL BASIS OF
A NEW SOCIETY

*God loves not only the Christians, but the whole world;
and all the revolutions of this world take place in some
fashion under God's providence to serve the final goals
of the Divine will of love.*

From the Report of the World Christian Study Conference
on Rapid Social Change, Thessalonica, 1959

Our study leads to the conclusion that Christian
thinking about society must be developed substantially to enable the
individual Christian as well as the Church to meet the challenge of
rapid social change. This difficult theological and intellectual task demands new understanding at three points: (1) the moral and spiritual
meaning of social and cultural change; (2) the criteria to be used in
developing a new social and political order; (3) the forms of action
and service which can express Christian justice in a changing world.
An examination of these three points reveals the kind of unresolved
issues on which the Church must now concentrate its thinking.

I. The Moral Dilemmas of Social Change

There is little unanimity in the Church today on its responsibility
in areas of rapid social change. On the contrary, there is profound
disagreement about the meaning of change. Christian youth tend to
equate social change and progress. Their elders tend to be suspicious

of the clamor for change, believing that it is based on profound moral and spiritual illusions. And even those Christians who do agree on the meaning and desirability of change often disagree on how and at what tempo that change is to be realized.

This disagreement is heightened by the fundamental moral dilemmas which many people see in change. These may be classified in three groups:

(1) The dilemmas created by the conflict between the different aims or values which underlie the search for new forms of society. The goals of progress, social justice, and freedom cannot be realized equally and simultaneously. A choice may be necessary, not only, for example, between economic growth and political freedom, but within freedom itself, between individual and national freedom. This is not a new dilemma for the churches, but it takes on fresh reality and intensity at the present time in Africa, Asia, and Latin America.

(2) The dilemmas created by the fact that technical change requires radical transformation of traditional social and cultural systems, though these may in fact contain much that is good. The resulting tension is augmented by the awareness that change is often an "all or nothing" proposition. Any major alteration in the highly integrated structures of cultural and social life threatens the collapse of the whole system.

(3) The dilemmas created by a growing realization that the outcome of change is not predictable, and that the choice is not between traditional and progressive, the old and the new, or between static and dynamic cultures, but between the inadequate past and the uncertain future. The breakup of old societies and the creation of new ones is costly in terms of human disorder, tensions, fears, and anxieties.

These dilemmas contribute to the conviction shared by many Christians that there is no positive meaning in change, that the "blind and contradictory strivings of our world" frustrate man's search for meaning; that the evils of change cancel out the good; that the noblest efforts of the children of God to develop a new and responsible society are practically impotent because of the sins of their fathers and the seemingly superhuman nature of the forces of this technical age.

Yet few Christians can accept this view of history and of social change. The Christian faith recognizes the element of ambiguity and contradiction in all human striving, but does not allow it to negate the meaning of history and men's efforts to discover and do the good. Moreover, since for the Christian the meaning of history is not dependent on the success or failure of particular social or political programs but on the conviction that in it God is working out His purpose of righteousness and truth, the struggle for social justice is not hopeless and futile but is of profound significance for man's ultimate destiny. It was this which led the World Council's Thessalonica conference on rapid social change to affirm that the "Christian understanding of man and community must lead to a radical interpretation of social change, which goes far beyond the usual pessimistic or optimistic evaluations." What does that imply for Christian attitudes to change in these lands?

In the past there was much Christian optimism about the possibility of "bringing light to darkness," of creating cultures and civilization which would be "Christian to the core." This optimism seems to have been based on a too hopeful evaluation of man's capacity to know and to do the good and a too uncritical attitude to Western culture as a guide to social change. The expectation was that Christian ideals would penetrate the life of the non-Christian peoples in much the same way that they had penetrated the cultures of Western countries and created there a "Christian civilization." This illusion was the product of both political and theological errors. The political miscalculation was to assume that these countries would remain for years under the control of Western "Christian" governments which would provide the umbrella for the Christianizing process. The theological mistake was to identify Christianity and a particular civilization. Today the umbrella of Christian culture has unexpectedly folded, and the Church has to reckon with the fact that its collapse was due as much to flaws in its own structure as to the storms of change without. There is in some Christian circles today, as a result of this experience, a tendency toward pessimism, a despair of any good coming from political or social change, and a fear that all human values will be lost in the rapid breakup of existing patterns of order and responsibility.

Many Christians in these young nations believe that a radically new Christian interpretation of change must be developed, based on an understanding of social justice which is not stated in wholly Western terms but formulated in relation to traditional cultural values. The basic question is, what is the possibility of a correlation between social justice and these traditional values?

II.   *The Criteria for Social Justice in non-Christian Societies*

In the past, Christian missions attempted to meet the need for social change very largely through social service: hospitals, schools, agricultural colleges, and other welfare and charitable work. Perhaps this was inevitable in a time when there was such great disparity in material conditions between the societies of the West and those of Africa, Asia, and Latin America. Today, however, social change has to be seen primarily in terms of social justice, because it requires the search for new social structures and the development of social welfare on a national rather than an individual or tribal basis; it also involves the creation of an international ethos which will encourage the rich nations to accept their responsibility for economic and social development in the new nations. It demands the churches' recognition that they are deeply implicated in the social revolution of these lands.

This Christian concern for social justice in Africa, Asia and Latin America is not new, but it has received scant attention in the past. Today it is being revived. The Indian study has defined the task of the Indian people in such a way that it could well apply to many other countries: "to find new patterns of social order and community living which help and do not hinder the nation in its efforts to develop new political and economic structures which do justice to the new urges for personal freedom and social justice."

The problem is that this Christian interpretation of social justice must be expressed in terms of traditional social values and cultures. What distinguishes the present social revolution from previous ones, and greatly complicates it, is that it involves not merely the formulation of new social goals and institutions, but also the rethinking of cultural and religious foundations. These nations want to make use of the social ideas and technological discoveries of the West, but within the context of their traditional culture and religion. This view is shared by Christians and non-Christians. The report of the rapid social change study in India declares:

> The task . . . is one of combining the values inherited from ancient and medieval India with the fresh influx of knowledge and experience from beyond the seas, with a view to creating a new outlook. It should mean a reinterpretation of all cultures on a new basis, if it is to produce a unified culture and not an incoherent mixture. The aim should be to provide the motivation necessary for a higher stand-

ard of material living, for rational ordering of life, for human individuality and social responsibility, for moral integrity and safeguards against the corruptions of power. Therefore, the culture we achieve should give positive value to the material world and technology, and recognize the dignity of human personality and its fulfilment in community. Most of all, it should be a culture which perceives man's accountability to the moral law and his freedom to transcend it, his capacities and incapacities for moral goodness, and his tendencies to use power and ideas to justify himself and exploit others.[1]

The Indian statement notes that "this cultural goal is not easily achieved." The question is, to what extent can it be achieved at all? How are the two elements of social justice and cultural renewal to be combined in a Christian view of responsible society without constant inner conflict and tension? Are there indigenous cultural values which will truly sustain the search for social justice? Such questions have arisen again and again in this study; they remain unanswered and pose one of the fundamental dilemmas of rapid social change. Change in community, family, and economic life is precarious and unstable if not supported by social ideas and sentiments embodied in the culture of the country. Yet is there not a basic incompatibility between a new individualistic, responsible, and national order of life and the traditional cultural patterns? For example, can the collectivism of traditional culture and society in Africa and Asia be so redefined as to provide the basis for the new democratic socialistic pattern of society with its emphasis on human rights? Can Christians help in the search to find within the traditional cultures and societies of Asia and Africa indigenous incentives which might sustain the whole process of nation-building and economic development?

For the Church such questions pose very difficult practical and theological problems. Would not such an undertaking in itself present the ultimate contradiction and are not Christians by definition precluded from taking part in such a re-evaluation of traditional cultures since they can only accept those facets which can be separated from their religious roots? The only answer to these questions thus far attempted points in the direction of a Christian contribution to a secular social philosophy.

[1] P. D. Devanandan and M. M. Thomas (editors), *Christian Participation in Nation-Building*, p. 246.

III. Can Christians Help to Develop a Social Philosophy of Change?

All the countries of Asia and Africa are engaged in some kind of effort to develop a new society combining Western socialist ideas and indigenous cultural and religious values. Some are seeking to create a synthesis of the new and the old. Others are developing a secular social philosophy in relation to political and economic life incorporating elements of the traditional culture. The best examples of this kind of secularization are the Pantjasila of Indonesia and the secular socialist state of India.

The Pantjasila embodies five principles or ideas which constitute the ideological basis for the Indonesian Republic: (1) The Almighty and One Godhead, (2) Respect for human values or humanity, (3) Democracy, (4) Social justice, and (5) Nationalism. As Dr. A. Th. van Leeuwen of Holland has pointed out, "the second up to the fifth principle inclusive are quite 'normal' foundations of a modern state. The crux is the first principle. . . . This rather vague term [Godhead] was purposely chosen that the connection between state and religion might be maintained while not proclaiming an Islamic state. In the Draft-Constitution the explicit declaration of this principle as the foundation of the state is closely linked up with the recognition of religious liberty, and President Sukarno has officially interpreted it as 'tolerance'."[2]

In India, the secular "socialistic pattern of society" involves a similar effort to combine goals of national development, which are largely Western, with historic Indian culture, though the process of secularization has been carried further.

In both India and Indonesia there is an attempt to affirm traditional culture, while insisting that in the interests of nation-building there must be acceptance of common social values. A secular social philosophy has resulted based on the idea that society and religion are, at least at certain points, distinct and separable, and should be so.

Can the Church support this secularizing process and what does it mean for its historic conception of its own contribution to changing

[2] A. Th. van Leeuwen, "The Response of Islam to the Impact of the West." (An address to a Christian study conference on *The Christian and the Contemporary Middle Eastern World*, Asmara, Ethiopia, April 1959. Report of the Conference, p. 18. Pantjasila is an old Javanese Sanskrit word which means, literally, "five principles."

societies? Many churches which have come to equate the secular with the nonreligious will feel that to support the secular society is practically anti-Christian. On what Christian grounds can it be defended? Mr. M. M. Thomas points out that secularization has two aspects:

a) It is necessary and desirable for the economic development of society. . . . Occupational mobility requires the break-up of occupational divisions (caste) sanctified by religion. Secularization of society is necessary for the liberation of the individual from authoritarian collective structure. The Hindu social code is sanctified by Hindu religion, and change in the former necessitates separation of society from religion. Secularization of society is also necessary for the sake of religious liberty. Society has to become secularized if coexistence and conversion are not to disturb social harmony. In the struggle for secularization of society, Christianity has an uneasy alliance with the reformed religion of the land and the secular faith, against religious and social orthodoxy.

b) The secularization of society involves perils also. Such perils are implied in demoralization, irresponsible individualism, growth of "secularism" and a moral vacuum which is filled by self-conscious militant (religious) orthodoxy or totalitarian communism.[3]

Elsewhere he justifies this limited secularization of society not only for practical but also for "valid Christian reasons," which may be summarized as follows: there is a divinely ordained separation of religion and society because God has implanted His Law in society and its institutions and they have therefore "purposes which are natural to them but distinct from those of religion." Thus society, the state, the university, the arts, and even the family, have a certain measure of autonomy which the Church must recognize. The nature of the true secular autonomy of society can be understood only in relation to its responsibility to the laws and purposes of God. The Church must not identify itself with society; its function is to remind society of the laws of God by which it can distinguish between true and false social purposes, and to help restore to society, through the Gospel of Redemption, its true and creative function.[4] When a religion seeks to organize society around itself, it inevitably corrupts both faith and society because it confuses ultimate truth with the limited truth which

[3] M. M. Thomas, "The Mission and Its Encounter with the Asian Revolution," an address to the East Asia Christian Conference, Prapat, Indonesia, 1957. See *The Common Evangelistic Task of the Churches in East Asia* (papers and minutes of the East Asian Christian Conference, Rangoon, 1957, pp. 81–82).

[4] *Christian Participation in Nation-Building*, pp. 154–55.

may be embodied in a particular social order and culture. To quote
M. M. Thomas:

> Secularism is a protest against this sacrifice of the fullness of life in
> the name of a man-made unity. Of course, secularism itself is in
> danger of setting up an ideological system as idolatrous as any other
> religious system or of degenerating into lawlessness and thus betray-
> ing its own protest. But there is a deep Christain truth in the secular
> protest, namely that the different spheres of human life have a real
> autonomy and must not be regimented into a narrow unity easily
> achieved through the religious integration of society. . . . Thus, in
> the Indian social situation, where religion has led society to stagnate
> in a static unity, there is clear justification for a large measure of
> secularization and even of separation of society from religion, when
> we are working for a more dynamic society.[5]

This interpretation would, according to Mr. Thomas, provide the
basis for practically unlimited Christian participation in the discussion of the new patterns of society and would create a neutral ground
where Christians and non-Christians alike could contribute their ideas.
The autonomy of state and society is essentially a Christian idea,
though in the pietist tradition the "secular world" has often been
interpreted to mean that lost area of life from which the individual
must be saved. However, in both Calvinist and Lutheran thought,
there is a positive recognition of the universal moral law as the basis
of government and social order, whether Christian or non-Christian.

A major objection to this view is that it may lead to unwarranted
optimism and hope in the human situation. It is just because the world
is such a broken world and because social change is so rapid that it is
hard to find even the minimal secular moral values on which all can
agree. Moreover while the secular state, as defined above, embodies
values and ideas which are akin to the Christian understanding of man
and society, can it also include moral ideas or social customs which
truly express the view of man in other religious systems? Without that,
what is its reality as the meeting-ground of all cultures? Or to turn
the question around, can we expect the non-Christian community,
which predominates in most areas of social change, to accept an interpretation of the secular society which is basically antithetical to its
whole conception of life? This points to the main difficulty with the
theory of "limited secularization" as a solution to the moral and spirit-

---

[5] *Christian Participation in Nation-Building*, pp. 155–56.

ual conflicts inherent in the struggle for a new society in Asia and Africa. It must in the last analysis rest upon some common assumptions about the nature of those "moral landmarks beyond the wills of men."[6]

And yet, in spite of these questions, the Church's efforts to understand and define the Christian responsibility for rapid social change must be carried on in close relationship to the non-Christian religions and cultures. There is no other way to find the common ground on which all can serve the welfare and dignity of man.[7] The area of common moral concern may be larger than many Western Christians believe and smaller than claimed by many Asian and African Christians, but large or small, it must be discovered.

There are a number of obstacles to such an encounter. The Christian stereotype of non-Christian religions is one. Some Christians may find it difficult to admit that today these religions can revise their views of man and society. Others may feel that efforts to realize a secular state will weaken the specifically Christian understanding of man and hinder the upbuilding and growth of Christ's Church. In this search for the spiritual and moral foundations of the state and society in Africa and Asia, the Christian is on the horns of the ultimate dilemma. Either he must emphasize the specific Christian view of man and society at the risk of cutting himself off from the discussion of political and social goals in a non-Christian situation, or he must take seriously his obligation to help create the basis of an ordered society at the risk of seeming to weaken his witness regarding the true foundations of all social order and nation-building. At this point the problem of rapid social change becomes very existential for the Church.

IV. *Christian Action for the World*

This unresolved dilemma affects every aspect of the life and witness of the Church and especially its social action and service in areas of

[6] This discussion in some respects parallels the problem of religious pluralism in the West and the conversation between Protestants, Catholics, and Jews regarding the moral basis of the secular or religiously neutral state. However, the problem is considerably more difficult in those situations where the areas of common moral agreement are far less apparent.

[7] This is not a call for a syncretistic ethical and religious system or the acceptance of every ethical system as equally valid, as advocated by Prof. Arnold Toynbee. See his statement, "No Chosen People, No Unique Truth" in *The Observer*, London, April 16, 1961. This approach results in the creation of a "new religion" to which most Christians must object.

rapid change. Indeed, this may explain the paralysis of Christian social action in Africa and Asia. By and large the churches and missions have not yet seen God at work in the social revolution and in the whole process of nation-building; they have seen His hand rather in the efforts of the Christian community to bring the benefits of civilization to "underdeveloped lands." There has consequently been a tendency for the Church to restrict itself to those areas of service and action where it can continue to hold to its conception of Christian fellowship and community with the least compromise. Its emphasis on schools, hospitals, and other technical services has been the outcome of this approach. The result of this strategy seems clear: constant withdrawal, leading to the eventual extinction of Christian social action when the technical services of the churches are no longer essential to the state. Such activity may place churches *alongside* the cultural-social revolution but it does not involve them *in* it.

In view of man's known capacity to betray the good he seeks, Christians cannot identify themselves completely with the revolution. The creative response of the churches to social change was defined as follows at the international ecumenical study conference in Thessalonica:

> . . . it will be quite clear that the Christian response . . . cannot be "withdrawal." The conviction that God is at work in this momentous revolution among men means a calling to the churches to work with Him in it. But it will also be clear that Christians cannot plunge with uncritical enthusiasm into all the historical situations in which they are working. To be critical in this sense does not mean to be hesitant. It means to live and work under God who is beyond all historical events, but who is in all the affairs of men in Christ, continuing his redemptive work in which it is the mission of the church to participate.[8]

The challenge to the Church today is to uncover new strategies and forms of action which will enable it to witness to Christ within this political, social, and cultural revolution. Some pioneering work is already being done: occupational evangelism for industrial worker groups in Japan; study guides on the Christian witness in politics in India; conferences on the role of women in church and society in Africa; leadership training for youth and students in the changing society of Latin America; the Christian center for Christians and Muslims to work out new patterns of community in Tunisia; Christian

---

[8] *Thessalonica Report, op. cit.,* p. 32.

work with landless peasants in the Philippines and Brazil. The younger churches are no longer bound by the concerns of Western missions, inhibited as they were by their "foreignness" and by conflicts of nationality and culture. At the same time, they need more than ever the perspective and help of the whole Church if they are to avoid the danger of social, ideological, and cultural syncretism which is constantly threatening in all such situations of revolutionary change.

The task before the churches is immense, but the power which Christ has given His Church is more than sufficient. It is already apparent in the earnest desire of the people of Africa, Asia, and Latin America to develop a society which will further the welfare and dignity of men and women; we see it in the struggle of people to free themselves from beliefs which cripple the human spirit, and where men dare to oppose unjust laws and racial barriers. The power of Christ is most strikingly evident in the lives of Christian laymen and women who are the leaders of the new nations and who must share in the responsibility for determining the direction of change.

The problem today is perhaps not so much to "find" new forms of Christian action as to open our eyes to what Christ is already doing and to share His burden of tragedy and victory in order that the whole of mankind may come to know its true destiny.

SELECTED BIBLIOGRAPHY

The difficulties in preparing a bibliography of Christian writing on problems of social change in Africa, Asia, and Latin America will be obvious to those who have worked in this field. While there is a great abundance of "secular" writing, there is a serious shortage of relevant Christian material, especially on specific topics; and much that was useful in the past is outdated by events.

Some helpful interpretations of the ethical problems of social change are to be found in novels by young writers in Asia and Africa. African writers particularly give much attention to the impact of Christianity on traditional society. Mention might be made of such titles as *Le Pauvre Christ de Bomba* (1956), by Mongo Beti of the Cameroun, who describes the struggles of a French priest and his eventual defeat by a rebellious and indifferent community; Peter Abrahams, the South African colored writer, describes in his *A Wreath For Udomo* (1956) the conflict in political life; Chinua Achebe's *Things Fall Apart* (1958) is a study of the coming of Christianity to a Nigerian village and its disintegrating social effects; his latest book, *No Longer At Ease* (1960), deals with the moral conflict of urbanization; T. M. Aluko's *One Man, One Wife* (1959) is another Nigerian novel which deals profoundly with the conflict of social ethics provoked by the impact of Christianity on traditional African society. *The Dark Child* by Camara Laye, a writer from Guinea, is an autobiographical account of his childhood in a Guinean village and the pull of Western life upon him. These thoughtful books by Africans give more of the "feel" of the conflict induced within the soul of the African by great social-cultural change than many sociological studies. However, I have not included a list of such novels. Such a compilation would be an assignment in itself.

The following bibliography does not include material on the response of Hinduism, Buddhism, Islam, and other religions to rapid social change. This is a most important field and an up-to-date bibliography is much needed.

Christian Periodicals on Rapid Social Change

There are now three bulletins in Asia which devote much attention to Christian responsibility for rapid social change. *Religion and Society* is a quarterly bulletin of the Christian Institute for the Study of Religion and Society, edited by P. D. Devanandan and M. M. Thomas and published in Bangalore, India; *Church and Society*, edited by M. M. Thomas, is a semiannual publication of the East Asia Christian Conference Committee on Church and Society. Also circulated through the East Asia Christian Conference is the *Church Labor Letter*, a brief mimeographed monthly paper dealing with the Christian witness in industrial society; Prof. M. Takenaka in Kyoto, Japan, is the editor.

The bulletin, *Iglesia Y Sociedad en America Latina*, mimeographed, is published twice yearly by a study group in Latin America in co-operation with the Department on Church and Society, WCC. The editor is Sr. Luis Odell, Montevideo.

Background Information on Church and Society, mimeographed, edited by the staff of the Department on Church and Society of the World Council of Churches, and published three times a year, contains much material on the problems of rapid social change.

The *Occasional Bulletin*, published by the Missionary Research Library, New York, also includes material on social questions.

*   *   *   *

I. Theological and Historical Interpretations of Churches, Missions, and Social Change in Africa, Asia, and Latin America.

A. GENERAL

The most important international missionary source materials on social questions are the official reports of the meetings of the International Missionary Council at Jerusalem (1928) and Tambaram, Madras (1938). For the Jerusalem meeting there are eight volumes, and three are of special interest to the student of rapid social change: Volume IV, *The Christian Mission in the Light of the Race Conflict*; Volume V, *The Christian Mission in Relation to Industrial Problems*; and Volume VI, *The Christian Mission in Relation to Rural Problems*. They include the preparatory papers as well as the statements of the meeting. These were published by Oxford University Press, London, 1928.

The reports for the Madras meeting are in seven volumes, of which Volume V, on *The Economic Basis of the Church* (compiled by J. Merle Davis), is concerned with social and economic problems. The reports arising out of the discussions at Madras are published in a separate volume entitled *The World Mission of the Church*, I.M.C., London and New York, 1939, and include the statements of Sections XIII., "The Church and the Changing Social and Economic Order"; XIV., "The Church and the International Order"; and XV., "The Church and State," as well as the reports of two special groups on "The Church and Rural Problems" and "Urban Problems."

Other studies of general interest are:

Bates, M. Searle, *Religious Liberty: An Inquiry*, I.M.C., New York and London, 1945.

Davis, J. Merle, *New Buildings on Old Foundations*, I.M.C., New York and London, 1945. A study of the relation of missions to cultural and social change; by the first director of the I.M.C.'s Department of Social and Economic Research and Counsel.

Dennis, James S., *Christian Missions and Social Progress*, Fleming H. Revell, three volumes (1897–1906), New York. Of historical interest as the first systematic survey of the social thought and work of missions.

Fleming, D. J., *Ethical Issues Confronting World Christians*, I.M.C., 1935.

Hocking, William Ernest, *Rethinking Missions: A Laymen's Inquiry After One Hundred Years*. Harper, New York, 1932. Contains much interesting information on the social action and work of missions at that time.

Hogg, William Richey, *Ecumenical Foundations* (A History of the International Missionary Council and its 19th Century Background). Harper, New York, 1952. Chapter VI, "A Decade of Crisis and Advance" (1928–38), tells the story of the I.M.C.'s social gospel period.

Kraemer, Hendrik, *The Christian Message in a Non-Christian World*, Edinburgh House Press, London, 1938.

McGavran, D. A., *Bridges of God*, World Dominion Press, London, 1955.

Mathews, Basil, *Roads to the City of God*, Edinburgh House Press, London, 1928. An account of the Jerusalem meeting of 1928 by one who was there and who describes it vividly.

Newbigin, Lesslie, *One Body, One Gospel, One World*, I.M.C, London and New York, 1958.

Oldham, J. H., *Christianity and the Race Problem*, Association Press, New York, 1924.

Paton, David, *Christian Missions under the Judgment of God*, S.C.M. Press, London, 1953.

Warren, M. A. C., *Caesar, the Beloved Enemy*, S.C.M. Press, London, 1955. The first of the three essays which make up this book, on a "theology of imperialism," has encouraged Asian Christians to develop a theology of nationalism!

Welborn, F. B., "The Missionary Culture" in *Essays in Anglican Self-Criticism*, edited by David M. Paton. S.C.M. Press, London, 1958.

B.   AFRICA

Busia, K. A., *Africa in Transition,* Project Paper No. 10, WCC, Geneva, 1957, 20 pp.

Carpenter, George W., *The Way in Africa,* The Friendship Press, New York, 1959.

Changing Africa and the Christian Dynamic, papers of a Seminar for Mission Board Executives, February 1960. The Center for the Study of the Christian World Mission, The Federated Theological Faculty, The University of Chicago. Mimeographed, January 1958.

The Church in Changing Africa, Report of the All-Africa Church Conference, I.M.C., New York, 1958. Contains speeches and reports of discussion on the Church and the economic and political questions.

Hutchinson, Bertram, "Some Social Consequences of Missionary Activity Among South African Bantu." *Africa, Journal of the International African Institute,* Vol. 27, No. 2, April 1957, pp. 167–75.

Karefa-Smart, Rena and John, *The Halting Kingdom, Christianity and the African Revolution.* Friendship Press, New York.

Oldham, J. H., *New Hope in Africa,* Longmans, Green, London, 1955.

Oliver, Roland, *The Missionary Factor in East Africa,* Longmans, Green, London, 1952. Illuminating history of missions in East Africa giving much attention to the social consequences of missionary work.

Orchard, R. K., *Africa Steps Out,* London, 1952.

Shepperson, George and Price, Thomas, *Independent African, John Chilembwe and . . . the Nyasaland Native Rising of 1915.* The University Press, Edinburgh, 1958. A fascinating study of an independent African Church and its leader seen as a social protest movement.

Sundkler, Bengt, *The Bantu Prophets in South Africa,* Lutterworth Press, London, 1948. A study of the independent Church movement in South Africa and the social forces which gave rise to it.

Taylor, John V., *The Growth of the Church in Buganda; An Attempt at Understanding,* S.C.M. Press, London, 1958.

C.   ASIA

The reports of the meeting of the East Asia Christian Conference established at Prapat (Indonesia) in 1957 contain important material on churches and rapid social change in Asia. See especially, the report of Inaugural Assembly of the East Asia Christian Conference on "The Witness of the Churches Amidst Social Change," in *Witnesses Together,* the official report of the Inaugural Assembly of the East Asia Christian Conference held at Kuala Lumpur, Malaya, May 1959; edited by U. Kyaw Than, pp. 60–74. The reports of other conferences are included under specific headings below.

Empiricus, *Social Change in an Asian Community*, Project Paper No. 12, WCC, Geneva, 1956.

Freytag, Walter, *Spiritual Revolution in the East*, Lutterworth, London, 1940.

Manikam, Rajah B., (editor), *Christianity and the Asian Revolution*, Friendship Press, New York, 1955.

Panikkar, K. M., *Asia and Western Dominance*, John Day Co., New York, 1954. This book includes a sharp and critical analysis of the political and social impact of Christian missions on Asian society.

Paton, William, *Christianity in the Eastern Conflicts*; A study of Christianity, Nationalism and Communism in Asia. Edinburgh House Press, London, 1937. A helpful survey of the efforts of the Church in the period before World War II to meet the oncoming crisis.

Sumiya, M., *Formation of Modern Japan and Christianity*, Project Paper No. 5, WCC, Geneva.

Takenaka, Masao, *Reconciliation and Renewal in Japan*, Friendship Press, New York, 1957.

Varg, Paul A., *Missionaries, Chinese, and Diplomats: The American Protestant Missionary Movement in China, 1890–1952*. Princeton University Press, Princeton, 1958.

D.   LATIN AMERICA

Barbieri, Sante Uberto, *Land of Eldorado*, Friendship Press, New York, 1961.

Bonino, Miguez, "Witness in a de-Christianized Continent," *Student World*, No. 1 and 2, 1961, pp. 96–110.

Camargo, G. B., *El Comunismo, el Christianismo y los Christianos*. Casa de Publicaciones, Mexico, 1960.

Camargo, G. B., and Grubb, K. G., *Religion in the Republic of Mexico*, World Dominion Press, London, 1935.

Rycroft, W. Stanley, *Religion and Faith in Latin America*, The Westminster Press, Philadelphia, 1958.

————— (editor), *Indians of the High Andes*, Report of the Commission appointed by the Committee on Cooperation in Latin America, New York, 1946, 330 pp.

II. Publications for the World Council of Churches' Rapid Social Change Study

A.   INTERNATIONAL

The purpose and scope of the World Council of Churches' study program is outlined in two printed statements on *The Common Christian Responsibility Toward Areas of Rapid Social Change*. The first was published in 1955 and the second in 1956 by the Department on Church and Society (WCC), Geneva. For an account of the operation of the study see *Progress Report* (1955–58). Mimeographed, 80 pp. A final report will be presented to the Third Assembly of the WCC, New Delhi, November 1961.

The findings of the International Ecumenical Study Conference on social change, held in Thessalonica, Greece in 1959, are published in the printed report, *Dilemmas and Opportunities, Christian Action in Rapid Social Change*, World Council of Churches, Geneva, 1959, 104 pp. A selection of addresses at the conference will be found in *Background Information on Church and Society*, No. 23, November 1959.

The two summary volumes published for the study are: Egbert de Vries, *Man in Rapid Social Change*, and Paul Abrecht, *The Churches and Rapid Social Change*. Doubleday, New York, 1961.

B. NATIONAL REPORTS

1. *Africa*

Copperbelt of Northern Rhodesia: *The Churches and Social Change in the Copperbelt of Northern Rhodesia*, by C. L. Van Doorn and Mrs. W. S. F. Van Doorn-Snijders. Mimeographed, 1959. This will be available soon in a printed edition.

Kenya: *The Social and Economic Conditions of Development* (tentative title), by Marion Forrester (to be published in 1961).

Liberia: *Changing Liberia, A Challenge to the Christian*, United Christian Fellowship Conference of Liberia, 1959, 121 pp., printed.

Nigeria: *Christian Responsibility in an Independent Nigeria*, a report by S. I. Kale and Herbert Hogan for the Christian Council of Nigeria, 1961, 132 pp.

South Africa: *Report From the Inter-Church Study Group, South Africa*, mimeographed. Issued for restricted circulation only. 1959.

Reports from other studies in Ghana and the Cameroons are not yet available.

2. *Asia*

Reports on two Asian regional discussions of rapid social change have been published: *The Social Goals of New Asia*, 1957, 39 pp., and *The Witness of the Churches Amidst Social Change in East Asia*, report of Commission I of the Inaugural Assembly of the East Asia Christian Conference, *op. cit.*

India: *Christian Participation in Nation-Building*, a summary volume compiled by M. M. Thomas and P. D. Devanandan. Published by the National Christian Council of India and the Christian Institute for the

Study of Religion and Society, 1960, 325 pp. Clearly the most substantial contribution to Christian thinking about rapid social change.

Japan: *The Common Christian Responsibility Toward Rapid Social Change in Japan.* Published by the National Christian Council of Japan, 1959, 50 pp.

(Smaller study projects have been held in West Pakistan, Indonesia, and Malaya, for which reports are not available.)

3. *Latin America*

Brazil: A *Igreja as Rapidas Transformacoes Sociais do Brasil,* Confederacao Evangelica do Brasil, 1958.

River Plate: *Rapid Social Change in Argentine, Chile, Uruguay,* report on Findings of the River Plate Study Conference. Project Paper, RSC Study, Geneva.

4. *The West*

Europe: *The Specific European Responsibilities in Relation to Africa and Asia.* Report from a European Ecumenical Consultation, Odense, Denmark, August 1958. Geneva, 16 pp. See also the mimeographed *Record of the Consultation,* 75 pp., Geneva, 1958.

The United States: See Section V on "Overseas Areas of Rapid Social Change," *Christian Responsibility on a Changing Planet.* Report of the Fifth World Order Study Conference, National Council of Churches, U.S.A., 1958.

III. Specific Issues.

A. RESPONSIBLE CITIZENSHIP

Chandran, J. R. and Thomas, M. M. (editors), *Religious Freedom.* Committee for Literature on Social Concerns, Bangalore, 1956.

Church and State. Statement adopted by the National Christian Council of Ghana, Accra, 1960.

Devanandan, P. D. and Thomas, M. M. (editors), *India's Quest for Democracy.* Y.M.C.A. Publishing House, Calcutta, 1955.

————, *Cultural Foundations of Indian Democracy.* Committee for Literature on Social Concerns, Bangalore, 1955.

————, *Human Person. Society and the State.* Committee for Literature on Social Concerns, Bangalore, 1957.

————, *Political Outlook in India Today.* Committee for Literature on Social Concerns, Bangalore, 1956.

Lopez, Mauricio, "Political Thinking Amongst Latin American Students," *Student World* (W.S.C.F.), No. 4, 1959.

Sithole, Ndabaningi, *African Nationalism.* Oxford University Press, Cape-
town, 1959.
Taylor, John V., *Christianity and Politics in Africa.* Penguin African
Series, London, 1957.
Teinonen, Seppo A., *Missio Politica Oecumenica.* Annals of the Finnish
Missiological Society. Published by the Institute for Missiology and
Ecumenics. University of Helsinki, 1961.
Thomas, M. M., "Indian Nationalism—A Christian Interpretation," *Re-
ligion and Society,* Vol. VI, No. 2, June 1959.
Wendland, H. D., *"Constructive" Nationalism As an Ecumenical Prob-
lem.* Mimeographed, Geneva, 1959.

B.   URBANIZATION AND INDUSTRIALIZATION

Bloy, P. P., *Aspects of the Growth of Industrial, Urban and Agricultural
Life in Nigeria.* Mimeographed, Church Missionary Society, London,
1959.
The Church in the Town. Report of a study conference convened by the
Christian Council of Ghana. 1955.
Devanandan, P. D. and Thomas, M. M., *Community Development in
India's Industrial Urban Areas.* Committee for Literature on Social
Concerns, Bangalore, 1958.
Davis, J. Merle, *Modern Industry and the African.* Macmillan, London,
1933.
First Asian Conference on Industrial Evangelism. Minutes and Report of
Proceedings, Manila, Philippines, 1958. Mimeographed, 268 pp.
*To Understand the Christian Responsibility in the Asian Industrial
Awakening.* Report of the First Asian Conference on Industrial Evan-
gelism. East Asia Christian Conference, Manila, 1958.
Jayakar, Samuel, *Rural Sweepers in the City.* Department of Social Re-
search, Leonard Theological College, 1952.
Jones, Henry D., "The Church and Industrial Society," Example: Japan,
International Review of Missions, Vol. 49, 1960, pp. 427–37.
Phillips, R. E., *The Bantu in the City.* Lovedale Press, South Africa, 1938.
Ranson, C. W., *A City in Transition.* Christian Literature Society for
India, Madras, 1938.

C.   RURAL CHANGE

The Christian Mission Among Rural People. A joint study. The Foreign
Missions Conference of North America. New York, 1949, second
abridged printing.
Comfort, Richard O., *The Village Church in West Pakistan.* West Pakistan Christian Council; Report of a survey printed for private use, 1957,
192 pp.

Hatch, D. Spenser, *Toward Freedom From Want From India to Mexico.* Bombay, Oxford University Press, 1949, 303 pp.

Moomaw, I. W., "Our Christian Mission to Rural People, 1910–1960." *The International Review of Missions,* Vol. XLIX, July 1960, pp. 273–280.

————, *Deep Furrows.* Agricultural Missions, New York, 1957.

Thomas, M. M., *The Pattern of Rural Community Development.* Report on a consultation, Allahabad Agricultural Institute and National Christian Council of India, 1956, 45 pp.

Wiser, W. H. and C. V., *Behind Mud Walls in India.* George Allen & Unwin, London, 1934.

D.   THE ETHICAL PROBLEMS OF WESTERN TECHNICAL ASSISTANCE AND ECO-
NOMIC AID

Bilheimer, Dr. Robert S., *Ethical Problems of Economic Aid and Technical Assistance.* Geneva, World Council of Churches. Printed as a *Project Paper* for the WCC study on rapid social change, 1957.

Ethical Problems of Foreign Aid and Technical Assistance. Religion and Society Bulletin of the Christian Institute for the Study of Religion and Society, Vol. IV, No. 1, 1957.

Maddox, James G., *Technical Assistance by Religious Agencies in Latin America.* University of Chicago Press, 1956, pp. xi, 139. A critical evaluation of the technical assistance services rendered by Christian missions in Latin America.

Munby, Denis, *God and the Rich Society.* Oxford University Press, London, 1961.